Prog
Business
Plan
for a
Boutique
Hotel

NON-DISCLOSURE AGREEMENT

_____ (Company)., and _____ (Person Name), agrees:

_____ (Company) Corp. may from time to time disclose to _____ (Person Name) certain confidential information or trade secrets generally regarding Business plan and financials of _____ (Company) corp.

_____ (Person Name) agrees that it shall not disclose the information so conveyed, unless in conformity with this agreement. _____ (Person Name) shall limit disclosure to the officers and employees of _____ (Person Name) with a reasonable "need to know" the information, and shall protect the same from disclosure with reasonable diligence.

As to all information which _____ (Company) Corp. claims is confidential, _____ (Company) Corp. shall reduce the same to writing prior to disclosure and shall conspicuously mark the same as "confidential," "not to be disclosed" or with other clear indication of its status. If the information which _____ (Company) Corp. is disclosing is not in written form, for example, a machine or device, _____ (Company) Corp. shall be required prior to or at the same time that the disclosure is made to provide written notice of the secrecy claimed by _____ (Company) Corp.. _____ (Person Name) agrees upon reasonable notice to return the confidential tangible material provided by it by _____ (Company) Corp. upon reasonable request.

The obligation of non-disclosure shall terminate when if any of the following occurs:
(a) The confidential information becomes known to the public without the fault of _____ (Person Name), or;
(b) The information is disclosed publicly by _____ (Company) Corp., or ;
(c) a period of 12 months passes from the disclosure, or;
(d) the information loses its status as confidential through no fault of _____ (Person Name).

In any event, the obligation of non-disclosure shall not apply to information which was known to _____ (Person Name) prior to the execution of this agreement.

Dated: _____

_____
_____ (Company) Corp.
_____(Person Name)

Business and Marketing Plan Instructions

1. If you purchased this Business Plan Book via Amazon's Print-on-Demand System, please send proof-of-purchase to Probusconsult2@Yahoo.com and we will email you the file.

2. Complete the Executive Summary section, as your final step, after you have completed the entire plan.

3. Feel free to edit the plan and make it more relevant to your strategic goals, objectives and business vision.

4. We have provided all of the formulas needed to prepare the financial plan. Just plug in the numbers that are based on your particular situation. Excel spreadsheets for the financials are available on the microsoft.com website and www.simplebizplanning.com/forms.htm
    http://office.microsoft.com/en-us/templates/

5. Throughout the plan, we have provided prompts or suggestions as to what values to enter into blank spaces, but use your best judgment and then delete the suggested values (?).

6. The plan also includes some separate worksheets for additional assistance in expanding some of the sections, if desired.

7. Additionally, some sections offer multiple choices and the word 'select' appears as a prompt to edit the contents of the plan.

8. Your feedback, referrals and business are always very much appreciated.

Thank you

Nat Chiaffarano, MBA
Progressive Business Consulting, Inc.
Pembroke Pines, FL 33027
ProBusConsult2@yahoo.com

"Progressive Business Plan for a Boutique Hotel"

Boutique Hotel
Business Plan
_____ (date)

Business Name: _____
Plan Time Period: 2017 - 2019

Founding Directors:
Name: _____
Name: _____

Contact Information:
Owner: _____
Address: _____
City/State/Zip: _____
Phone: _____
Cell: _____
Fax: _____
Website: _____
Email: _____

Submitted to: _____
Date: _____
Contact Info: _____

Boutique Hotel Business Plan: Table of Contents

Section	Description	Page

1.0 Executive Summary

Industry Overview

Boutique hotel is a term popularized in North America and the United Kingdom to describe hotels which often contain luxury facilities of varying size in unique or intimate settings with full service accommodations. Boutique hotels began appearing in the 1980s in major cities like London, New York, and San Francisco. Typically boutique hotels are furnished in a themed, stylish and/or aspirational manner. Boutique hotels are often individual and focused on offering their services in a comfortable, intimate, and welcoming setting, so they are very unlikely to be found amongst the homogeneity of large hotels.

Guest rooms and suites may be fitted with telephone and Wi-Fi Internet, air-conditioning, honesty bars and often cable/pay TV but sometimes none of these, focusing on quiet and comfort rather than gadgetry. Guest services are often attended to by 24 h hotel staff. Many boutique hotels have on-site dining facilities, and the majority offer bars and lounges that may also be open to the general public.

Boutique hotels have typically been unique properties operated by individuals or companies with a small collection. However, their successes have prompted multi-national hotel companies to try to establish their own brands in order to capture a market share. Notable example include Starwood Hotels & Resorts Worldwide's W Hotels, ranging from large boutique hotels, such as the W Union Square NY, to the W 'boutique resorts' in the Maldives, and Epoque Hotels among many others. There is some overlap between the concept of a small boutique hotel and a bed and breakfast.

In the United States, New York remains an important centre of the boutique hotel phenomenon, as the original Schrager-era boutique hotels remain relevant and are joined by scores of independent and small-chain competitors, mainly clustered about Midtown and downtown Manhattan. For the last couple of years, the hospitality industry has been following the general "no-frill chic" consumer trend, with affordable or budget boutique hotels sprouting and thriving all around the world.

Business Overview

_____ (company name) is a Boutique Hotel establishment that is scheduled to begin operations on _____ (date). _____ (company name) will provide high quality accommodation for leisure travelers, business clients and visitors to _____ (primary area attractions) in the city of _____. Accommodation at _____ (company name) will consist of ___ (#) comfortably and uniquely furnished rooms, each with queen-sized beds. Full breakfast will be served according to menu selections that will be made the night before.

Our boutique hotel will be designed to create a specifically unique experience for a highly targeted audience with an interest in _____. Our boutique hotel will be considered on the leading edge of design innovation. We will offer truly creative spatial solutions, while not losing the intimacy of a truly hospitable stay.

We will identify the type of guest we want to attract and do in-depth market research to know what those guests really want from their hospitality experience. The space in which our targeted guests stay, sleep, relax or work we be designed specifically for them, with their style in mind, emphasizing amenities and features that matter to them.

This level of specificity will provide a real opportunity to have a distinctive approach to design and service. It will also allows for creativity, exploration and innovation in honing and refining the experiential essence that will attract these guests. The targeted guest population, and others who want to feel like they are part of that group, will influence our general design approach. There will also be a variety of design materials, colors, sounds, aromas and lighting options that will be used to emphasize our boutique hotel's character within its historical context, and make the hotel environment truly memorable.

The surrounding area has beautiful scenery, numerous attractions and recreational activities. Guests will have many opportunities to enjoy themselves in this area, which is also well suited for weekend and holiday getaways.

_____ (company name) will be a ____ (state) based corporation that will provide customers with an outstanding resort experience that will consist of the following:
1.   Premium hotel lodgings   (select/add)
2.   An onsite restaurant
3.   A full service health club and day spa.
4.   A state-of-the-art fitness room and business center.
5.   Corporate Meeting Rooms
6.   Uniquely themed rooms
7.   _____

_____ (company name) will become the best choice in the _____ area for lodging by creating a differentiated experience capitalizing on personal service, the historical nature of the _____ building, and its unique location in one of the most attractive parts of the _____ region. We plan to be more than a great Boutique Hotel. We plan to create an environment of pampered luxury that surpasses the standard fare for _____ (city). Expanding our exposure via the Internet and introducing the _____ (island/community) to people that have not yet discovered this year-round paradise will allow us to maintain a higher than average occupancy rate and above average profits.

We believe that we can become the Boutique Hotel lodging provider of choice in the _____ area for the following reasons:
1.   We will make guests feel as though our home is their home away from home.
2.   We will provide a gourmet breakfast menu that features locally grown organic produce.
3.   We will become the contact point for all of our guest activities in the area.

Our goal is to become a luxury Boutique Hotel by offering a lot of facilities and activities to customers, such as sport, water sport, mini club for kids, tours, onsite nightclubs and fine dining restaurants. The target of our luxury Boutique Hotel will be businessmen seeking locations for seminars and conferences, and people wanting an all-inclusive package to create a special "experience" for their holidays.

In order to succeed, _____ (company name) will have to do the following:
1.   Make superior guest service and their interest sharing our number one priority.
2.   Stay abreast of trends in the Boutique Hotel industry.
3.   Precisely assess and then exceed the expectations of all guests.
4.   Form long-term, trust-based relationships with guests to secure profitable repeat business and referrals.
5.   Develop process and purchasing efficiencies to achieve and maintain rate affordability.
6.   Deliver a unique experience each time the guest returns for a stay.

Critical Risks

Management recognizes there are several internal and external risks inherent in our business concept. Quality and uniqueness of experience will be key factors in the guests' decision to utilize our Boutique Hotel on a continual basis. Also, consumers must be willing to accept the services offered in order for the company to meet its sales projections. A strong marketing strategy and careful screening of guests and contracted service providers will mitigate these risks. Building a loyal and trusting relationship with our guests and referral partners is a key component to the success of____ (company name).

Customer Service

We will take every opportunity to help the guest, regardless of what the short-term profitability might be. We will outshine our competition by doing something "extra" and offering added-value. We will treat guests with respect and help them like we would help a friend. We will take a long-term perspective and focus on the guest's possible lifetime value to our business.

Plan Objective

The purpose of this document is to provide a strategic business plan for our company. The plan has been adjusted to reflect the particular strengths and weaknesses of _____ (company name). Actual financial performance, guest satisfaction, referrals and repeat business will be tracked closely and the business plan will be adjusted when necessary to ensure that full profit potential is realized.

The Company

The business _____ (will be/was) incorporated on _____ (date) in the state of _____ , as a _____ (Corporation/LLC), and intends to register for Sub-chapter 'S' status for federal tax purposes. This will effectively shield the owner(s) from personal liability and double taxation. After start-up and a brief period of becoming established, _____ (company name) will diverse our range of products and services

to ensure a steady flow of patrons (tourists and locals) through its doors.
or
_____ (company name) will be a partnership, equally owned by _____ and
_____. _____ (owner name) will reside on the property, managing and
maintaining the business and satisfying _____ (state) license requirements.

Business Goals
Our business goal is to continue to develop the _____ (company name) brand
name. To do so, we plan to execute on the following:
1.   Offer quality Boutique Hotel lodging at a competitive price.
2.   Focus on quality controls and ongoing operational excellence.
3.   Recruit and train the very best, background checked employees with a flare for
       delivering extraordinary customer service.
4.   Create a marketing campaign with a consistent brand look and message content.

Location
_____ (company name) will be located in the _____ (estate name) on
_____ (street address) in _____ (city), ____ (state). The _____
(purchased/leased) space is easily accessible and provides ample parking for ____ (#)
quests and staff. The location is attractive due to its historic heritage and the area
demographics, which reflect our target guest profile.   _____ (city name) is also
home to the _____ (hospital/university), which will serve as an excellent referral
base for our lodging services.

Mission Statement   (optional)
Our mission is to become a premier resort location and address the following guest pain
points or unmet needs and wants, which will define the opportunity for our business:
_____
In order to satisfy these unmet needs and wants, we will propose the following unique
solutions, which will create better value for our customers:
_____

Products and Services
The property was originally built in ____ (year) and ____ (may/will) qualify for an
_____ (historic?) designation in the near future. The structure has undergone a number
of restorations and uses since the _____ ceased operation in ____ (year). With
construction completed, it now has the potential of ____ (#) rental units, with owner-
occupancy _____ (in an unused room or on the first floor).

_____ (company name) will feature ___ (#) rooms, a health club and day spa, a fully
equipped fitness club, and a ___ (5?) star restaurant onsite. At this time, Mr. _____, the
owner is scouting the potential location for the boutique hotel. He expects that the
facilities will aggregately require approximately ___ (#) acres of property. The business
will have multiple revenue streams, which will allow the business to achieve maximum
profitability by providing all the vacation, recreational and/or business support services

that a guest could want from one location.

Each of our rooms will be equipped with ___ (two?) double beds or a queen bed, and rooms with a second bedroom or kitchenette will be available. We will have a _____ (full-service restaurant?), and ____ . We will be putting in full-service coin-operated laundry facilities along with a self-serve car wash. The _____ (company name) will also have an on-site 24/7 front desk service. We plan to add __ (#) more Boutique Hotel units in ____(year).

The diversity of attractions in _____ County have always drawn a significant number of tourists to the _____ area. In addition to providing information about such locations, we plan to collaborate with tour agencies and businesses throughout the area and offer uniquely targeted packages and special rates.

As the Boutique Hotel becomes established through the peak season, we plan to expand our services to the residents of _____ , in time for the off-season. The adjoining common areas are open creating a large area, ideal for formal or informal gatherings, weddings, and meetings.

Competitive Edge

_____ (company name) will compete well in our market by offering competitive prices, high-quality guest services and a unique ambiance. Our boutique hotel will stand apart from most properties in _____ City because of the value-added amenities that will be hallmarks of our brand of hospitality. These include private club rooms with books, newspapers, magazines, free Wi-Fi, and computer stations; complimentary refreshments throughout the day including Continental breakfast each morning and wine and cheese receptions, evenings from 5 to 8 p.m., complimentary bottles of water in the room, and many other thoughtful touches. Technology will play a major role in our hotels' creative offerings, with a loaded iPad stocked in every room and select rooms will allow guests usage of a Samsung Galaxy S3 smartphone. Internet service will be complimentary on both devices. Each room will feature either Queen or King beds, all with private baths. Each bed will have a leather-tufted headboard, luxury high thread count bed linens, fluffy down pillows, and ultra soft cotton bamboo blankets. Flat screen televisions with DirecTV included, USB compatible electrical outlets, individual refrigerators, and single brew Keurig Coffeemakers will be included in all bedrooms. All rooms will also feature electric fireplaces. Each shower will feature glass mosaic tiling and an ultra-luxurious spa shower. In keeping with our Green efforts all toilets will be low flow to conserve water. Each guest will be provided an RFID keycard to allow them to access the Hotel and their individual room. Security cameras will be placed throughout the property both inside and out for guests' safety and comfort. Furthermore, we will maintain an excellent reputation for trustworthiness and integrity with the community we serve.

The location of _____ (company name) is ideal for a weekend getaway. It is far enough from the city to feel as if a couple is somewhere special, but not so far as to be a tiring journey. The area provides a number of attractions and recreational activities, including _____ and _____ .

____ (company name) has been designed to provide the comfort of a home with the option to partake in the company of the owners or retreat to the seclusion of a comfortable room. The building will retain its historic heritage, while offering the modern amenities expected for a comfortable stay, such as _____ and _____.

We will feature our extensive and well-equipped MICE facilities, including our Meeting Rooms, Incentive, Conference Rooms and Exhibition Halls.

Target Market
Our market research indicates that our target market are travelers between the ages of ___ (25) and ___ (55), married with moderate to high incomes, and homeowners. About 75% of them will have booked accommodations before leaving home and will stay two nights as a getaway from either of ___ (#) urban centers. In addition, there is the potential in this area for business travelers as well as small conferences.

Our target market strategy is based on becoming a destination choice for the people in the _____ area who are looking for a place to relax or recharge. We plan to target the following markets:

1.	Leisure Travelers	2.	Honeymooners
3.	Family reunions	4.	Hunters/Skiers
5.	Drop-in customers	6.	Business travelers

A modest projection for increased unit rental is ___% per year, and since there is no competition within ___ (#) miles. This projection is without any significant increase in advertising or exposure, but is based on the general average increase in tourism.

Subscriptions to various Web directory services will provide international exposure to potential customers for nominal annual fees, plus we will have a website. _____ (company name) will likely see a ___% increase in customers on a yearly basis. Our Boutique Hotel will be quick to develop an excellent reputation because of the work experiences of our owner, _____ (owner name) who has worked in the lodging industry for the last _____ (#) years.

Boutique Hotels, along with other short-term lodging in _____ (city), have been a substantial factor in the area's tourism business. Of the short-term lodgings in _____ (city), _____ (#) are categorized as hotels, ___ (#) as long-term lease facilities (rentals, condos, and houses) and only ___ (#) as hotels, including our business. _____ (Hotels/hotels?) constitute the largest percentage of rental properties in the city in terms of units.

Licensing Requirements
Our company will be licensed by the State of _____. We have already initiated the licensure, permit and insurance certification processes and expect to easily meet the guidelines for providing guest lodging in _____ region of _____ (state).

Marketing Strategy

With the help of an aggressive marketing plan, _____ (company name) expects to experience steady growth. Our promotional strategy includes membership in local and national lodging industry associations. This will enable inclusion into their registries and guidebooks. _____ (company name) also plans to attract its customers through the use of local newspaper advertisements in the getaway weekend section, circulating brochures to tourism offices and travel agents, a systematic series of direct mailings, news releases in local newspapers, a website, online reservation directories, networking with local professional organizations and destination institutions, and Yellow Page ads. We will also become an active member of the local Chamber of Commerce and B&B association.

Return customers and referrals constitute a valuable source of revenue in the lodging industry. We will encourage this by offering exceptional service and maintaining a guest database. We will also offer our past customers special rates and referral incentives. Research indicates that it will also be very important to network with other Boutique Hotel owners and innkeepers in the area and establish a policy to refer customers to one another when alliance partner rooms are full and they can't take on additional guests. It will also be critical to work with the local Convention & Visitors Bureau to get established as a travel destination.

Pricing Strategy

Pricing will be set competitively with a similar business in the first year, but will be raised by ___ (5?)% per year over the next ___ (#) years to reflect our better service and location. Our rooms can be booked by phone, in person, through commissioned travel agents, sales agents or over the internet.

A modest projection for increased unit rental is ___% per year. Competitors in the city have averaged ___% + rental increases over the past _____ (#) years, and the Chamber is forecasting ___% increases for the next ___ (#) years before hitting full capacity. This projection is without any significant increase in advertising or exposure, but is based on the general average increase in tourism. Our two major guest segments are tourists from _____ who traditionally prefer the cozy environment of hotels, and local patrons who need our facilities for various events. Subscriptions to various Web services will provide national and international exposure to potential customers for nominal annual fees.

The Management Team

_____ (company name) will be lead by _____ (owner name) and _____ (co-owner name). _____ (owner name) has a _____ degree from ___ (institution name) and a ____ background within the industry, having spent _____ (#) years with ____ (former employer name or type of business). During this tenure, ___ (he/she) helped grow the business from $_____ in yearly revenue to over $___. ____ (co-owner name) has a ___ background, and while employed by __ was able to increase operating profit by __ percent. These acquired skills, work experiences and educational backgrounds will play a big role in the success of our Boutique Hotel. Additionally, our president, _____ (name), has an extensive knowledge of the _____ area and has identified a niche market retail opportunity to make this venture highly successful, combining his ___ (#) years of work experience in a variety of businesses. _____ (owner name) will manage all aspects of the business and service development to ensure effective customer responsiveness while monitoring day-to-day operations. Qualified and trained sales associates personally trained by _____ (owner name) in customer service skills will provide additional support services. Support staff will be added as seasonal or extended hours mandate.

Recap of Past Successful Accomplishments
_____ (company name) is uniquely qualified to succeed due to the following past successes:
1.   **Entrepreneurial Track Record**: The owners and management team have helped to launch numerous successful ventures, including a _____.

2.   **Key Milestones Achieved**: The founders have invested $___ to-date to staff the company, build the core technology, acquire starting inventory, test market the _____ (product/service), realize sales of $_____ and launch the website.

Start-up Funding

_____ (owner name) will financially back the new business venture with an initial investment of $ _____, and will be the principal owner. Additional funding in the amount of $_____ will be sought from _____, a local commercial bank, with a SBA loan guarantee. This money will be needed to start the company. This loan will provide start-up capital, financing for a selected site lease, remodeling renovations, inventory supply purchases, pay for permits and licensing, purchase furnishings and working capital to cover expenses during the first year of operation.

Financial Projections

We plan to open for business on _____ (date), and start with an initial registration of ___ guests. _____ (company name) is forecasted to gross in excess of $___ in sales in its first year of operation, ending ___ (month/ year). Profit margins are forecasted to be at about ____ percent. Second year operations will produce a net profit of $___. This will be generated from an investment of $___ in initial capital. It is expected that payback of our total invested capital will be realized in less than __ (#) months of operation. It is further forecasted that cash flow becomes positive from operations in year ___ (one/two?). We project that our net profits will increase from $___ to over $ __ over the next three years.

We are assuming an initial capital start-up of $_____ for operating expenses. We estimate average monthly fixed costs to be at $_____ ($_____ for expenses and $_____ for interest payments). Peak and off-season will have significant impact on the monthly earnings. For the first year, on-season revenues will offset off-season losses. As _____ (company name) builds its market position among the local patrons, we anticipate that off-season revenues will be enough to break even during that season.

Financial Profile Summary

Key Indicator	2017	2018	2019
Total Revenue			
Expenses			
Gross Margin			
Operating Income			
Net Income			
EBITDA			

EBITDA = Revenue - Expenses (excluding tax, interest, depreciation and amortization)
EBITDA is essentially net income with interest, taxes, depreciation, and amortization added back to it, and can be used to analyze and compare profitability between companies and industries because it eliminates the effects of financing and accounting decisions.

Gross Margin (%) = (Revenue - Cost of Goods Sold) / Revenue

Net Income = Total revenue - Cost of sales - Other expenses - Tax

Financial Projections Key Assumptions

Initial Capital Required:
    $____K including $____K for building improvement $___K for equipment and the remainder for start-up working capital.

Revenue Growth:
    Brisk growth in years 1 and 2 for _____ (type of product or service) and wholesale business due to small revenue base.

Labor Expenses:
    Cash burn rate for labor expenses is approximately $____K per month, which is ___ (60?)% of total. This includes all employees. Labor expenses include payroll taxes and health benefits for employees.

Operating Expenses:
    Inventory Cost of Goods Sold (ICOGS) is modeled starting at ___ (35?)% of revenue, narrowing to ___ (31?)% by year 3. Remaining expenses represent predictable fixed costs such as rent, utilities, insurance and equipment maintenance. We have a small amount of discretionary marketing expenses that is less that ___ (5?)% of total cash burn.

Balance Sheet Considerations:
    Accounts payable and accounts receivable aging assumes net 30 for ___ (75?)% of balances with the remaining paid in ___ (15?) days.

Working Capital:
    Initial working capital of $____K is enough to cover six months fixed costs (people and non-ICOGS). A working capital infusion will be needed in Year 2 that is modeled as equity but could be financed via debt (line of credit) with _____ (company name).

Exit Strategy

If the business is very successful, ____ (owner name) may seek to sell the business to a third party for a significant earnings multiple. Most likely, the Company will hire a qualified business broker to sell the business on behalf of _____ (company name). Based on historical numbers, the business could generate a sales premium of up to __(#) times earnings.

Summary
Through a combination of a proven business model and a strong management team to guide the organization, _____ (company name) will be a long lasting, profitable business. We believe our ability to create future product and service opportunities and growth will only be limited by our imagination and our ability to attract talented people who understand the concept of branding.

1.1.0   Tactical Objectives   (select - 3)

The following tactical objectives will specify quantifiable results and involve activities that can be easily tracked. They will also be realistic, tied to specific marketing strategies and serve as a good benchmark to evaluate our marketing plan success. (Select Choices)

1. Obtain a bank loan of $_____ to cover selected renovations, furnishing purchases start-up and initial operating costs for _____ (company name).
2. Open the _____ (company name) as a "turn key operation" on _____ (date).
3. Demonstrate a minimum of ___(70)% occupancy averaged throughout year ____.
4. Through incentives and increased exposure on the Internet, we plan to increase off-season occupancy by ____ (30?)% the _____ (second) year.
5. To create a company whose primary goal is to exceed guest expectations.
6. To develop a cash flow that is capable of paying all salaries , as well as grow the business, by the end of the _____ (first?) year.
7. To be an active networking participant and productive member of the community by _____ (date).
8. Create over _____ (30?) % of business revenues from repeat customers by _____ (date).
9. Achieve an overall guest satisfaction rate of ____ (98?) % by _____ (date).
10. Get a business website designed, built and operational by _____ (date), which will include an online shopping cart.
11. Achieve total sales revenues of $_____ in _____ (year).
12. Achieve ____ (30)% occupancy in the first year of operation.
13. Realize gross margins higher than _____ (85?) percent by _____ (date).
14. Achieve net income more than ___ (10?) percent of net sales by the ____ (#) year.
15. Increase overall sales by _____ (20?) percent from prior year through superior service and word-of-mouth referrals.
16. Reduce the cost of new guest acquisition by ___ % to $ ___ by _____ (date).
17. Turn in profits from the _____ (#) month of operations.
18. Expand our marketing campaign to include all of the _____ (city) area, including _____, _____ and _____.
19. To pursue a growth rate of ____ (20?) % per year for the first ____ (#) years.
20. The reservation of at least ___ (#) different families in the first _____ (#) months.
21. Maintain a ____ percent occupancy rate throughout the ____ (first/second) year.

22. Maintain a ____ (85?)% occupancy rate during the peak periods.
23. Enable the owner to draw a salary of $ _____ by the end of year ____ (one?).
24. To reach cash break-even by the end of year ____ (one?).
25. Increase market share to ___ percent over the next ___ (#) months.
26. Become one of the top ___ (#) players in the emerging _____ category in __ (#) months.
27. Increase Operating Profit by ___ percent versus the previous year.
28. Achieve market share leadership in the Boutique Hotel category by ____ (date).
29. Achieve a room occupancy rate higher than _____ (70?) percent.
30. Achieve an Average Daily Rate (ADR) rate of $ _____ (200.00?).

1.1.1   Strategic Objectives

We will seek to work toward the accomplishment of the following strategic objectives: (Select)
1. Improve the overall quality of Boutique Hotel services.
2. Make the Boutique Hotel experience better.
3. Improve access for seniors.
4. Strengthen personal relationships with guests.
5. Maintain affordability.
6. Give guests more control over their package options.
7. Foster a spirit of innovation.
8. Increase exposure using Internet technology and direct advertising to _____ regions of the United States.
9. Increase off-season use by investing into other uses for property (cater parties, receptions, weddings, etc.).
10. Maintain positive, steady growth each quarter.
11. Experience a growth in new guests who are turned into long-term customers.
12. Realize an increase in occupancy rates each subsequent year.
13. Achieve double digit growth rate for each future year.
14. Reduce the variable costs per guest.
15. Continue to decrease the fixed costs.

1.2.0   Mission Statement   (select)

Our Mission Statement is a written statement that spells out our organization's overall goal, provides a sense of direction and acts as a guide to decision making for all levels of management. In developing the following mission statement we will encourage input from employees, volunteers, and other stakeholders, and publicize it broadly in our website and other marketing materials.

The following are guidelines for preparing our mission statement:
1. Use terms that are understandable to employees.

2. Word our mission to inspire the human spirit, as a person should read the statement and feel good about working for the hotel.
3. Catchy (but not cliché) slogans can help people remember the mission.
4. Keep the mission statement as short as possible.
5. Widely distribute the mission.
6. Communicate the mission to employees regularly.

Source:
http://scholarship.sha.cornell.edu/cgi/viewcontent.cgi?article=1295&context=articles

The mission of _____ (company name) is to provide the finest Boutique Hotel experience. Our services will exceed the expectations of our customers. We will realize 100% guest satisfaction, and generate long-term profits through professional referrals and repeat business.

Our mission of _____ (company name) is to become the number one Boutique Hotel of choice with visitors to _____ area. To become a recognized leader on a national level for its expansive, original, amazing, sensual, social, discovery filled, intriguing, and luxurious boutique hotel accommodations.

Our mission is to successfully build, promote and provide quality Boutique Hotel accommodations for the _____ region. Our goal is to set ourselves apart from the competition by making guest satisfaction our number one priority and to provide guest service that is responsive, informed and respectful. We are committed to giving our guests a family friendly, personalized, affordable, and a uniquely joyful experience. We value each customer and are constantly striving to keep our facilities in the best possible condition. We believe in personable, prompt, respectful, and attentive service at all times. It is our goal to employ competent , caring and well-informed individuals who are responsible to the needs of our guests, and the communities we serve. Our mission is to create an environment of pampered luxury that surpasses the standard fare for ____ (city).

1.2.1   Mantra

We will create a mantra for our organization that is three or four words long. Its purpose will be to help employees truly understand why the organization exists. Our mantra will serve as a framework through which to make decisions about product and business direction. It will boil the key drivers of our company down to a sentence that defines our most important areas of focus and resemble a statement of purpose or significance.
Our Mantra is _____

1.2.2   Core Values Statement

The following Core Values will help to define our organization, guide our behavior, underpin operational activity and shape the strategies we will pursue in the face of various challenges and opportunities. We will fulfill our mission through our commitment to:

Being respectful and ethical.

Building enduring partnerships with networking associates, local businesses, etc.

Forging long-term, mutually beneficial relationships with guests.

Seeking innovation in our boutique hotel industry.

Practicing accountability to our colleagues and stakeholders.

Pursuing continuous learning as individuals and as a business entity.

Performing tasks on time to satisfy the needs of our internal and external clients.

Taking active part in the organization to meet the objectives and the establishment of continuous and lasting relationships.

Offering professional treatment to our guests, employees, shareholders, and the community.

Continuing pursuit of new technologies for the development of the projects that add value for our guests, employees, shareholders, and the community.

1.3 Vision Statement   (select)

The following Vision Statement will communicate both the purpose and values of our organization. For employees, it will give direction about how they are expected to behave and inspires them to give their best. Shared with customers, it will shape customers' understanding of why they should work with our organization.

_____ (company name) will strive to become one of the most respected and favored Boutique Hotel lodging providers in the _____ area. It is our desire to become an historic landmark business in _____ (city), ____ (state), and become known not only for the quality of our personalized guest services, but also for our community and charity involvement.

_____ (company name) is dedicated to operating with a constant enthusiasm for learning about the Boutique Hotel business, being receptive to implementing new and creative ideas, and maintaining a willingness to adapt to changing target market needs and wants. To develop new strategies for the delivery of Boutique Hotel services and the management of scarce resources. To be an active and vocal member of the community, and to provide continual reinvestment through participation in community activities and financial contributions.

In five years,_____ (company name) will be an area leader in the Boutique Hotel industry, and plans will be developed and implemented to pursue national business through the franchising of our unique business model concept.

1.4 Keys to Success

In broad terms, the success factors relate to providing what our clients want, and doing what is necessary to be better than our competitors. The following critical success factors are areas in which our organization must excel in order to operate successfully and achieve our objectives:

1. Treat the guest properly so they are amazed at the level of attention that they receive.
2. Continue to build brand awareness which will drive new customers.
3. Gain operating efficiencies.
4. Develop a strong relationship with the local University.
5. Service our client needs with personalized attention and expert knowledge.
6. Launch a website to showcase our services and guest testimonials, provide helpful information and facilitate online registrations.
7. Local community involvement and business partnerships.
8. Conduct a targeted and cost-effective marketing campaign that seeks to differentiate our Boutique Hotel services from traditional offerings.
9. Institute a program of profit sharing among all employees to reduce employee turnover and improve productivity.
10. Control costs and manage budgets at all times in accordance with company goals.
11. Institute management processes and controls to insure the consistent replication of operations.
12. Recruit screened employees with a passion for delivering exceptional service.
13. Institute an employee training to insure the best techniques are consistently practiced.
14. Network aggressively within the community, as word of mouth will be our most powerful advertising asset.
15. Maintaining a highly regarded reputation for excellence in guest service   and community involvement.
16. Adhere to our strategic business plan for growth and expansion, and reinvesting in the business and its employees.
17. Competitive pricing in conjunction with a differentiated service business model.
18. Effective collaboration with other community service providers.
19. Build our brand awareness, which will drive customers to increase their usage of our services and make referrals.
20. Business planning with the flexibility to make changes based on gaining new insightful perspectives as we proceed.
21. Build trust by circulating and adhering to our Code of Ethics and Service Guarantees.
22. Be consistently available to solve problems and provide personalized support.
23. Get the following basics right to generate repeat business: a really comfortable bed, a high level of cleanliness, excellent breakfast and a warm welcome.
24. Must ask guests how they found our Boutique Hotel to focus marketing dollars.
25. Must clearly define family and guest areas and publish operating policies.
26. Offer guests something upon their arrival, to make them feel at home and to allow

you to answer any questions they may have.

27. Keep the outside grounds and the rooms as clean and litter-free as possible.
28. Invest in landscaping and parking that create an inviting environment.
29. Hire a reliable staff that is well versed in guest service in order to maintain a good reputation and build referrals and repeat business.
30. Have friendly staff manning the front desk and greeting your visitors.
31. Recognize that different seasons tend to draw different leisure travelers with different wants and needs.
32. Interview representatives of the local visitor bureau, Chamber of Commerce and local event and attraction operators to learn about local leisure demand.
33. Strategize the right combination of amenities, atmosphere, location, and services that will be right for our targeted customers.
34. Develop a company culture based on a hospitality mindset, and putting the needs and wants of the guests first.
35. Continuously improve every aspect of our service quality and hospitality experience by keeping up with technology.
36. Appoint of a full-time Training Manager who is dedicated to training the staff on soft skills and all other skill sets needed to excel in the hospitality industry.
37. Recognize that our people are the most important asset of our business.
38. Nothing is more important to a guest checking into a hotel than a clean room.
39. Getting the right team in place at the front desk will transform how our hotel operates.
40. Stay true to the chosen positioning strategy, by determining which segments of the market are viable for our hotel, to ensure that all marketing strategies are cost effective and actually reach the target audience.
41. The impeccable guest service is expected to be consistent.
42. Celebrate the distinctive decor, ambiance, culinary traditions and hospitality of the local culture in which the boutique hotel is situated. Be reflective of the context which attracts visitors to the destination in the first place by immersing the hotel in the local, organic culture.
43. Provide additional options for customers booking, by creating partnerships with local attractions, tours, restaurants,… and offer them as add-ons after the customer has booked with us.
Source: https://hetras.wordpress.com/2013/03/15/7-digital-marketing-tips-to-differentiate-your-hotel-online/
44. The boutique model depends more on filling rooms than a big hotel does, because in a smaller building, every dollar must be wrung out of the facility and there are fewer economies of scale opportunities.
45. There is a need to not only to deliver a brand experience with continuity, but also with a brand story.
46. Do everything possible to understand would-be guests, including listening to what the customers want via surveys, holding focus groups, researching broader trends in the market, and evaluating the competitive set to form a clear, coherent set of goals.

47. Make local residents feel like they are welcome even if they are not staying at our boutique hotel by making a connection to the look and feel of the neighborhood and building a restaurant and temporary office space on the ground floor.

48. Because, boutique hotels do not provide enough amenities to be destinations in themselves, they must rely on finding the right location to blend into and complement.

49. Travelers expect the service to match the culture of the country and the specific area.

50. Provide guests with a well-trained and engaging staff.

51. Employ marketing designed to keep the memories alive before, during and after each guest's stay.
Resource: http://madiganpratt.com/about/approach.html

52. Make use of the fact that the small hotel audience relies more strongly on offers and recommendations via platforms such as TripTdvisor, laterooms.com, lastminute.com, Groupon, Facebook, and blogs.
Source: https://www.reviewpro.com/blog/small-hotel-marketing/

53. Explore ways to improve your ranking on TripAdvisor.com
Source: https://www.reviewpro.com/segments/hotels/#demoblock

54. Always remembers that the largest driving force in return customers or repeat business is an overemphasis on service.
Source: www.inc.com/guides/2010/10/how-to-start-a-boutique-hotel.html

55. Use your online booking engine or front desk or other designated area to take advantage of point-of-sale up-sell and cross-sell opportunities, such as car rentals or tickets to special events or spa treatments, and/or excursions and tours.

2.0   Company Summary

_____(company name) is a start-up _____ (Corporation/Limited Liability Company) consisting of __(#) principle officers with combined industry experience of __ (#) years.

The owner of the company will be investing a significant amount of ___ (his/her) own capital into the company and will also be seeking a loan to cover start-up costs and future growth.

_____ (company name) will be located in a ___ (purchased/rented) ____(suite/complex) in the _____on _____ (address) in ____ (city), _____ (state). The facilities _____ (will be/were designed) to meet strict design standards, under the supervision of the _____ County Health Department an Fire Safety Commissioner.

The _____ (company name), located in the recently opened _____ area, will have ___ (#) ____(#)-bedroom units with adjacent parking, fully-equipped kitchens, laundry facilities and stone fireplaces. Our intimate-feeling boutique hotel will cater to people who want personalized service, accommodations that fit their lifestyle, and/or are eager to try something new.

The company plans to use its existing contacts and guest base to generate short-term sales. Its long-term profitability will rely on focusing on referrals, networking within community organizations and a comprehensive marketing program that includes public relations activities and a structured referral program.

Sales are expected to reach $_____ within the first year and to grow at a conservative rate of ____ (20?) percent during the next two to five years.

Facilities Renovations
The necessary renovations will begin on _____ (date) and are itemized as follows:

	Estimate
Create landscape/garden	_____
Upgrade heating, air conditioning & ventilation systems.	_____
Install ceiling fans in every room.	_____
Kitchen Upgrade	_____
Bathroom Additions	_____
Expand water heater capacity	_____
Flooring Installations	_____
Noise Control/soundproofing	_____
Install bathroom safety devices.	_____
Install handicap accessibility features.	_____
Install fire protection and security devices.	_____
Build storage areas.	_____
Install guest closet organization systems.	_____
Install gas fireplaces in every room.	_____
Interior painting and other general room repairs	_____

Exterior Painting _____
Install adequate interior and exterior lighting. _____
Install cable, DSL and phone lines to every room. _____
Install office equipment. _____
Create exercise room _____
Create library/media room. _____
Create morning/breakfast dining room. _____
Create covered porch _____
Redecorate _____
Other _____ _____
Total: _____

Operations

_____ (company name) will open for business on _____ (date) and will maintain the following check-in/check-out business hours:

Monday through Thursday:	_____	(7 to 7 ?)
Friday:	_____	(7 to 8 ?)
Saturday:	_____	(8 to 5 ?)
Sunday:	_____	(?)

The company will invest in guest relationship management software (CRM) to track sales and collect guest information, including names, email addresses, key reminder dates and preferences. This information will be used with email, e-newsletter and direct mail campaigns to build personalized fulfillment programs, establish guest loyalty and drive revenue growth.

2.0.1   Traction   (optional)

We will include this section because investors expect to see some traction, both before and after a funding event and investors tend to judge past results as a good indicator of future projections. It will also show that we can manage our operations and develop a business model capable of funding inventory purchases. Traction will be the best form of market research and present evidence of guest acceptance.

Period	_____
Product/Service Focus	_____
Our Sales to Date:	_____
Our Number of Users to Date:	_____
Number of Repeat Users	_____
Number of Pending Orders:	_____
Value of Pending Orders:	_____
Reorder Cycle:	_____
Key Reference Sites	_____
Mailing List Subscriptions	_____
Competitions/Awards Won	_____

Notable Product Reviews   _____

Actual Percent Gross Profit Margin   _____

Industry Average: GPM   _____

Actual B/(W) Industry Average   _____

Note: Percent Gross Profit Margin equals the sales receipts less the cost of goods sold divided by sales receipts multiplied by 100.

2.1 Company Ownership

_____ (company name) is a _____ (Sole-proprietorship /Corporation/Limited Liability Corporation (LLC)) and is registered to the principal owner, _____ (owner name). The company was formed in _____ (month) of ____ (year).

It will be registered as a Subchapter S to avoid double taxation, with ownership allocated as follows: _____ (owner name) ____ % and _____ (owner name) ____ %.

The owner is a _____ (year) graduate of _____ (institution name), in _____ (city, ____ (state), with a _____ degree.

He/she has ____ years of executive experience in the _____ (?) industry as a _____, performing the following roles: _____
_____.

His/her major accomplishments include: _____
_____.

Ownership Breakdown:

Shareholder Name	Responsibilities	Number and Class of Shares	Percent Ownership

The remainder of the issued and outstanding common shares are retained by the Company for ___(future distribution / allocation under the Company's employee stock option plan).

Shareholder Loans

The Company currently has outstanding shareholder loans in the aggregate sum of $_____. The following table sets out the details of the shareholder loans.

Shareholder Name	Loan Amount	Loan Date	Balance Outstanding

Directors

The Company's Board of Directors, which is made up of highly qualified business and industry professionals, will be a valuable asset to the Company and be instrumental to its development. The following persons will make up the Board of Directors of the Company:

Name of Person	Educational Background	Past Industry Experience	Other Companies Served

Note: As owners of the real estate property, we plan to lease the property to our Boutique Hotel Corporation, and collect a monthly rent from the business.

2.2   Company Licensing & Liability Protection

The business will consider the need to acquire the following types of insurances. This will require extensive comparison shopping, through several insurance brokers, listed with our state's insurance department:

1. Workman's Compensation,
2. B &B Commercial Coverage: Property & Liability Insurance
3. Health insurance.
4. Commercial Auto Insurance
5. Household Personal Property Insurance
6. State Unemployment Insurance
7. Surety Bonds
8. Disability Income Protection

Workman's compensation covers employees in case of harm attributed to the workplace. The property and liability insurance protects the building from theft, fire, natural disasters, and being sued by a third party. Employee health insurance will be provided for the full time employees. Professional Liability Insurance is important when a business is involved with contracts.

Disability Income Protection-a form of health insurance in case you become disabled.
Liability Insurance includes protection in the face of day-to day accidents, unforeseen results of normal business activities, and allegations of abuse or molestation, food poisoning, or exposure to infectious disease.
Property Insurance - Property Insurance should take care of the repairs less whatever deductible you have chosen.
Loss of Income Insurance will replace our income during the time the business is shut-down. Generally this coverage is written for a fixed amount of monthly income for a fixed number of months.

To help save on insurance cost and claims, management will do the following:

1. Stress employee safety in our employee handbook.
2. Screen employees with interview questionnaires and will institute pre-employment drug tests and comprehensive background checks.
3. Videotape our equipment and inventory for insurance purposes.
4. Create an operations manual that shares safe techniques.
5. Limit the responsibilities that we choose to accept in our contracts.
6. Consider the financial impact of assuming the exposure ourselves.
7. Establish loss prevention programs to reduce the hazards that cause losses.
8. Consider taking higher deductibles on anything but that which involves liability insurance because of third-party involvement.
9. Stop offering services that require expensive insurance coverage or require signed releases from clients using those services.
10. Improve employee training and initiate training sessions for safety.
11. Require Certificate of Insurance from all subcontractors.
12. Make staff responsible for a portion of any damages they cause.
13. We will investigate the setting-up of a partial self-insurance plan.
14. Convince underwriters that our past low claims are the result of our ongoing safety programs and there is reason to expect our claims will be lower than industry averages in the future.
15. At each renewal, we will develop a service agreement with our broker and get their commitment to our goals, such as a specific reduction in the number of incidents.
16. We will assemble a risk control team, with people from both sides of our business, and broker representatives will serve on the committee as well.
17. When an employee is involved in an accident, we will insist on getting to the root cause of the incident and do everything possible to prevent similar incidents from re-occurring.
18. At renewal, we will consult with our brokers to develop a cost-saving strategy and decide whether to bid out our coverage for competitive quotes or stick with our current carrier.
19. We will set-up a captive insurance program, as a risk management technique, where our business will form its own insurance company subsidiary to finance its retained losses in a formal structure.
20. Review named assets (autos and equipment), drivers and/or key employees identified on policies to make sure these assets and people are still with our company.
21. As a portion of our business changes, that is, closes, operations change, or outsourcing occurs, we will eliminate unnecessary coverage.
22. We will make sure our workforce is correctly classified by our workers' compensation insurer and liability insurer because our premiums are based on the type of workers used.
23. We will become active in Trade Organizations or Professional Associations, because as a benefit of membership, our business may receive substantial insurance discounts.
24. We will adopt health specific changes to our work place, such as adopting a no smoking policy at our company and allow yoga or weight loss classes to be held

in our break room.
25. We will consider a partial reimbursement of health club membership as a benefit.
26. We will find out what employee training will reduce rates and get our employees involved in these programs.
27. Hire a full-time security and safety manager and stay OSHA compliant.

The required business insurance package will be provided by _____ (insurance carrier name) . The business will open with a ____ (#) million dollar liability insurance policy, with an annual premium cost of $ _____ ..

All required licenses to own and operate a Boutique Hotel business will be obtained through the local city and county government offices. Each state has its own guidelines for the hospitality staff qualifications, proper physical environment, and proper health and safety practices. Additionally, any zoning restrictions will need to be addressed, including the fact that our clients should be considered as guests, with pre-screened reservations, rather than boarders. Contact your local economic development center, chamber of commerce, county Cooperative Extension Service office, small business development center, or local community or technical school.

In some states, a Boutique Hotel may have to purchase a hotel license. The purpose of this license is to make sure that any lodgings with five or more bedrooms comply with the state fire marshal requirements for safety. Check with your state fire marshal's office to see if a special hospitality license is required for a Boutique Hotel.

The Boutique Hotel business will need to acquire the following special licenses, accreditations, certifications and permits:
1. A sales tax license is required through the State Department of Revenue.
2. Occupancy and/or room taxes.
2. A County and/or City Occupational License.
3. Business License from State Licensing Agency
4. Permits from the Fire Department and State Health Department.
5. Building Code Inspections by the County Building Department.
6. Adequacy of off-street parking.
7. Sign Permit

As a Resort Hotel we will need to research the following types of required State License(s):
1. Room rentals are subject to a __% use tax license.
   Contact your state's Department of Treasury or Revenue
2. Personalized sales tax returns
   Contact Department of Treasury
3. Permits for cigarettes, tobacco, and motor fuel sales
   Department of Treasury
4. License for public swimming and spa pools
   Contact Department of Environmental Quality, Water Bureau, Drinking Water and Environmental Health Section

5. License for restaurant facilities
   Contact local health department or Department of Agriculture.
6. License for sales of beer, wine or liquor
   Contact Liquor Control Commission for a Resort Liquor License
   Department of Licensing and Regulatory Affairs
7. Ski-lift safety license
   Contact Department of Licensing and Regulatory Affairs
8. Construction Permits
   Contact Bureau of Construction Codes
   Department of Licensing and Regulatory Affairs
   Department of Environmental Quality about land use
   Transportation Department for road alteration permits
   Local building inspector for general approval.
9. Tourism groups may add a "surcharge" to all room rentals in their market
   area to pay for tourism promotion activities.
10. Cabaret Dance Floor License
11. Spa Treatments
    Contact Health Department for sanitary inspections.

Note: In most states, you are legally required to obtain a business license, and a dba certificate. A business license is usually a flat tax assessment and a percentage of your gross income. A dba stands for Doing Business As, and it is the registration of your trade name if you have one. You will be required to register your trade name within 30 days of starting your business. Instead of registering a dba, you can simply form an LLC or Corporation and it will have the same effect, namely register your business name.

Resources:
Workers Compensation Regulations
   http://www.dol.gov/owcp/dfec/regs/compliance/wc.htm#IL
New Hire Registration and Reporting
   www.homeworksolutions.com/new-hire-reporting-information/
State Tax Obligations
   www.sba.gov/content/learn-about-your-state-and-local-tax-obligations

Notes: If we plan to offer guided tours of the area in our vehicle, we will need to secure a chauffeur's license and livery insurance.
   If we are unable to secure a license to cook for guests, breakfast will consist of fruits, cereals, pastries and coffee.
   Compliance with the American Disabilities Act will require ramps, wheelchair access, and special bathing facilities.

Note: Check with your local County Clerk and state offices or Chamber of Commerce to make sure you follow all legal protocols for setting up and running your business.

Note: To find out about your local business licensing office, visit SBA.gov. This government website compiles information on business licenses and permits at the state level.

Note: Facilities like hotels often require review by a City Planning Commission before a business license will be granted.

Resources:

Block Insurance   www.blockinsurance.com
Insurance Information Institute   www.iii.org/individuals/business/
National License Directory   www.sba.gov/licenses-and-permits
The Society & Fidelity Association of America   www.surety.org
Markel Insurance Company   www.inninsurance.com/Pages/default.aspx
Find Law   http://smallbusiness.findlaw.com/starting-business/starting-business-
                licenses-permits/starting-business-licenses-permits-guide.html
Business Licenses   www.iabusnet.org/business-licenses
National Association of Surety Bond Producers   www.nasbp.org
Legal Zoom   www.legalzoom.com

Resort Hotel Association (RHA)   www.rhainsure.com/
A not-for-profit insurance association. Specializes in insurance programs that address the risks unique to independent resorts, hotels, city clubs and spas. Coverages include:

Casualty Insurance: General Liability, Business Auto and Umbrella Liability
Commercial General Liability Insurance
Coverage for numerous exposures unique to the hospitality/resort industry, including
        Garagekeepers Legal Liability
        Liquor Liability
        Innkeepers Liability
        Saddle Animals, Spas, Watercraft, and Winter Sports Activities
        Terrorism Coverage
Business Automobile Insurance
Coverage for vehicles registered or leased by the resorts, including private passenger
        vans, buses, and even antique automobiles. Coverage included for hired and non-
        owned vehicles.

Executive Liability Program
This Executive Liability Program includes:
        Directors & Officers (D&O)
        Employment Practices Liability Insurance (EPLI)
        Fiduciary Liability

Group Personal Umbrella
This program provides coverage to the policy-holder for their and their family's everyday activities that could put personal assets at risk – driving personal autos, activities in the home or service on a not-for-profit board, to name only a few.
        Coverage included for:
                multiple residences
                vehicles
                watercraft

youthful drivers

Personal coverage available to resort owners, shareholders, directors, officers and employees of RHA member properties

Coverage for non-profit board participation.

Pollution Insurance

Pollution Legal Liability Insurance covers key exposures, including:

Mold / Microbial Matter

Legionella

Dry-cleaning / Laundry Operations

Dining / Food Service Operations

Golf Courses

Landscaping / Pesticide Application

Underground Storage Tanks / Financial Responsibility Requirements

2.3   Start-up To-Do Checklist

1. Describe your business concept and model, with special emphasis on planned multiple revenue streams and services to be offered.
2. Create Business Plan and Opening Menu of Products and Services.
3. Determine our start up costs for a Boutique Hotel business, and operating capital and capital budget needs.
4. Seek and evaluate alternative financing options, including SBA guaranteed loan, equipment leasing, social networking loan (www.prosper.com) and/or a family loan (www.virginmoney.com).
5. Do a name search: Check with County Clerk Office or Department of Revenue and Secretary of State to see if the proposed name of business is available.
6. Decide on a legal structure for business.
   Common legal structure options include Sole Proprietorship, Partnership, Corporation or Limited Liability Corporation (LLC).
7. Make sure you contact your State Department of Revenue, Secretary of State, and the Internal Revenue Service to secure EIN Number and file appropriate paperwork. Also consider filing for Sub-Chapter S status with the Federal government to avoid the double taxation of business profits.
8. Protect name and logo with trademarks, if plan is to go national.
9. Find a suitable location with proper zoning.
10. Research necessary permits and requirements your local government imposes on your type of business. (Refer to: www.business.org)
11. Call for initial inspections to determine what must be done to satisfy Fire Marshall, and Building Inspector requirements.
12. Adjust our budget based on build-out requirements.
13. Negotiate lease or property purchase contract.
14. Obtain a building permit.
15. Obtain Federal Employee Identification Number (FEIN).
16. Obtain State Sales Tax ID/Exempt Certificate.

17. Open a Business Checking Account.
18. Obtain Merchant Credit Card /PayPal Account.
19. Obtain City and County Business Licenses
20. Create a prioritized list for equipment, furniture and décor items.
21. Comparison shop and arrange for appropriate insurance coverage with product liability insurance, public liability insurance, commercial property insurance and worker's compensation insurance.
22. Locate and purchase all necessary equipment and furniture prior to final inspections.
23. Get contractor quotes for required alterations.
24 Manage the alterations process.
25. Obtain information and price quotes from possible supply distributors.
26. Set a tentative opening date.
27. Install 'Coming Soon' sign in front of building and begin word-of-mouth advertising campaign.
28. Document the preparation, project and payment process flows.
29. Create your accounting, purchasing, payroll, marketing, loss prevention, employee screening and other management systems.
30. Start the employee interview process based on established job descriptions and interview criteria.
31. Contact and interview the following service providers: uniform service, security service, trash service, utilities, telephone, credit card processing, bookkeeping, cleaning services, etc.
32. Schedule final inspections for premises.
33. Correct inspection problems and schedule another inspection.
34. Set a Grand Opening date after a month of regular operations to get the bugs out of the processes.
35. Make arrangements for website design.
36. Train staff.
37. Schedule a couple of practice lessons for friends and interested prospects.
38. Be accessible for direct guest feedback.
39. Distribute comment cards and surveys to solicit more constructive feedback.
40. Remain ready and willing to change your business concept and offerings to suit the needs of your actual customer base.

2.3.1 EMPLOYER RESPONSIBILITIES CHECKLIST

1. Apply for your SS-4 Federal Employer Identification Number (EIN) from the Internal Revenue Service. An EIN can be obtained via telephone, mail or online.
2. Register with the State's Department of Labor (DOL) as a new employer. State Employer Registration for Unemployment Insurance, Withholding, and Wage Reporting should be completed and sent to the address that appears on the form. This registration is required of all employers for the purpose of determining whether the applicants are subject to state unemployment insurance taxes.

3. Obtain Workers Compensation and Disability Insurance from an insurer. The insurance company will provide the required certificates that should be displayed.
4. Order Federal Tax Deposit Coupons – Form 8109 – if you didn't order these when you received your EIN. To order, call the IRS at 1-800-829-1040; you will need to give your EIN. You may want to order some blanks sent for immediate use until the pre-printed ones are complete. Also ask for the current Federal Withholding Tax Tables (Circular A) – this will explain how to withhold and remit payroll taxes, and file reports.
5. Order State Withholding Tax Payment Coupons. Also ask for the current Withholding Tax Tables.
6. Have new employees complete an I-9 Employment Eligibility Verification form. You should have all employees complete this form prior to beginning work. Do not send it to Immigration and Naturalization Service – just keep it with other employee records in your files.
7. Have employees complete aW-4 Employees Withholding Allowance Certificate.

2.4.0   Company Location

_____ (company name) will be located at _____ (address) in _____ (city), ___ (state). It is situated on a _____ (turnpike/street/avenue) just minutes from _____ (benchmark location), in the neighborhood of _____.

The location has the following demand generating advantages:
(Select Choices)
It is easy to locate and accessible to a number of major roadways.
High lodging demand in the area.
Adequate off-street parking.
Proximity to _____ convention centers and tourist attractions.
Proximity to _____ college/institution events.
Proximity to businesses in same affinity class with same ideal client profiles.
Reasonable rent.
Proximity to _____ festivals.
Proximity to _____ recreational and entertainment activities.
Shortage of lodging providers in the area.
Similar businesses have had a good track record in this area.
Limited number of direct competitors.

Our chosen location will be attractive, accessible and offer unspoiled natural features including lakes, streams, forest, etc. Surrounding land uses that affect area aesthetics, noise, safety and accessibility to local attractions and businesses will be beneficial to our Boutique Hotel.

We will use the following parameters to describe our location: **Description**
1.   Lake quality (water quality, fishing reputation, aesthetic, size)   _____

2.	Weather conditions (temperatures and snow conditions)	_____
3.	Aesthetics of property (trees, privacy, grass, waterfront)	_____
4.	Adjacent land uses	_____
5.	Proposed developments in area	_____
6.	Services available nearby (food, fuel, shopping)	_____
7.	Tourist attractions (museums, historical sites, recreation)	_____
8.	Zoning restrictions	_____
9.	Local events (sports tournaments, festivals, conventions)	_____
10.	Accessibility of resort	_____
11.	Quality of roads leading to the resort	_____

2.4.1   Company Facilities

_____ (company name) signed a _____ (#) year lease for _____ (#) square foot of space with the owners of the home. The cost is very reasonable at $____/sq. foot. We also have the option of expanding into an additional _____ sq. ft. of space.

The facilities will greatly influence the market image of our resort and the amount visitors are willing to pay for accommodation and services. Our facility will present a warm charm, innovative appearance, excellent condition, and a diversity of types of units.

The following will be a description of our facilities:
1. Age of facilities   _____
2. Charm and character of facilities   _____
3. Exterior appearance and condition   _____
4. Interior appearance and condition   _____
5. Types of units   _____
6. Cleanliness   _____
7. ADA requirements   _____

It will be very important to create an interesting and welcoming environment in our guest rooms. We will use the following approaches to create a distinctive guest room look:
1. Ornamentation   2. Quality flooring materials
3. Luxury bed linens   4. Bathroom amenities
5. Selection of novels and magazines   6. A single stem vase with a flower
7. Tea and coffee making facilities.   8. Wall Decor
8. Quality Furniture

The facility will feature the following in-room amenities:
1. DSL Access   2. Cable TV
3. DVD Player   4. Ceiling Fans
5. Computer Workstation   6. _____

Our facility will offer the following services and amenities: (select/add/describe)
1. Swimming pools   _____

2. Beach access _____
3. Quality of service and hospitality _____
4. Recreational amenities _____
5. Fitness room _____
6. Food and beverage service _____
7. Boat and motor rental _____
8. Ski Equipment rental _____
9. Groceries, gasoline and oil sale _____
10. Bait and fishing equipment sale _____
11. Recreational activities and programs _____
12. Nature programs _____
13. Outdoor skills teaching _____
14. Children's programs and childcare _____
15. Evening entertainment _____
16. Game rooms/video arcade _____
17. Library/Magazines/Books/DVDs _____
18. Theater/Live Performances _____

2.4.2   Facility Design

Our property will have unique stylistic design qualities due in part to its historical context and the resulting use of materials and workmanship that would be financially out-of-reach today, such as hand-laid tile work, crown moldings, marble floors and columns. All such elements will have a distinctive aesthetic based on the age, history, and place of our building. Both the location and pre-existing stylistic look of the building will contribute to the unique character of our boutique hotel, which simply cannot be easily replicated in new construction and will lend itself to a one-of-a-kind experience.

The design of the boutique will come from the intersection of the desired guest experience and the existing building character. Because our building has "good bones," there will be an opportunity for creative solutions to architectural challenges that result in doing things that one would not typically do in the course of designing a new building. For this reason, our boutique hotel will be considered on the leading edge of design innovation, which in and of itself will be attractive to many guests. There will be floor plate configuration and atypical structural bays, which will present a unique design opportunity.

The lobby will be designed for business people and vacation lingerers, with flexible chill-out or work spaces, with screened desks and alcoves, and very comfortable relaxation chairs. The lobby will be transformed into hubs of kinetic energy with "socialization areas" and "productivity pods" that work as mobile offices, with nooks for meetings and computer access. The lobby will also have the feel of an art gallery cum exhibition space, with myriad seating areas, and a library devoted to art and lifestyle. Changing images of the local tourist attractions and scenic areas will be projected on to the walls.

The lobby will be designed for a new generation of travelers. A touchscreen map will feature the best places to eat and see in the city, tables will go from work stations to presentation tables with video screens, and there will be a communal area with a charging mat that reveals where others at the hotel have travelled to recently.

When it comes to furniture, the key will be not to chase trends, because a typical hotel will go five to seven years before updating its rooms. We will have partially exposed cement walls, giving them a slightly artistic look, which also cost less. This will allow our designers to put more money into statement furniture like a trendy chair that can be easily swapped out to update the look, without a major overhaul. The rooms will also feature local art to enrich the visitor's experience. The bathrooms will have spa-like features with waterfall showers, over-sized bathtubs, his & hers sinks, giant towels, beauty items and plenty of space.

We will also place an emphasis on 'green' features with over-sized windows for natural lighting, natural building materials, green walls and green roofs, recycling bins for guests, electronic water faucets, locally grown food for cooking and graywater recycling.

Resource:
http://freshome.com/2013/08/20/the-11-fastest-growing-trends-in-hotel-interior-design/

Examples:
www.telegraph.co.uk/travel/destinations/europe/united-kingdom/england/somerset/
    articles/the-best-boutique-hotels-in-somerset/

2.5   Start-up Summary

The start-up costs for the Boutique Hotel business will be financed through a combination of an owner investment of $ _____ and a short-term bank loan of $ _____. The total start-up costs for this company are approximately $ _____ and can be broken down in the following major categories:

1.	Computer hardware & software	$ _____
2.	Equipment	$ _____
3.	Office Furniture, Work Tables and Fixtures	$ _____
4.	Inventory: Food and Office Supplies	$ _____
5.	Working Capital	$ _____
	For day-to-day operations, including payroll, etc.	
6.	Boutique Hotel Renovations/Buildout	$ _____
	Includes architect, lighting update, flooring, etc.	
7.	Marketing/Advertising Expenses	$ _____
	Includes sales brochures, direct mail, opening expenses.	
8.	Rent and Utility Deposits	$ _____
9.	Furnishings	$ _____
10.	Shops Set-up	$ _____

11.	Property Downpayment	$	_____
12.	Contingency Fund	$	_____
13.	Other (Includes training, legal expenses, software, etc.)	$	_____
Total:		$	_____

In terms of start-up costs, buying an existing property and renovating to fit our needs will be more cost-effective than developing an entirely new project. Cost will also vary based on how many rooms in our building, as well as the types of additional amenities offered. This is considered a per key basis, or how much money is spent on the boutique hotel compared to how many room keys exist. According HVS and their 2009 end-of-year study, the cost per room (when factoring in land costs, site improvements, soft costs and working capital) could be anywhere from $75,000-$400,000, depending on the hotel and location. To determine the local per-key sales figures, we will check out the HVS study or find a local hotel industry consultant in the market we are targeting to figure out the going rate.

Resources: http://www.hotelinvestmentadvisors.com/
               http://www.rsbaswig.com/

The company will require $_____ in initial cash reserves and additional $_____ in assets. The start-up costs are to be financed by the equity contributions of the owner in the amount of $ _____ , as well as by a _____ (#) year commercial loan in the amount of $ _____. The funds will be repaid through earnings. These start-up expenses and funding requirements are summarized in the tables below.

2.5.1   Inventory

Inventory:	Supplier	Qty	Unit Cost	Total
Food Supplies				
Bed Linens				
Towels				
Cleaning Supplies				
Office Supplies				
Computer Supplies				
Marketing Materials				
Product Inventory				
Misc. Supplies				
Totals:				

Furnishings:

Beds				
Mattresses and box springs				
Nightstands				
Reading Lamps				
Armchairs				
Sofa or loveseat				

Dressers	_____
Luggage Rack	_____
Full-length Mirror	_____
Blankets/Sheets/Pillows	_____
Televisions	_____
Mini-refrigerators	_____
Other	_____
Totals:	_____

2.5.2   Supply Sourcing

We will search for and contact several wholesale suppliers for our _____. We will first contact the National Association of Wholesaler-Distributors, and ask our contact person if they can supply a list of _____ wholesalers. We will also visit the Tradepub.com website, and order some free trade publications on retailing. We will read through the classified ads for potential _____ wholesalers. We will consider the wholesalers that offer the best mix of lowest unit cost of _____ products, the fastest re-order turnaround service, and the best open credit terms. We will meet up with suppliers and inquire if we can avail discounted prices if we buy in bulk.

Initially, _____ (company name) will purchase all of its equipment and supplies from _____, the _____ (second/third?) largest supplier in _____ (state), because of the discount given for bulk purchases. However, we will also maintain back-up relationships with two smaller suppliers, namely _____ and _____. These two suppliers have competitive prices on certain products.
Resource: http://www.blla.org/suppliers.htm

Input Products	Description	Source	Back-up	Cost

2.5.3   Supplier Assessments
We will use the following form to compare and evaluate suppliers, because they will play a major role in our procurement strategies and significantly contribute to our profitability.

	Supplier #1	Supplier #2	Compare
Supplier Name			
Website			
Address			
Contacts			
Annual Sales			
Distribution Channels			
Memberships/Certifications			

Quality System	_____
Positioning	_____
Pricing Strategy	_____
Payment Terms	_____
Discounts	_____
Delivery Lead-time	_____
Return Policy	_____
Rebate Program	_____
Technical Support	_____
Core Competencies	_____
Primary Product	_____
Primary Service	_____
New Products/Services	_____
Innovative Applications/Uses	_____
Competitive Advantage	_____
Capital Intensity	_____
State of Technology	_____
Capacity Utilization	_____
Price Volatility	_____
Vertical Integration	_____
References	_____
Overall Rating	_____

2.5.4   Equipment Leasing

Equipment Leasing will be the smarter solution allowing our business to upgrade our equipment needs at the end of the term rather than being overly invested in outdated equipment through traditional bank financing and equipment purchase. We also intend to explore the following benefits of leasing some of the required equipment:

1. Frees Up Capital for other uses.
2. Tax Benefits
3. Improves Balance Sheet
4. Easy to add-on or trade-up
5. Improves Cash Flow
6. Preserves Credit Lines
7. Protects against obsolescence
8. Application Process Simpler

List Any Leases:

Leasing Company	Equipment Description	Monthly Payment	Lease Period	Final Disposition

Resource:

LeaseQ   www.leaseq.com

An online market place that connects businesses, equipment dealers, and leasing companies to make selling and financing equipment fast and easy. The LeaseQ Platform is a free, cloud based SaaS solution with a suite of on-demand software and data solutions for the equipment leasing industry. Utilizes the Internet to provide business process optimization (BPO) and information services that streamline the purchase and financing of business equipment across a broad array of vertical industry segments.

Innovative Lease Services   http://www.ilslease.com/equipment-leasing/
This company was founded in 1986 and is headquartered in Carlsbad, California. It is accredited by the Better Business Bureau, a long standing member of the National Equipment Finance Association and the National Association of Equipment Leasing Brokers and is the official equipment financing partner of Biocom.

2.5.5   Funding Source Matrix

Funds Source	Amount	Interest Rate	Repayment Terms	Use

2.5.6   Distribution or Licensing Agreements (if any)

Note: These are some of the key factors that investors will use to determine if we have a competitive advantage that is not easily copied.

Licensor	License Rights	License Term	Fee or Royalty

2.5.7   Trademarks, Patents and Copyrights (if any)

Our trademark will be virtually our branding for life. Our choice of a name for our business is very important. Not only will we brand our business and services forever, but what may be worthless today will become our most valuable asset in the years to come. A trademark search by our Lawyer will be a must, because to be told down the road that we must give up our name because we did not bother to conduct a trademark search would be a devastating blow to our business. It is also essential that the name that we choose suit the expanding product or service offerings that we plan to introduce.

Note: These are some of the key factors that investors will use to determine if we have a proprietary position or competitive advantage that is not easily copied.

Resources: Patents/Trademarks www.uspto.gov / Copyright   www.copyright.gov

2.5.8   Innovation Strategy   (optional)

____ (company name) will create an innovation strategy that is aligned with not only our firm's core mission and values, but also with our future technology, supplier, and growth strategies. The objective of our innovation strategy will be to create a sustainable competitive advantage . Our education and training systems will be designed to equip our staff with the foundations to learn and develop the broad range of skills needed for innovation in all of its forms, and with the flexibility to upgrade skills and adapt to changing market conditions. To foster an innovative workplace, we will ensure that employment policies facilitate efficient organizational change and encourage the expression of creativity, engage in mutually beneficial strategic alliances and allocate adequate funds for research and development. Our radical innovation strategies include _____ to achieve first mover status. Our incremental innovation strategies will include modifying the following _____ (products/services/processes) to give our customers added value for their money.

2.5.9   Summary of Sources and Use of Funds

Sources:
Owner's Equity Investment $ _____
Requested Bank Loans $ _____
Total: $ _____

Uses:
Capital Equipment $ _____
Beginning Inventory $ _____
Start-up Costs $ _____
Working Capital $ _____
Total: $ _____

2.5.9.1   Funding To Date   (optional)

To date, _____'s (company name) founders have invested $_____ in _____ (company name), with which we have accomplished the following:
1.   _____ (Designed/Built) the company's website
2.   Developed content, in the form of ____ (#) articles, for the website.
3.   Hired and trained our core staff of __(#) full-time people and ___ (#) part-time people.
4.   Generated brand awareness by driving ___ (#) visitors to our website in a ___(#) month period.
5.   Successfully _____ (Developed/Test Marketed) ___ (#) new _____ (products/services), which compete on the basis of _____.
6.   _____ (Purchased/Developed) and installed the software needed to _____ (manage _____ operations?)

7. Purchased $ _____ worth of _____ (supplies)
8. Purchased $ _____ worth of _____ equipment.

2.6 Start-up Requirements

Start-up Expenses:		Estimates
Legal	_____	400
Accountant	_____	300
Accounting Software Package	_____	300
Licenses & Permits	_____	300
Market Research Survey	_____	300
Office Supplies	_____	500
Mattresses, sheets, blankets	_____	2000
Marketing Materials	_____	2000
Logo Design	_____	500
Advertising (2 months)	_____	2000
Consultants	_____	1000
Insurance	_____	1200
Property downpayment	_____	
Facility Renovation	_____	
Utility Deposit	_____	600
DSL Installation/Activation	_____	100
Telephone System Installation	_____	200
Telephone Deposit	_____	200
Direct TV	_____	
Data Processing Expenses	_____	
Expensed Kitchen Equipment	_____	1000
Website Design/Hosting	_____	2000
Reservation Service Commissions	_____	200
Reservation Service Annual Fee	_____	75
Used Office Equipment/Furniture	_____	1500
Property Maintenance Expenses	_____	
Boutique Hotel Org. Memberships	_____	300
Facility Renovations/Buildout	_____	5000
Guest Room Furnishings	_____	8000
Guest Transportation Expenses	_____	
Vending Expenses	_____	
Cleaning Supplies	_____	200
Breakfast Preparation Supplies	_____	500
Training Materials	_____	
Front Entrance Sign	_____	1000
Other	_____	
Total Start-up Expenses	_____ (A)	

Start-up Assets:

Cash Balance Required	_____	(T) 5000
Start-up Equipment	_____	See schedule
Start-up Inventory	_____	See schedule
Other Current Assets	_____	
Long-term Assets	_____	
Total Assets	_____	**(B)**
Total Requirements	_____	(A+B)

Start-up Funding

Start-up Expenses to Fund	_____	(A)
Start-ups Assets to Fund	_____	(B)
Total Funding Required:	_____	**(A+B)**

Assets

Non-cash Assets from Start-up	_____	
Cash Requirements from Start-up	_____	(T)
Additional Cash Raised	_____	(S)
Cash Balance on Starting Date	_____	(T+S=U)
Total Assets:	_____	**(B)**

Liabilities and Capital

Short-term Liabilities:

Current Borrowing	_____	
Unpaid Expenses	_____	
Accounts Payable	_____	
Interest-free Short-term Loans	_____	
Other Short-term Loans	_____	
Total Short-term Liabilities	_____	**(Z)**

Long-term Liabilities:

Commercial Bank Loan	_____	
Other Long-term Liabilities	_____	
Total Long-term Liabilities	_____	**(Y)**
Total Liabilities	_____	**(Z+Y = C)**

Capital

Planned Investment

Owner		_____	
Family		_____	
Other		_____	
Additional Investment Requirement		_____	
Total Planned Investment		_____	**(F)**
Loss at Start-up (Start-up Expenses)	**(-)**	_____	**(A)**
Total Capital	**(=)**	_____	**(F+A=D)**
Total Capital and Liabilities		_____	**(C+D)**
Total Funding		_____	(C+F)

2.6.1 Capital Equipment List

Equipment Type	Model	Quantity	Unit Cost	Total	Est.
Computer System					800
Printer					300
Fax Machine					200
Digital Camera					500
Copy Machine					600
Phone System					300
Security System					
Answering Machine					200
TV and DVD Player					
Surge Protector					35
Accounting Software					
Boutique Hotel Management Software					
Microsoft Office Equipment					
Cleaning Equipment					
Washing Machines					
Clothes Dryers					
Kitchen Equipment					
Credit Card Terminal					
File Cabinets					100
Postage Meter					50
Electronic Scale					
Telephone headsets					
Calculator					
Gift Item Display Cases					
Signs					
Paper Shredder					
Broadband Internet Connection					
Refrigerator					
Microwave					
Accident Investigation Kit					
Other					

Total Capital Equipment _____

Note: Equipment costs are dependent on whether purchased new or used or leased.
All items that are assets to be used for more than one year will be considered a
long-term asset and will be depreciated using the straight-line method.

The following equipment will be included in our accident investigation kit:

1. Backpack for carrying kit items.
2. Legal Pad and clipboard.
3. Digital Camera or a disposable camera.
4. 25-foot tape measure to triangulate the accident scene.
5. Markers: 2x2 orange flags on a 12inch wire rod for accident scene triangulation.
6. Tape Recorder for recording names and addresses of witnesses, or recording distances to be plotted later, as part of accident scene triangulation.
7. Miscellaneous: roll of surveyor's tape, pair of disposable gloves and a medical waste bag/bodily fluid spill kit, and can of spray paint.
8. Investigative forms to document the details at time of the accident.

2.7.0   SBA Loan Key Requirements

In order to be considered for an SBA loan, we must meet the basic requirements:
1. Must have been turned down for a loan by a bank or other lender to qualify for most SBA Business Loan Programs. 2. Required to submit a guaranty, both personal and business, to qualify for the loans. 3. Must operate for profit; be engaged in, or propose to do business in, the United States or its possessions; 4. Have reasonable owner equity to invest; 5. Use alternative financial resources first including personal assets.

All businesses must meet eligibility criteria to be considered for financing under the SBA's 7(a) Loan Program, including: size; type of business; operating in the U.S. or its possessions; use of available of funds from other sources; use of proceeds; and repayment. The repayment term of an SBA loan is between five and 25 years, depending on the lift of the assets being financed and the cash needs of the business.
Working capital loans (accounts receivable and inventory) should be repaid in five to 10 years. The SBA also has short-term loan guarantee programs with shorter repayment terms.

A Business Owner Cannot Use an SBA Loan:

To purchase real estate where the participant has issued a forward commitment to the developer or where the real estate will be held primarily for investment purposes. To finance floor plan needs. To make payments to owners or to pay delinquent withholding taxes. To pay existing debt, unless it can be shown that the refinancing will benefit the small business and that the need to refinance is not indicative of poor management.

SBA Loan Programs:
Low Doc: www.sba.gov/financing/lendinvest/lowdoc.html
SBA Express   www.sba,gov/financing/lendinvest/sbaexpress.html
Basic 7(a) Loan Guarantee Program
   For businesses unable to obtain loans through standard loan programs.
   Funds can be used for general business purposes, including working
   capital, leasehold improvements and debt refinancing.

www.sba.gov/financing/sbaloan/7a.html
Certified Development Company 504 Loan Program
Used for fixed asset financing such as purchase of real estate or machinery.
www. Sba.gov/gopher/Local-Information/Certified-Development-Companies/
MicroLoan 7(m) Loan Program
Provides short-term loans up to $35,000.00 for working capital or
purchase of fixtures.
www.sba.gov/financing/sbaloan/microloans.html

2.7.1   Other Financing Options

1.   Grants:
Health care grants, along with education grants, represent the largest percentage
of grant giving in the United States. The federal government, state, county and
city governments, as well as private and corporate foundations all award grants.
The largest percentage of grants are awarded to non-profit organizations, health
care agencies, colleges and universities, local government agencies, tribal
institutions, and schools. For profit organizations are generally not eligible for
grants unless they are conducting research or creating jobs.

A.   Contact your state licensing office.
B.   Foundation Grants to Individuals: www.fdncenter.org
C.   US Grants   www.grants.gov
D.   Foundation Center   www.foundationcemter.org
E.   The Grantsmanship Center   www.tgci.com
F.   Contact local Chamber of Commerce
G.   The Catalog of Federal Domestic Assistance is a major provider of
business grant money.
H.   The Federal Register is a good source to keep current with the continually
changing federal grants offered.
I.   FedBizOpps is a resource, as all federal agencies must use FedBizOpps to
notify the public about contract opportunities worth over $25,000.
J.   Fundsnet Services   http://www.fundsnetservices.com/
K.   SBA Women Business Center
www.sba.gov/content/womens-business-center-grant-opportunities

Local Business Grants
Check with local businesses for grant opportunities and eligibility requirements.
For example, Bank of America sponsors community grants for businesses that
endeavor to improve the community, protect the environment or preserve the
neighborhood.
Resource:
www.bankofamerica.com/foundation/index.cfm?template=fd_localgrants

Green Technology Grants
If you install green technology in the business as a way to reduce waste and make the business more energy efficient, you may be eligible for grant funding. Check your state's Economic Development Commission. This grant program was developed as part of the American Recovery and Reinvestment Act.
Resource: www.recovery.gov/Opportunities/Pages/Opportunities.aspx

2.	Friends and Family Lending	www.virginmoney.com
3.	National Business Incubator Association	www.nbia.org/
4.	Women's Business Associations	www.nawbo.org/
5.	Minority Business Development Agency	www.mbda.gov/
6.	Social Networking Loans	www.prosper.com
7.	Peer-to-Peer Programs	www.lendingclub.com
8.	Extended Credit Terms from Suppliers	30/60/90 days.
9.	Consignment Terms from Suppliers	Contract statements.
10.	Community Bank	
11.	Prepayments from Customers	
12.	Seller Financing: When purchasing an existing Boutique Hotel.	
13.	Business Funding Directory	www.businessfinance.com
14.	FinanceNet	www.financenet.gov
15.	SBA Financing	www.sbaonline.sba.gov
16.	Micro-Loans	www.accionusa.org/
17.	Private Investor	

18. Use retirement funds to open a business without taxes or penalty. First, establish a C-corporation for the new business. Next, the C-corporation establishes a new retirement plan. Then, the owner's current retirement funds are rolled over into the C-corporation's new plan. And last, the new retirement plan invests in stock of the C-corporation. Warning: Check with your accountant or financial planner. Resource: http://www.benetrends.com/

19. Business Plan Competition Prizes
www.nytimes.com/interactive/2009/11/11/business/smallbusiness/Competitions-table.html?ref=smallbusiness

20. Unsecured Business Cash Advance based on future credit card transactions.
www.merchantcreditadvance.com

21.	Kick Starter	www.kickstarter.com
22.	Tech Stars	www.techstars.org
23.	Capital Source	www.capitalsource.com

www.msl.com/index.cfm?event=page.sba504
Participates in the SBA's 504 loan program. This program is for the purchase of fixed assets such as commercial real estate and machinery and equipment of a capital nature, which are defined as assets that have a minimum useful life of ten years. Proceeds cannot be used for working capital.

24. Commercial Loan Applications   www.c-loans.com/onlineapp/
www.wellsfargo.com/com/bus_finance/commercial_loans

25. Sharing assets and resources with other non-competing businesses.

26. Angel Investors   www.angelcapitaleducation.org

27. The Receivables Exchange   http://receivablesxchange.com/

28. Bootstrap Methods: Personal Savings/Credit Card/Second Mortgages

29. Community-based Crowd-funding   www.profounder.com
                                           www.peerbackers.com
A funding option designed to link small businesses and entrepreneurs with pools of prospective investors. Crowdfunding lenders are often repaid with goods or services.

30. On Deck Capital   www.ondeckcapital.com/
Created the Short Term Business Loan (up to $100,000.00) for small businesses to get quick access to capital that fits their cash flow, with convenient daily payments.

31. Royalty Lending   www.launch-capital.com/
With royalty lending, financing is granted in return for future revenue or company performance, and payback can prove exceedingly expensive if a company flourishes.

32. Stock :Loans   Southern Lending Solutions, Atlanta. GA.
                                      Custom Commercial Finance, Bartlesville, OK
A stock loan is based on the quality of stocks, Treasuries and other kinds of investments in a businessperson's personal portfolio. Possession of the company's stock is transferred to the lender's custodial bank during the loan period.

33. Lender Compatibility Searcher   www.BoeFly.com

34. Strategic Investors
Strategic investing is more for a large company that identifies promising technologies, and for whatever reason, that company may not want to build up the research and development department in-house to produce that product, so they buy a percentage of the company with the existing technology.

35. Bartering

36. Small Business Investment Companies   www.sba.gov/INV

37. Cash-Value Life Insurance

38. Employee Stock Option Plans   www.nceo.org

39. Venture Capitalists   www.nvca.org

40. Initial Public Offering (IPO)

41. Meet investors through online sites, including LinkedIn (group discussions), Facebook (BranchOut sorts Facebook connections by profession), and CapLinked (enables search for investment-related professionals by industry and role).

42. SBA Community Advantage Approved Lenders
                     www.sba.gov/content/community-advantage-approved-lenders

43. Small Business Lending Specialists
https://www.wellsfargo.com/biz/loans_lines/compare_lines
http://www.bankofamerica.com/small_business/business_financing/
https://online.citibank.com/US/JRS/pands/detail.do?ID=CitiBizOverview
https://www.chase.com/ccp/index.jsp?pg_name=ccpmapp/smallbusiness/home/pa
        ge/bb_business_bBanking_programs

44. Startup America Partnership   www.s.co/about
Based on a simple premise: young companies that grow create jobs. Once startups apply and become a Startup America Firm, they can access and manage many

types of resources through a personalized dashboard.
45. United States Economic Development Administration   www.eda.gov/
46. Small Business Loans   http://www.iabusnet.org/small-business-loans
47. Tax Increment Financing (TIF)
A public financing method that is used for subsidizing redevelopment, infrastructure, and other community-improvement projects. TIF is a method to use future gains in taxes to subsidize current improvements, which are projected to create the conditions for said gains. The completion of a public project often results in an increase in the value of surrounding real estate, which generates additional tax revenue. Tax Increment Financing dedicates tax increments within a certain defined district to finance the debt that is issued to pay for the project. TIF is often designed to channel funding toward improvements in distressed, underdeveloped, or underutilized parts of a jurisdiction where development might otherwise not occur. TIF creates funding for public or private projects by borrowing against the future increase in these property-tax revenues. Currently, thousands of TIF districts operate nationwide in the US, from small and mid-sized cities, to many states, including California and Illinois.
48. Gust   https://gust.com/entrepreneurs
Provides the global platform for the sourcing and management of early-stage investments. Gust enables skilled entrepreneurs to collaborate with the smartest investors by virtually supporting all aspects of the investment relationship, from initial pitch to successful exit.
49. Goldman Sachs 10,000 Small Businesses   http://sites.hccs.edu/10ksb/
50. Earnest Loans   www.meetearnest.com
51. Biz2Credit   www.biz2credit.com

Resources: www.sba.gov/category/navigation-structure/starting-managing-business/starting-business/local-resources

http://usgovinfo.about.com/od/moneymatters/a/Finding-Business-Loans-Grants-Incentives-And-Financing.htm

3.0   Products and Services

In this section, we will not only list all of our planned products and services, but also describe how our proposed products and services will be differentiated from those of our competitors and solve a real problem or fill an unmet need in the marketplace.

Services:
_____ (company name) will offer guests ___ (#) 1-bedroom units and ___ (#) 2-bedroom units. ___ (#) units will have a kitchenette and ___ (#) units can be used together as a suite. Each unit is equipped with ____ (#) ____ (single/double?) beds or a queen bed. We will have a _____ (full-service restaurant?).

_____ (company name) will be a ___ (#) unit Boutique Hotel in _____ (city), _____ (state), designed to provide guests with high quality accommodations, full breakfast and spectacular views at reasonable rates, while _____ (vacationing/attending to business) in the _____ area. Two cots will be available for over-flow bookings or family groups.

The Company will offer a Boutique Hotel room on a nightly basis for travelers and a weekly basis for leisure customers. As the Company expands, Management intends to offer more amenities and services so that we can consistently add value for the customers' experience. Our resort will be designed for any type of traveler, with a highly personalized approach to the treatment of all guests.

Our boutique hotel will stand apart from most properties in _____ City because of the value-added amenities that will be hallmarks of our brand of hospitality. These include private club rooms with books, newspapers, magazines, free Wi-Fi, and computer stations; complimentary refreshments throughout the day including Continental breakfast each morning and wine and cheese receptions, evenings from 5 to 8 p.m., complimentary bottles of water in the room, and many other thoughtful touches. Technology will play a major role in our hotels' creative offerings, with a loaded iPad stocked in every room and select rooms will allow guests usage of a Samsung Galaxy S3 smartphone. Internet service will be complimentary on both devices. Each room will feature either Queen or King beds, all with private baths. Each bed will have a leather-tufted headboard, luxury high thread count bed linens, fluffy down pillows, and ultra soft cotton bamboo blankets. Flat screen televisions with DirecTV included, USB compatible electrical outlets, individual refrigerators, and single brew Keurig Coffeemakers will be included in all bedrooms. All rooms will also feature electric fireplaces. Each shower will feature glass mosaic tiling and an ultra-luxurious spa shower. In keeping with our Green efforts all toilets will be low flow to conserve water. Each guest will be provided an RFID keycard to allow them to access the Hotel and their individual room. Security cameras will be placed throughout the property both inside and out for guests' safety and comfort.

Activities and attractions in the area include: **(select)**
1.   Nature walks   2.   Museum tours
3.   Shopping tours   4.   Historic Site Tours

5.	Art Festivals	6.	Sporting Events
7.	Casinos/Gambling	8.	Nightclubs
9.	Golf Course	10.	_____

Optional Services:

We plan to offer the following optional services:

1.	Dietitian Services	2.	Private-Duty Personal Care
3.	Companion Services	4.	Homemaker Services
5.	Nutrition Counseling	6.	Child Care/Baby Sitting
7.	Special Interest Tours	8.	Real Estate Sales
9.	Breakfast in Bed	10.	Shopping Tours
11.	Picnic Lunches	12.	Errand Services
13.	Concierge Services	14.	Office Services
15.	Cooking Lessons/Classes	16.	Horse Boarding/Grooming
17.	Walking Tours	18.	Wardrobe Consulting
19.	Laundry/Dry Cleaning Services	20.	Dog Walking
21.	Therapeutic Massages	22.	Psychic Readings
23.	Facilities Rentals for Events	24.	Spa Treatments
25.	Wine Tasting Events	26.	Gourmet Cooking Lessons
27.	Picnic Lunch Baskets	28.	Custom Gift Baskets
29.	Recreational Equipment Rentals	30.	Front Desk Concierge Svc.
31.	Wedding Ceremonies	32.	Health Club
34.	Corporate Meeting Place		

Products:

The following products will be made available to our guests via our on-site gift shop and also be incorporated into our lobby décor:

1. Craft and Collectibles Sales
2. Antiques for sale
3. Cosmetics Sales
4. Souvenir Guidebooks and Maps
5. Local Artwork and Photo Sales
6. Basic hygiene supplies including toothbrushes, toothpaste, and hair care products.
7. Newspapers and magazines
8. Bottled water, energy drinks and soda
9. Food and healthy snacks.
10. Equipment Sales (Golf/Skiing/Hunting/etc.)
11. Gift items
12. Logo Imprinted Clothing Sales
13. Hotel Branded Linens

3.0.1   Amenities

1.	Free Wireless Internet Service	2.	Recently Renovated Pool
3.	Elevator Service	4.	Flat Screen TV's in all units
5.	In-room telephones	6.	Fully air-conditioned and heated

7.	Fully equipped kitchen	8.	Soundproof and Fireproof
9.	Daily Maid Service	10.	Hair Dryer, Blender and Iron
11.	Ironing Boards in All Units	12.	Smoke Alarms in All Units
13.	Hospitality Room	14.	Gas Barbecue Access
15.	Ice Machine	16.	Washer/Dryer (Coin Operated)
17.	Crib Rentals Available	18.	Free Parking (ONE car space/unit)
19.	Conveniently/Centrally Located.	20.	Office Hours: 8:00 a.m. to 11 p.m.
21.	Fax Service Available	22.	Safe Deposit Boxes
23.	Handicap Accessible	24.	Gift Certificates Available
25.	Loaded iPads	26.	Yoga mat in every room,

27. Full concierge and business services
28. Overnight shoeshine, laundry and dry cleaning service
29. Personalized room preferences
30. Complimentary high-speed internet access
31. Hosted wine reception
32. Complimentary morning coffee and tea service from 6 to 11 a.m. daily
33. Complimentary morning newspaper
34. Valet parking is $30/overnight, with full in-and-out privileges
35 Acclaimed restaurant and bar, featuring flavorful regional cuisine
36. 24-hour room service
37. Onsite 24-hour business center with printer and copier
38. Complimentary kayak and bicycle rentals
39. Express checkout
40. Fully accessible hotel for people with disabilities; ADA compliant
41. Onsite 24/7 fitness center

3.1   Service Description

In creating our service descriptions, we will provide answers to the following types of questions:
1. What does the service do or help the customer to accomplish?
2. Why will people decide to buy it?
3. What makes it unique or a superior value?
4. How expensive or difficult is it to make or copy by a competitor?
5. How much will the service be sold for?

Rental of Hotel Rooms
The Boutique Hotel facility intends to operate as a four or five star rated facility that will feature a number of amenities commonly found in comparably priced resorts. The Company expects that the final facility will feature ___ (#) suite style rooms. Each room will have a king or two full sized beds, access to high speed internet, a luxurious bathroom with whirlpool bath, full cable access, a desk with chair, reading lamps, and other quality amenities.

Health Club and Spa

Guests will be able to re-energize in our state-of-the-art Health Club and rejuvenate in our tranquil Spa and Salon. Our Wellness program will provide treatments, methods and lectures toward positive change for optimum health and well-being. Our Spa & Health Club will offer some of the most advanced fitness equipment in our area. We will provide only the finest exercise apparatus, friendly attentive service, all in our luxurious fitness center. Our goal will be to provide a refreshingly positive workout experience and change the way people view health clubs. Our guests will enjoy an atmosphere of relaxation and cleanliness in our well-maintained facility, while being treated with respect by our professional staff. Our Full Service Health Club and Spa will be a _____ (#) square foot facility and offer the following amenities:

1.	Free weights	2.	Snack Bars
3.	Tanning Beds	4.	Treadmills
5.	Stationary Bikes	6.	Personal Trainers
7.	Sauna	8.	Steam Room
9.	Indoor/Outdoor Pool	10.	Hair and Nail Salons

Corporate Meeting Place
_____ (company name) will be a full-service Hotel and Resort hosting corporate meetings and conferences. We will offer the best of ____ (city) Catering services along with a variety of conference halls and meeting rooms to suit any need. We will set up rooms to the client's specification, whether they need classroom style, auditorium style, banquet style or a U-Shaped format. We will also provide all of the state of the art audio-visual (A/V) equipment to make the event a success.

Our services will deliver the following benefits to guests:
1. The optimal amount of personalized service.
2. All rooms provide a separate living or work space.
3. Each unit will have a private bathroom.
4. Each bathroom has a whirlpool tub.

_____ (company name) will maintain high service standards and will provide guests with the following:
1. Well-appointed clean rooms.
2. Prompt response to reservation requests.
3. Resource materials on local culture, history, geography and events.
4. Warmth of welcome and hospitality.
5. Flexibility of meal content and timing.
6. Reminder services.

3.2 Alternative Revenue Streams

1.	Classified Ads in our Newsletter	2.	Vending Machine Sales
3.	Errand Running/Concierge Service	4.	Exercise and Yoga Classes
5.	Product sales and rentals.	6.	Website Banner Ads
7.	Content Area Sponsorship Fees	8.	Online Survey Report Fees

9.	Innkeeper Consulting Services	10.	Recreational Equipment Rentals
11.	Conference Room Rentals	12.	ATM Machines

3.3 Production of Products and Services

It is expected that in the first year, there will be no need for extra help involved in the duties required for running the Boutique Hotel. If the need arises for extra cleaning help, the service will be locally contracted out. This expense is variable and will be tied to the volume of business and be covered by an increase in revenue.

The plan is to furnish and decorate each bedroom in a different style in order to differentiate the theme of each living area and create a unique selling point for our guests.

We also plan to create a landscape that is interesting in all seasons and to add a gazebo for thoughtful reflection and wedding photo opportunities. The backyard is in view from all areas of the house, and will be an integral part of the guests' accommodation experience.

We will use the following methods to locate the best suppliers for our business:
- Attend trade shows and conferences to spot upcoming trends, realize networking
        opportunities and compare prices.
   Boutique Hotel Investment Conference   www.bllaevents.com,
                                              www.hospitalitynet.org/news/4065649.html

- Subscribe to appropriate trade magazines, journals, newsletters and blogs.
   - Cornell Hotel and Restaurant Quarterly
   - Hotel & Boutique Hotel Management and Lodging
   - Resort Management
   - Hotel & Motel Management
   - Lodging (AHMA)
   - Hospitality Net   www.hospitalitynet.org/search.html
   - Hotel Chatter   www.hotelchatter.com
        A daily web magazine chronicling hotel stories worldwide and dedicated to
        covering everything related to hotels and lodging around the world, covers hotel
        deals and reviews, which celebrities are staying where, hotel industry news, tips
        for booking online, the hotels to stay away from, the hotels people should book,
        and more
   - Hotel News Now   www.hotelnewsnow.com
   - Boutique Hotel News   www.boutiquehotelnews,com
   - Boutique Lodging Magazine   www.boutiquelodgingmagazine.com/home.html
   - Daily Travel News Int'l   www.traveldailynews.com
   - Hotel News Resource   www.hotelnewsresource.com
   - Hotel Executive   https://hotelexecutive.com
   - Luxury Hoteliers Magazine
                www.luxuryhotelassociation.org/luxury-hoteliers-magazine/
   - Boutique Hospitality Management   www.boutique-hospitality.com

- Bedtimes Magazine   www.bedtimesmagazine
    BedTimes is the only trade and business journal dedicated exclusively to the global
    mattress industry. It is published by the International Sleep Products Association.

- Join our trade association to make valuable contacts, get listed in any online
    directories, and secure training and marketing materials.

Boutique And Lifestyle Lodging Association   **www.blla.org**
BLLA is an association created to be the unifying voice of this distinctive, yet extremely
fragmented sector, within the hospitality industry. Its goal is to unite the world's
collection of boutique and lifestyle properties and the suppliers that sustain them, offering
them the opportunity to successfully compete on a level playing field with major hotel
companies, as well as market themselves to meet the ever-increasing demand from
discerning boutique-seeking clients.

American Hotel & Lodging Association
International Hotel and Restaurant Assoc.   www.ih-ra.com/
    We will join this association to stay abreast of new ideas and changes in the
    industry that could affect our business. We will use participation in the seminars,
    conferences and meetings as an opportunity to build partnerships with other
    Boutique Hotel owners and to find opportunities for training support.
American Resort Development Association   www.arda.org
International Luxury Hotel Association   www.luxuryhotelassociation.org

3.4   Competitive Comparison

According to _____ County Records, the city of _____, _____ (state)
has only ____(#) lodging facilities and ___ (#) Boutique Hotel businesses. We expect to
filling the growing local market need for this vital service.

_____ (company name) will differentiate itself from its local competitors by
offering a superior range of high-quality, personalized services, and uniquely designed
products, at a competitive prices. We plan to feature a comprehensive breakfast menu
that will easily surpass the dietary and esthetic requirements of all of our guests.

_____ (company name) has been designed to provide the comfort of a home with
the option to partake in the company of the owners or other guests, or retreat to the
seclusion of a comfortable room. The building will retain its heritage appeal, while
offering the modern amenities expected for a comfortable stay, including whirlpool tubes
and room balconies.

Local attractions and events include:
1. _____
2. _____

By forming strategic referral alliances with local service providers, we plan to become the local market leader in high quality, one-stop lodging services.

3.5 Sales Literature

_____ (company name) has developed sales literature that illustrates a professional organization with vision. _____ (company name) plans to constantly refine its marketing mix through a number of different literature packets. These include the following:
- direct mail with introduction letter and product price sheet.
- product information brochures
- press releases
- new product/service information literature
- email marketing campaigns
- website content
- corporate brochures

A copy of our corporate informational brochure is attached in the appendix of this document. This brochure will be available to provide referral sources, leave at seminars, and use for direct mail purposes.

3.6 Fulfillment

The key fulfillment and delivery of services will be provided by our owners and limited staff. The real core value is the industry expertise of the founder, and _____ (his/her) ability to develop unique lodging experiences for guests.

3.7 Technology

_____ (company name) will employ and maintain the latest technology to enhance its programs, office management, reservation scheduling, payment processing and record keeping systems.

Our goal will be to have a unique guest experience by working on all aspects of technology in our boutique hotel. An elaborate touch-screen system that is situated near the bed will be able to change the notification that usually hangs from the outside doorknob to familiar messages that reads "do not disturb" or "please make up the room. We will also make videoconferencing equipment available to our hotel quests.
The new technology will also allow front-desk staff to stage a room based on check-in times, so the room will be set when guests arrive.
Resource:
Veraview LLC   www.veraview.com

ALICE   **http://info.aliceapp.com/product**

Joins all the departments of a hotel onto a single operations platform for internal communication and task management, ALICE helps staff act as a team to provide consistently excellent service. ALICE"s main product - ALICE Suite - brings together the front office, concierge, housekeeping, and maintenance teams, and connects guests to the hotel with their app and SMS tools. The ALICE platform is also available as specialized software and mobile applications for the staff (ALICE Staff), the concierge (ALICE Concierge) and the guests (ALICE Guest). Each module is fully integratable with PMS, POS, and all other third party management systems. Provides exceptional service through mobile staff technology and guest communication channels. Third-party service providers also leverage the ALICE API.
Source: https://www.hospitalitynet.org/news/4083126.html

Booking Platforms
We will critique the following booking platforms, before deciding which one to utilize:

BookingSuite
A software-as-a-service website platform where hotels can build effective, and inexpensive responsive websites. There are no upfront costs, and the subscription-based model ensures hoteliers receive timely updates to their websites built by a team of developers, as opposed to bespoke code which can be cumbersome.

Stayful
A booking platform that allows travelers to negotiate nonrefundable rates one-on-one with hoteliers in unique boutique and independent hotels. The goal is to help those hoteliers unload the inventory that sits unused every day, and at a lower cost to owners. Stayful charges a 10% commission.

HotelsByDay
This booking platform has been described as "the sharing economy for hotels." The site allows hoteliers to sell their perishable inventory for hours-long blocks in the morning, mid-day and afternoon, allowing guests to crash somewhere after a red-eye flight, recharge mid-day or have an afternoon base of operations before a big meeting, for instance. The commission structure is half of the typical online travel agency at around 7.5%. Hoteliers are still able to sell those rooms for the traditional overnight stay.
Source:
www.hotelnewsnow.com/Article/16440/Hoteliers-critique-3-new-booking-platforms

Resources:
IDeaS Revenue Solutions   **www.ideas.com**
A leading provider of pricing and revenue management software, services and consulting. Helping hotels that are under tremendous pressure to maximize revenues from their perishable capacity, products, and services. Founded in 1989 the Company, offers industry-leading revenue management Software, Services, and Consulting to the hospitality industry. Headquartered in Minneapolis, IDeaS has technology, support, sales and distribution offices in North and South America, the United Kingdom, Europe, the Middle East, Africa, Greater China, Australia and Asia.

HeBS Digital   www.hebsdigital.com
Founded in 2001, HeBS Digital is the industry's leading digital technology, full-service hotel digital marketing, website design and direct online channel consulting firm based in New York City. HeBS Digital has pioneered many of the best practices in hotel digital marketing, social and mobile marketing, and direct online channel distribution. The firm has won over 250 prestigious industry awards for its digital marketing and website design services, including numerous Adrian Awards, Davey Awards, W3 Awards, WebAwards, Magellan Awards, Summit International Awards, Interactive Media Awards, and IAC Awards. A diverse client portfolio of top tier major hotel brands, luxury and boutique hotel brands, resorts and casinos, hotel management companies, franchisees and independents, and CVBs are profiting from HeBS Digital's hospitality digital marketing expertise.

Hotel Reservation Software   http://ResortHotel-reservation.qarchive.org/
Reservation Master is a reservations software package developed for use in Hotels, motels, Guest Houses, B&Bs, Lodges & hotels worldwide. It offers an easy to use, economically priced, yet robust solution for reservations, front desk, unlimited history, easy reporting.

Fiesta Hotel Management Software   www.fiestahms.com
An integrated and cost effective one-stop solution to fit the various needs of Boutique Hotels. It is organized around an Operational Management and Business Office Management model and is complemented comprehensive on-line inquiries & reports which support all management & decision making information needs of a hotel operation. It provides the information required by managers for efficient day to day operations, as well as, a treasure-trove of information to enable the analysis of past trends for accurate forecasting.

Hotelogix   www.hotelogix.com
A cloud-based, end-to-end, hospitality technology solution, built to seamlessly manage hotels, resorts, serviced apartments or multi-location hotel chains, by providing a single window to manage all hotel operations and bookings (online and offline). Hotelogix also integrates with travel agent networks and external booking sites, providing a wider inventory distribution, along with real-time integration with partner sites, group booking websites, and other central reservation systems. Hotelogix is used by both new hotels, hotels previously unable to afford such 360 degree technology, and hotels looking to replace legacy systems with a web-based SaaS solution, which gives greater functionality and a higher level of integrations for distribution of inventory. Hotelogix offers 24x7 live support and transparent pricing plans to its customers, and is hosted on highly reliable and secured cloud services.

HotelScienz
An affordable high performing demand based revenue management system for hotels. It provides **a** proven methodology to hotel yield through advanced algorithms which highlight demand trends, to support daily rate decisions and revenue management strategy.

Mobile Phone Credit Card Reader   https://squareup.com/

Square, Inc. is a financial services, merchant services aggregator and mobile payments company based in San Francisco, California. The company markets several software and hardware products and services, including Square Register and Square Order. Square Register allows individuals and merchants in the United States, Canada, and Japan to accept offline debit and credit cards on their iOS or Android smartphone or tablet computer. The app supports manually entering the card details or swiping the card through the Square Reader, a small plastic device which plugs into the audio jack of a supported smartphone or tablet and reads the magnetic stripe. On the iPad version of the Square Register app, the interface resembles a traditional cash register.

Google Wallet   https://www.google.com/wallet/

A mobile payment system developed by Google that allows its users to store debit cards, credit cards, loyalty cards, and gift cards among other things, as well as redeeming sales promotions on their mobile phone. Google Wallet can be used near field communication (NFC) to make secure payments fast and convenient by simply tapping the phone on any PayPass-enabled terminal at checkout.

Apple Pay   http://www.apple.com/apple-pay/

A mobile payment and digital wallet service by Apple Inc. that lets users make payments using the iPhone 6, iPhone 6 Plus, Apple Watch-compatible devices (iPhone 5and later models), iPad Air 2, and iPad Mini 3. Apple Pay does not require Apple-specific contactless payment terminals and will work with Visa's PayWave, MasterCard's PayPass, and American Express's ExpressPay terminals. The service has begun initially only for use in the US, with international roll-out planned for the future. Resource: www.wired.com/2018/01/shadow-apple-pay-google-wallet-expands-online-reach/

WePay   https://www.wepay.com/

An online payment service provider in the United States. WePay's payment API focuses exclusively on platform businesses such as crowdfunding sites, marketplaces andsmall business software. Through this API, WePay allows these platforms to access its payments capabilities and process credit cards for the platform's users.

Chirpify

Connects a user's PayPal account with their Twitter account in order to enable payments through tweeting.

3.8   Future Products and Services

_____ (company name) will continually expand our offering of services based on Boutique Hotel industry trends and changing guest needs. We will not only solicit feedback via one-on-one interviews, surveys and comments cards from guests on what they need in the future and what they would like to see improved, but will also work to develop strong relationships with all of our guests to improve our repeat business percentage.

We plan to pursue niche markets by developing themed rooms that match the interests and lifestyles of targeted groups.

Examples:
Bridal Suite	Newlyweds
Library Suite	Literary Enthusiasts
Victorian Suite	European History Buffs.
Garden Suite	Gardeners
NASCAR Suite	Auto Racing Fans

We also plan to develop the following types of themed packages, with strategic alliance partners, for guests looking for a specific experience.

- Spa Pampering Package
- Romantic Candlelight Dinner Package
- Picnic Basket Nature Walk Package
- Local Sightseeing Package
- Getaway Weekend Package
- Mother and Daughter Package

We are also planning the following facility upgrades:
1. The inclusion of a country garden into the landscape.
2. A commercial kitchen capable of making full dinner meals.
3. Addition of luxury features to the bathrooms, such as whirlpool tubs.
4. The addition of an in-ground, heated swimming pool.
5. The addition of an miniature outdoor putting green.
6. Equip on-site mini-fitness center.
7. Develop snowmobile/nature walking trail on property.
8. Add a full service coin-operated laundry facility (washing, drying, and optional folding).

Business Travelers Club
We plan to start a 'Business Travelers Club' that will provide business travelers with the following benefits, for a minor $____ annual membership fee.
1. ____ (48?) hour Cancellation Policy
2. Free in-room High Speed DSL Internet and computer access
3. Local Fitness Gym access at a ____ (50?)% discounted rate.
4. Pick-up and delivery of laundry/dry cleaning services.
5. Flexible breakfast scheduling.
6. Flexible check-in and check-out processing.
7. Frequent Guest Discount Points Program.

We will publish a brochure that lists all local tourist attractions, restaurants and retail shops, and charge these businesses to place advertisements in the booklet.
We plan to develop an in-house hospitality school, that will provide a steady supply of fresh talent and a new revenue stream.

Expanded Service Offerings

We plan to expand our range of travel products and services to include complementary products, such as air ticketing, ground handling and transfers, and sightseeing tours and transportation packages.

Conference Center

We plan to add a conference center, which will enable our company to generate revenues from the following types of events;
1.   Business Meetings
2.   Conventions
3.   Seminar and Workshop Presentations
4.   News Conferences
5.   Special Events

Specialty Common Rooms

Our plan is to become a destination for guests who want to celebrate anything from birthdays and family reunions to anniversaries and weddings. We will create meeting and banquet rooms to accommodate corporate and private events.

Outdoor Patio

We plan to build a landscaped courtyard that will be available for private event rental.

Tourist Attraction

We plan to set up a museum on the site, as well as a cafe and bistro to become even more of a tourist attraction.

We plan to build a boutique hotel with a _____ (sports/classic car) theme so we can market to _____ (Sports/Classic Car) Clubs throughout the _____ area.
Example: Beachwalk
Resource:
www.nytimes.com/2017/04/19/realestate/designs-for-a-fast-paced-market.html?_r=0

Lobby Makeover

We plan to make the lobby more friendly to traveling business people and working vacationers. We will respond to the trend that the working area is moving out of the office and into public space, such as coffee shops, bars, and hotel lobbies. Our lobby will become a version of the town square or a social work space, frequented as much by locals who live around the corner as by guests who are actually staying overnight. In the lobby, we will create a space that is conducive to working, with a next-gen desk that is spacious, comfortable, stylish, and practical, and bookable in advance, by the hour. There will be room for colleagues to gather and collaborate. The Wi-Fi will be fast and free, and the lobby will be fully equipped with the required technology..
Example: www.TravelBrilliantly.com.

Personalized Rooms

To make the stay truly memorable, we will personalize the theme of the room according to the interests and styling preferences of the guest. As an example, a hotel with a Hollywood movie theme, might stage a room with a James Bond theme using artwork, movie posters, soundtrack music, video clips and replicas of movie set props.
Source:
http://freshome.com/2013/08/20/the-11-fastest-growing-trends-in-hotel-interior-design/

Catering Sales
We will develop a plan to maximize catering revenues and optimize sales productivity. because catering sales in boutique hotels can conservatively, represent 50% of the total food and beverage revenues.
Source: http://fieldsandcompany.net/articles/hotel-online.Jul04_CateringBoutique.html

Point-of-sale Opportunities
We will use our front desk or other designated areas to take advantage of point-of-sale opportunities, such as selling tickets to local attractions and theatrical events, renting cars, etc.

Hotel/Retailer Alliances
Retailers are seeing the exposure that the hotel and retail partnerships can provide by allowing retailers to showcase their products within guestrooms and hotel common areas. The introduction of boutique hotels sponsored or owned by retailers now immerses travelers into a brand and provides them with the unique opportunity to see and try products while traveling. The ultimate goal is that guests will purchase these products to bring the vacation experience to their own homes long after their hotel stay is over. This innovative approach to brand and product marketing will allow retailers to reach new and different customers, thereby increasing their market share.

Example:
West Elm, a division of William-Sonoma, has partnered with a leading hospitality management team, DDK, to create West Elm Hotels which will feature West Elm products throughout the facilities. With more than 60 years of combined hospitality and investment experience, DDK is an ideal partner for this venture. In addition to the use of West Elm's products, they plan to commission local artists to produce work to display at the properties and local chefs to provide the appropriate dining experiences. West Elm Hotels will debut the first five boutique properties in late 2018. The initial hotels will be located in the cities of Detroit, Minneapolis, Savannah, Charlotte, and Indianapolis, which are all cities where the brand has little or no retail presence. West Elm executives view hotels as a way to build their brand by creating exceptional customer experiences without over saturating markets with new stores.

Example:
Restoration Hardware is in the process of obtaining permits to renovate a building in the meatpacking district of New York in order to open a 14 room boutique hotel there which will use its entire line of products.

Source:
www.lexology.com/library/detail.aspx?g=e51f45ab-f75a-4225-9570-98d907002217

Hotel Branded Product Sales
We will add a new revenue stream by making available for purchase branded hotel products like towels, bed linens, soaps, lotions, grooming and hygiene products, and shampoos.
Source:
https://hmghotelsblog.com/2013/11/05/30-ways-hotels-can-increase-revenues-decrease-
costs-and-boost-their-bottom-line/

4.0 Market Analysis Summary

Our Market Analysis will serve to accomplish the following goals:
1.   Define the characteristics, and needs and wants of the target market.
2.   Serve as a basis for developing sales, marketing and promotional strategies.
3.   Influence the e-commerce website design.

_____ (company name) will focus on quality, luxurious, yet affordable, lodging for business clients and vacationers interested in exploring _____ (city) and the surrounding regions of _____.

The _____'s (company name) target market strategy is based on becoming a destination choice for families, business people and hunters in the greater _____ region who are looking for a place to _____ (conduct business, relax, stage a reunion, recreate, hunt or recharge). The target markets that we are going to pursue are people looking for a vacation or hunting destination, and drop-in customers.

Boutique Hotel development and operation in the _____ area has been very profitable and successful due to the economic upturn experienced in the early and mid 90's. Time-share / Boutique Hotel development and investments into _____ resorts nationwide are currently starting to recover from the 2007 recession. In the past two years, sales of time-shares in the _____ area have increased by over ___ percent. There are ___ (#) condominiums, lodges, inns and hotels within _____ (#) miles of the resort. Each year, room occupancy is close to ____% during the peak ___ (skiing/hunting/racing?) season.

The setting and our facilities make the _____ (company name) a natural destination choice for people. We would like to see a ___ % increase in customers on a yearly basis.

The consumer base for _____ (company name) will be guests referred by the following:
1.   Tourism Offices   2.   Wedding Planners
3.   Travel Agents   4.   Online Reservation Services
5.   Community Centers   6.   Hospital Volunteers
7.   University Counselors   8.   Reunion Organizers

_____ (company name) performed a market study to access the feasibility of our venture and point out key factors that would contribute to our success. The market study was conducted using the following methods and sources:
1.   Tourism and hospitality industry studies.
2.   Innkeeper's association literature.
3.   _____ (year) U.S. Census Data
4.   Internet websites.
5.   Interviews with owners of similar establishments in other regions.
6.   Surveys and interviews with likely guests.
7.   Suggestion card system.

We will use the following checklist to complete our market analysis:
Area Tourism and Recreational Activities
1.   Park visitation   _____
2.   Museum visitation   _____
3.   Amusement and attraction visitation   _____
4.   Casino visitation   _____
5.   Festivals and events visitation   _____
6.   Snowmobile trail usage (weather forecasts) _____
7.   Boating activity   _____
8.   Hunting and fishing activity   _____
9.   Golf course usage   _____
10.   Biking/biking trail usage   _____
11.   Antique shop patronage   _____
12.   Shopping activities   _____
13.   Restaurants in the area   _____

Local Economic and Demographic Characteristics
14.   Local sales tax collections   _____
15.   Room tax collections   _____
16.   Local population   _____
17.   Household income distribution   _____

4.1   Secondary Market Research

We will research demographic information for the following reasons:
1.   To determine which segments of the population, such as Hispanics and the elderly, have been growing and may now be underserved.
2.   To determine if there is a sufficient population base in the designated service area to realize the company's business objectives.
3.   To consider what products and services to add in the future, given the changing demographic profile and needs of our service area.

We will pay special attention to the following general demographic trends:
1.   Population growth has reached a plateau and market share will most likely be increased through innovation and excellent customer service.
2.   Because incomes are not growing and unemployment is high, process efficiencies and sourcing advantages must be developed to keep prices competitive.
3.   The rise of non-traditional households, such as single working mothers, means developing more innovative and personalized programs.
4.   As the population shifts toward more young to middle aged adults, ages 30 to 44, and the elderly, aged 65 and older, there will be a greater need for child-rearing and geriatric mobile support services.
5.   Because of the aging population, increasing pollution levels and high unemployment, new 'green' ways of dealing with the resulting challenges will need to be developed.

We will collect the demographic statistics for the following zip code(s):

_____

This information will be used to decide upon which targeted programs to offer and to make business growth projections.

Resource: www.sbdcnet.org/index.php/demographics.html

Snapshots of consumer data by zip code are also available online:
http://factfinder.census.gov/home/saff/main.html?_lang=en
http://www.esri.com/data/esri_data/tapestry.html
http://www.claritas.com/MyBestSegments/Default.jsp?ID=20

1.	**Total Population**	_____
2.	**Number of Households**	_____
3.	**Population by Race:**	White ____% Black ____%
		Asian Pacific Islander ___% Other ____%
4.	**Population by Gender**	Male ____% Female ____%
5.	**Income Figures:**	Median Household Income $_____
		Household Income Under $50K ____%
		Household Income $50K-$100K ____%
		Household Income Over $100K ____%
6.	**Housing Figures**	Average Home Value - $_____
		Average Rent $_____
7.	**Homeownership**:	Homeowners % _____
		Renters % _____
8.	**Education Achievement**	High School Diploma % _____
		College Degree % _____
		Graduate Degree % _____
9.	**Stability/Newcomers**	Longer than 5 years % _____
10.	**Marital Status**	___% Married ___% Divorced ___% Single
		___% Never Married ___% Widowed ___% Separated
11.	**Occupations**	___%Service ___% Sales ___% Management
		___% Construction ___% Production
		___% Unemployed ___% Below Poverty Level
12.	**Age Distribution**	___%Under 5 years ___%5-9 yrs ___%10-12 yrs
		___% 13-17 yrs ___%18-years
		___% 20-29 ___% 30-39 ___% 40-49 ___% 50-59
		___% 60-69 ___% 70-79 ___% 80+ years
13.	**Prior Growth Rate**	_____% from _____ (year)
14.	**Projected Population Growth Rate**	_____%

Other demographic factors to consider include:

Business and Economic Characteristics

      - Room tax collections   _____

      - Eating and drinking place sales   _____

- Retail sales   _____
- Employment (levels, types, major employers, trends)   _____
- Office/Industrial space occupied   _____
- Business and plant closings   _____
- New businesses planned   _____

Tourism and Recreation Characteristics
- Park visitation   _____
- Museum visitation   _____
- Casino visitation   _____
- Festivals and events visitation   _____
- Attractions visitation   _____
- Snowmobile trail usage   _____
- Boating activity   _____
- Hunting and fishing licenses issued   _____
- New tourism attractions planned   _____

Transportation Factors
- Distance from major cities   _____
- Distance from airport   _____
- Traffic volume   _____
- Airport volume   _____
- Ferry volume   _____
- Passenger rail volume   _____

Demographic Conclusions:
This area will be demographically favorable for our business for the following reasons:
_____

Resources:
www.allbusiness.com/marketing/segmentation-targeting/848-1.html
http://www.sbdcnet.org/industry-links/demographics-links
http://factfinder2.census.gov/faces/nav/jsf/pages/index.xhtml

4.1.1   Primary Market Research

We plan to develop a survey for primary research purposes and mail it to a list of local home, senior and parenting magazine subscribers, purchased from the publishers by zip code. We will also post a copy of the survey on our website and encourage visitors to take the survey. We will use the following survey questions to develop an Ideal guest Profile of our potential client base, so that we can better target our marketing communications. To improve the response rate, we will include an attention-grabbing ____ (discount coupon/ dollar?) as a thank you for taking the time to return the questionnaire.

1.   What is your zip-code?   _____
2.   Are you single, divorced, separated, widowed or married?   _____

3.   Are you male or female?   _____
4.   What is your age?   _____
5.   What is your approximate household income?   _____
6.   What is your educational level?   _____
7.   What is your profession?   _____
8.   Are you a dual income household?
9.   Do you have children? If Yes, what are their ages?   _____
10. What are your favorite magazines?   _____
11. What is your favorite local newspaper?   _____
12. What is your favorite radio station?   _____
13. What are your favorite television programs?   _____
14. What clubs or organizations are you a member of?   _____
15. Does our community have adequate Boutique Hotel facilities?   Yes / No
16. Is your family currently enrolled in home health care program?   Yes / No
17. What are the ages of your children?
18. Do you travel on business?   Yes / No
19. How often?
20. Where do you travel on business?
21. Do you travel for pleasure?   How often?
22. Where do you travel for pleasure?
23. Where do you normally stay?

     ___ Family member   ___ Hotel

     ___ Boutique Hotel   ___ B & B

     ___ Campground   ___ Other _____

24. What are their strengths as lodging providers?
25. What are their weaknesses or shortcomings?
26. What would it take for us to earn your lodging business?
27. What is the best way for us to market our Boutique Hotel lodging services?
28. What is your general need for Boutique Hotel lodging services?

Circle Months: J F M A M J J A S O N D

Circle Days: S   M   T   W   T   F   S

Indicate Hours: _____

Indicate Occasions: _____

Indicate Average Length of Stay: _____

29. How much do you currently pay as a per-night lodging room rate?
30. Would you be willing to pay a higher fee for better Boutique Hotel services or
     amenities?
31. Are you satisfied with your current lodging arrangements?
32. How frequently would you use the services of a Boutique Hotel?
33. Do you live in _____ community?
34. Do you work or study in _____ community?
35. Do you think you will be in need of a Boutique Hotel in the near future?
36. What type of lodging arrangements would you prefer?
37. Describe your experience with other lodging providers.
38. Please rank (1 to 18) the importance of the following factors when choosing
     a Boutique Hotel:

___ Cancellation Policy	___ Hours of service
___ Convenient location	___ Staff Responsiveness
___ guest Service	___ Breakfast Menu Selection
___ Scheduling Convenience	___ Value Proposition

___ Price   ___ Referral

___ Amenities   ___ Other _____

39.   Please rank the importance of the following amenities (1 to 14):

___ In-room Fireplace	___ Whirlpool Tub
___ Private bathroom	___ Swimming pool
___ Evening snacks	___ Suites
___ Breakfast Menu	___ Cable TV/DVD Player
___ Internet Access	___ View
___ Private kitchen	___ Library
___ Antiques	___ BBQ Grill
___ Other _____	

40.   What information would you like to see in home health care newsletter?

41.   Which online social groups have you joined? Choose the ones you access.

___ Facebook	___ MySpace
___ Twitter	___ LinkedIn
___ Ryze	___ Ning

42.   What types of new Boutique Hotel packages would most interest you?

43.   What are your suggestions for realizing a better Boutique Hotel guest experience?

44.   Are you on our mailing list? Yes/No   If No, can we add you?   Yes / No

45.   Can you supply the name and contact info of person who might be interested in our Boutique Hotel services?

46.   What is your average stay length in a Boutique Hotel in our area?

47.   What types of unique values and deals would you be interested in?

48.   What types of room amenities are you most interested in ?

49.   How do you typically make a Boutique Hotel reservation?

50.   What room rate range is acceptable?

Please note any comments or concerns about Boutique Hotel services.

We very much appreciate your participation in this survey. If you provide your name, address and email address, we will sign you up for our e-newsletter, inform you of our survey results, advise you of any new Boutique Hotel facilities opening in your community, and enter you into our monthly drawing for a free

_____.

Name   Address   Email   Phone

4.1.2   Voice of the Customer

To develop a better understanding of the changing needs and wants of our Boutique Hotel guests, we will institute the following ongoing listening practices:

1. Focus Groups

   Small groups of customers (6 to 8) will be invited to meet with a facilitator to answer open-ended questions about priority of needs and wants, and our company, its products or other given issues. These focus groups will provide useful insight into the decisions and the decision making process of target consumers.

2. Individual Interviews

   We will conduct face-to-face personal interviews to understand guest thought processes, selection criteria and entertainment preferences.

3. guest Panels

   A small number of customers will be invited to answer open-ended questions on a regular basis.

4. Guest Tours

   We will invite customers to visit our facilities to discuss how our processes can better serve them.

5. Visit with Customers

   We will observe customers as they actually use our products and services to uncover the pains and problems they are experiencing during usage.

6. Trade Show Meetings

   Our trade show booth will be used to hear the concerns of our customers.

7. Toll-free Numbers

   We will attach our phone number to all products and sales literature to encourage the guest to call with problems or positive feedback.

8. Guest Surveys

   We will use surveys to obtain opinions on closed-ended questions, testimonials, constructive feedback, and improvement suggestions.

9. Mystery Shoppers

   We will use mystery shoppers to report on how our employees treat our customers.

10. Salesperson Debriefing

    We will ask our salespeople to report on their guest experiences to obtain insights into what the guest faces, what they want and why they failed to make a sale.

11. Guest Contact Logs

    We will ask our sales personnel to record interesting guest revelations.

12. Guest Serviceperson's Hotline

    We will use this dedicated phone line for service people to report problems.

13. Discussions with competitors.

14. Installation of suggestion boxes to encourage constructive feedback. The suggestion card will have several statements customers are asked to rate in terms of a given scale. There are also several open ended questions that allow the guest to freely offer constructive criticism or praise. We will work hard to implement reasonable suggestions in order to improve our service offerings as well as show our commitment to the guest that their suggestions are valued.

4.2   Market Segmentation

Market segmentation is a technique that recognizes that the potential universe of users may be divided into definable sub-groups with different characteristics. Segmentation enables organizations to target messages to the needs and concerns of these subgroups. We will segment the market based on the needs and wants of select customer groups. We will develop a composite customer profile and a value proposition for each of these segments. The purpose for segmenting the market is to allow our marketing/sales program to focus on the subset of prospects that are "most likely" to purchase our Boutique Hotel products and services. If done properly this will help to insure the highest return for our marketing/sales expenditures.

Our targeted customers are mainly locals looking and paying for a distinctive experience and not a hotel room that will look and feel identical to any other hotel room of an established brand. The target market for boutique hotels can be described as follows:
1.   Guests in the early 20's to mid-50's.
2.   Have a mid to upper income average.
3.   Majority of guests' are male (61%)
4.   63% of the subsector's business mix is from corporate travel

The average stay of a guest to a boutique hotel is between one to two nights. Theses guests continually seek new and unique experiences different from standardized hotels in which the property itself becomes the destination location and their tourism purchase patterns are becoming polarized, both of which favors boutique hotels as they are experience focused upscale properties. Additionally, symbolic meaning behind premium brands, such as prestige associated with boutique and lifestyle hotels are used to express the visitors' self-concept of themselves or express their self-actualization needs.

We will pursue the following market segments: (select)
1.   **Tourists**
      These are the vacationers in search of a good time. This market can be extremely seasonal, unless you are located in an urban area.
2.   **Business Travelers**
      This is more popular in urban areas, but many rural areas feature one or two major corporations that can produce a fair amount of business travel.
3.   **Romantic Getaways**
      The focus here is on romantic weekend getaways. Involves setting up a reminder service to help celebrate the arrival of spouse birthdays and anniversaries.
4.   **Wedding Receptions**
      Install a photogenic gazebo in the backyard and set-up a dessert buffet, and you will add a whole new dimension to your Boutique Hotel operations.
5.   **Colleges and Universities**
      Involves handling the visitors to sporting events, homecomings, academic conferences and graduations.
6.   **Hospitals**
      Hospitals draw bedside visitors and visiting physicians, lecturers and conference

attendees.

7. **Local Patrons/Extra Bedroom**
   Involves promoting your Boutique Hotel as the extra bedroom for locals with an overwhelming influx of family members.

8. **Town Meetings**
   Diversify your revenue stream by renting part of your facility to organizations and clubs that want to conduct teas, meetings and other get-togethers.

9. **Leisure Travelers**
   We will establish relationships with the local visitor bureau, Chamber of Commerce and local event and attraction operators.

10. **Group Meeting Travelers:**
    Leisure groups include bus tours, school activities, athletic events, etc. Tour groups are often brought to an area for sightseeing and attending special events. Local attractions that appeal to leisure tour groups may have records of the numbers and names of tour operators who have visited their attractions. We will contact The National Tour Association and American Bus Association for information on tour activity. Business group meetings are typically associated with conferences, board meetings, training programs, seminars, trade shows, and other gatherings. We will contact the sponsoring organization because they will typically be from the local area. Information on the group meeting market will be obtained through state chapters of Meeting Planners International and the American Society of Association Executives.

11. **Recreational _____ (Skiers/Hunters/Cyclists/Chefs?)**
    This area is quickly becoming one of the best ____ (ski?) resorts in the U.S. The resort is located ___ (#) miles from _____ Airport and is easily accessible.

12. **Summer Visitors.**
    During the summer months, the _____ area is a beautiful wilderness retreat with over ___ (#) hiking trails and other outdoor recreational activities.

Composite Ideal guest Profile:

By assembling this composite guest profile we will know what guest needs and wants our company needs to focus on and how best to reach our target market. We will use the information gathered from our guest research surveys to assemble the following composite guest profile:

Ideal guest Profile

Who are they?
- age _____
- gender _____
- occupation _____
  location: zip codes _____
- income level _____
  marital status _____
  ethnic group _____
  education level _____
  family life cycle _____
  number of household members _____

household income	_____
homeowner or renter	_____
association memberships	_____
leisure activities	_____
hobbies/interests	_____
core beliefs	_____
Where are they located (zip codes)?	_____
Most popular product/service purchased?	_____
Lifestyle Preferences?	Trendsetter/Trend follower/Other _____
How often do they buy?	_____
What are most important purchase factors?	Price/Brand Name/Quality/Financing/Sales Convenience/Packaging/Other_____
What is their key buying motivator?	_____
How do they buy it?	Cash/Credit/Terms/Other_____
Where do they buy it from (locations)?	_____
What problem do they want to solve?	_____
What are the key frustrations/pains that these customers have when buying?	_____
What search methods do they use?	_____
What is preferred problem solution?	_____

Table: Market Analysis

		Number of Potential Customers		
Potential Customers	Growth	2017	2018	2019
Tourists	10%			
Local Patrons/Extra Bedroom	10%			
Business Travelers	10%			
Romantic Getaways	10%			
Weddings	10%			
Colleges and Universities	10%			
Hospitals	10%			
Business Meetings	10%			
Recreational Golfers	10%			
Other	10%			
Totals:	10%			

4.3   Target Market Segment Strategy

Our target marketing strategy will involve identifying a group of customers to which to direct our Boutique Hotel products and services. Our strategy will be the result of intently listening to and understanding customer needs, representing customers' needs to those responsible for product production and service delivery, and giving them what they want. In developing our targeted customer messages we will strive to understand things like: where they work, worship, party and play, where they shop and go to school, how they spend their leisure time, what magazines they read and organizations they belong to, and where they volunteer their time. We will use research, surveys and observation to uncover this wealth of information to get our product details and brand name in front of our customers when they are most receptive to receiving our messaging.

Target Market Worksheet   (optional)

Product Benefits: Actual factor (cost effectiveness, design, performance, etc.) or perceived factor (image, popularity, reputation, etc.) that satisfies what a customer needs or wants. An advantage or value that the product will offer its buyer.

Products Features: One of the distinguishing characteristics of a product or service that helps boost its appeal to potential buyers. A characteristic of a product that describes its appearance, its components, and its capabilities. Typical features include size and color.

Product or Service	Product/ Service Benefits	Product/ Service Features	Potential Target Markets

We plan to aggressively pursue guests from _____ while introducing _____ (area) to the local under-tapped market population. We also plan to use the Boutique Hotel for local patrons by opening it for catered parties, receptions, etc. Subscriptions to various Web services will provide international exposure for nominal annual fees. Committing to staying in the building to book reservations and opening the Boutique Hotel to diverse groups of people will also increase bookings.

The target market for _____ (company name) are travelers between the ages of 25 and 55, married with moderate to high income. Three quarters will have booked accommodations before leaving home and will stay two nights as a getaway from one of the ____ (#) urban centers.

Referral marketing, direct-mail campaigns and community activities will be the primary types of marketing strategies employed. Enhancing our reputation for trust with families and in the community will be crucial in establishing our brand image and obtaining the planned market share growth that we have forecasted. To this end, we will draft and publish our associated modeled Code of Ethics and any service guarantees that we decide to offer.

Our customers can be broadly divided into the following groups:

1. **Weekend getaway customers**
    These people are from the region and are looking to get away, be pampered and escape from daily stress. Requires advertising in the romantic getaway sections of local newspapers and regional editions of lifestyle magazines. We also require

setting up special romantic package deals, such as arranging for an optional catered in-room candlelit dinner, flower delivery and a horse-drawn carriage ride.

2. **Leisure Travelers**

    These people are passing through ____ (city) and prefer to stay in an affordable Boutique Hotel instead of a luxury hotel. Travelers that thoroughly plan their excursions will pre-register through reservation service organizations. They will be looking for a unique blend of socialization, security and privacy.

3. **Destination travelers**

    The ____ (university/hospital) brings a large number of people through ____ (city) and __ (company name) believes that a good portion of business will be from the ____ (attraction name). Occasions include parents weekend, orientation, parents visiting, and graduation. These guests will be referred by their contacts at the destination institutions, so it will be important contact with these influencers.

4. **Weddings**

    It will be important to establish mutual referral relationships with other bridal service providers, including wedding planners, photographers and bridal shops. We will advertise on internet wedding directories and set-up booths at bridal center exhibitions. It is also critical to set-up a sign-in registy form to collect names and addresses from guest attendees for the in-house mailing list.

5. **Business Travelers**

    We will personally call upon the human resource executives at the local corporations and make them aware of our Boutique Hotel service offerings.

6. **Clubs and Organizations**

    We will help clubs to form around specialized interests and charge a rental fee for the use of our facility as a meeting place and the housing of materials related to their topic of interest.

7. **Local trade organizations**

    We will offer special rates to members.

8. **Exhibition spaces or conference venues**

    We will special discounts to delegates and exhibitors

9. **Target Drop-ins**

    When rooms are available we will welcome the drop-in customer who is looking for a place to stay for the night. Our lite sign can be seen from Route ____ (#), a main thoroughfare, and we expect to get quite a few drop-ins.

10. **Targeted Niche Markets:**

Target Realtors

Realtors often need to make overnight lodging arrangements for out-of-town buyers and want potential buyers to meet with local business owners and residents.

Target Learning Fanatics

We will schedule regular fee-based seminars and workshops to teach things such as crafting, cooking, gardening and scrap booking. We will promote these workshops in our sales brochure and provide information about them to our reservation service organizations.

Target Dog Lovers

We will offer special amenities for guests with dogs, including an in-room cage and free dog-walking services. We will advertise in dog magazines and pet supply and grooming businesses.

Target Families with Children

We will promote the fact that we have made our facility 'kid friendly' and installed playground equipment in our backyard. We will also help local businesses to advertise their kid attractions. We will offer our guests a babysitting service.

Target Romantic Couples

We will promote our Boutique Hotel as a romantic getaway destination. We will advertise on websites that promote romantic hotels, such as bestromanticinns.com and bnblist.com.

Target Historic Heritage Tourists

We will help our guests to appreciate the historic design of our building. We will advertise in magazines such as Victorian Homes and Colonial Homes, and on websites such as victorianinns.com, and become a member of the local historic preservation society. Resources: National Register of Historic Places (www.nps.gov/nr/)
BBonline (www.bbonline.com/historic.html)

Target Health, Beauty, Outdoor and Fitness Enthusiasts

We will develop a menu that includes vegetarian dishes and organically grown produce. We will set-up a spa room on our premises and hire independent contractors to perform therapeutic massages, pedicures, manicures and facials. We will stock one room with fitness equipment and make arrangements for the rental of mountain bikes and other tpes of equipment for field can canoeing trips. We will make a mailing to our existing guest database, and advise them of our new service and rental offerings. We will also place classified ads in related magazines and offer to give free seminars on topics related to these new targeted offerings and special interests.

Target Cyclists

We will target cyclists by adding a bicycle shop to the premises that repairs and rents bicycles. We will advertise in the newsletters of bicycle clubs and rent a mailing list of subscribers of bicycle themed magazines by area zip code. We will also organize bicycle tours of our area.

Target Business Guests

We will become a member of the Chamber of Commerce and welcome speaking engagement opportunities, where we will discuss our ability to accommodate the specialized needs of business travelers.

Target Millennials (ages 21 to 34)

Millennials represent a quarter of the U.S. population, more than $200 billion in annual buying power and $500 billion in indirect spending, which considers their impact on

other generations. They account for 21 to 25 percent of consumer discretionary purchases, and that is going to increase has they acquire more earning power. Millennials number more than 75 million in the United States, and the Census Bureau projects they will surpass baby boomers as the nation's largest generation in 2017. Presently, millennial buyers are struggling with higher prices, and tighter mortgage-lending procedures. Research also indicates that Millennials are willing to sacrifice comfort for cheaper travel. U.S. millennials plan to spend about $226 billion in 2017 on travel, according to a Harris Poll survey. Millennials are reaching out to social networks and observing behaviors of their friends to look for new, novel, authentic experiences. Millennials don't look exclusively to their friends for information. They also process information from lots of sources, because they do want an accurate, authoritative portrayal of an experience they are hoping to enjoy. As marketers, we will provide useful information to potential clients via social networking sites. In fact, JWT data from March 2014 suggests that millennial travelers are more likely to grab their smartphones to access their social networks, Yelp reviews or foursquare users to garner real-time suggestions and find local information while on the go. We will provide these types of "concierge-like" services to reach millennials. And to gain the initial trust of these customers, we will join social media conversations, participate in forums and comment on blogs, already in progress, rather than interrupt them in order to start and control conversations of our own. We will also practice nostalgia marketing to connect with millenials and use content that reminds them how they have changed from their common, shared experiences in the 90s.
Resource:
http://hotelmarketing.com/index.php/content/article/what_the_hospitality_
        industry_can_learn_from_airbnb

Our objective will be to attract millennial travelers with super-fast WiFi connections, Bluetooth sound systems and communal lobby areas. The Internet speed will be super fast, and the Wi-Fi will be free. Power outlets and USB ports will dot the walls, especially near the bed to accommodate binge watching. This will help us to target the millennial traveler, ages 18 to 34, who likes to stay connected online, eat on the run and commune with other millennials. We will place a heavy focus on technology, including kiosk driven check-in systems, keyless room entry and smartphone apps to let guests adjust the room temperature or make restaurant reservations without talking to a human. We will also respond to their need for healthy food-to-go choices in the lobby, and spacious gathering areas with communal tables, couches and comfy chairs. We will also test the concept of outdoor gathering spots with fire pits and picnic areas, and introduce design concepts and artwork by local artisans.
Example: Billionaire Sir Richard Branson has a new millennial-oriented chain, called Virgin Hotels.
Resource:
www.adweek.com/brand-marketing/how-hotels-are-luring-millennials-era-airbnb-
        172136/

Target Women Business Travelers
We will get involved with women business organizations, such as the American Business

Women's Association (www.abwa.org). We will install computer workstations that feature printers, fax and copy machines, and DSL access, and create a separate sales brochure that targets the need of this market segment and highlights our security measures.

Target Retired People and Seniors
This group may have mobility and anxiety problems, and the desire to relax in the tranquility of a private home. They can be reached through community and daycare centers. These women require more help with both personal care needs and routine needs, and are less likely to have a spouse available to help them. They will be more appreciative of the personalized and support services offered by our Boutique Hotel. It will be important to identify creative approaches to connecting with the social and community causes that are important to women and reinforce the role of a total wellness and lifestyle solution, rather than a product-centric or service-centric brand approach.

Target Local Ethnic Groups
Ongoing demographic trends suggest that, in the coming decades, early childhood programs will be serving a population of children which is increasingly diverse in economic resources, racial and ethnic background, and family structure. Our plan is to reach out to consumers of various ethnic backgrounds, especially Hispanics, who comprise nearly 13 percent of the country's total population. In addition to embarking on an aggressive media campaign of advertising with ethnic newspapers and radio stations, we will set up programs to actively recruit bilingual employees and make our Boutique Hotel more accessible via signage printed in various languages based on the Boutique Hotel's community. We will accurately translate our marketing materials into other languages. We will enlist the support of our bilingual employees to assist in reaching the ethnic people in our surrounding area through a referral program. We will join the nearest _____ (predominate ethnic group) Chamber of Commerce and partner with _____ (Hispanic/Chinese/Other?) Advocacy Agencies. We will also develop programs that reflect cultural influences and brand preferences.

Helpful Resources:
U.S. census Bureau Statistics   www.census.gov
U.S. Dept. of Labor/Bureau of Labor Statistics   www.bls.gov/data/home.htm
National Hispanic Medical Association

4.3.1   Market Needs

The recent demand for boutique hotels is credited to the growing interest of consumers in learning about the fine arts and culture. In comparison to other lodging subsectors, boutique hotels are able to deliver both aspects of design and local culture to guests; hence, successfully attracting more guests and charging higher room rates. The increasing polarization of tourists today is also fuelling development in this subsector. Boutique hotels normally have at least a four star rating and operate between mid to luxury markets due to added value for guests from the nature of the lodging product and to their higher level of services and amenities.

Supply side growth for boutique hotels is fuelled by outperformance of the subsector compared to overall regional lodging sector performance. This subsector has consistently outperformed the overall sector in terms of occupancy rate, ADR and RevPAR. The boutique concept is successful at differentiating itself from other lodging products, while better addressing guest needs and creating value for them. This trend was expected to continue strong but has been restrained due to the recent financial crisis. Deloitte noted boutique hotels yielded weaker performance and slower growth through the recessionary phase, pulling down the sector's overall performance averages (Deloitte, 2010).

Similar to tourists who choose to stay in traditional hotels, customers who patronize Boutique Hotels seek relaxation, fun and stress management while on vacation. However, this type of guest also prefers comfortable accommodations in a trendy, hip, cool, inspiring, sensual, joyful, romantic, intriguing. aspirational environment. These patrons are more social, they love meeting new people while at the same time require sufficient privacy to enjoy their vacation.

Our guests have the following needs:
1.   Room Selection (joyful ambiance)
2.   Accessibility (reasonable driving distance)
3.   Exceptional guest Service (personalized service)
4.   Competitive Pricing   (value-based)
5.   Security (women business travelers)
6.   Guests Hobbies and Interests Aligned with our boutique hotel theme.

_____ (company name) has all the necessary facilities to attract such customers.

4.4   Buying Patterns

A Buying Pattern is the typical manner in which /buyers consumers purchase goods or services or firms place their purchase orders in terms of amount, frequency, timing, etc. In determining buying patterns, we will need to understand the following:
     - Why consumers make the purchases that they make?
     - What factors influence consumer purchases?
     - The changing factors in our society.

Many guests who travel to the same destination more than once often stay at the same hotel. In that vein, our boutique hotel will attract guests who not only want consistency in service, amenities, and rewards, but also want to be excited by the experience of staying in a different room with a new design, layout and aesthetic each time. Our boutique hotel, with its varying layouts and creative spatial solutions, will be able to meet this demand time and time again without losing the intimacy of a truly hospitable stay.

Our targeted guests will appreciate a property where they can feel special, where owners and operators can differentiate their personalized offerings and where architects can challenge themselves and the constructs of modern hospitality design to create something that is truly unique in both function and aesthetics. Given all the choices a traveler today has, including ultra-high end resorts, mixed-use urban towers and flagship chains, only a boutique hotel such as ours, can combine the qualities of differentiation, distinction, discernment and even a flare for the daring into a truly unique and memorable stay.

The Boutique Hotel industry offers a unique lodging environment, which caters to an ever-increasing group of travelers. Successful hotels create a climate of home, where guests become temporary members of a larger family. The Boutique Hotel opens itself to guests, allowing them to participate and share in the richness of a community, while still allowing whatever degree of privacy is preferred. Breakfast meals can be shared with the other travelers allowing new relationships to be created and old ones enriched, or meals can be taken in the privacy of the guest's room.

A variety of settings available in the Boutique Hotel are situated to enable individuals or small groups to locate the perfect setting for whatever mood or activity one is pursuing (reading, watching television, playing board games, etc.).

At _____ (company name) guests will have the right mix of membership and privacy. Being dutiful without being intrusive is a delicate balance and one that owners have mastered in their various walks of life.

The top reasons for staying at a hotel are as follows:
1.   Personal touch   (82%)
2.   Building Charm   (79%)
3.   Scheduled Getaway   (70%)
4.   Décor   (69%)
5.   Romance   (64%)

The top attributes that played the most important role in the guest purchase decision were as follows:
1.   Friendliness of the manager   (82%)
2.   Private bathrooms   (61%)
3.   Full breakfast   (52%)
4.   Fireplace in room   (45%)
5.   Nearby activities/shopping   (45%)
6.   Historical building or area   (29%)
7.   Credit cards accepted   (28%)
8.   Afternoon/evening refreshments   (20%)

On average, about 15% of Boutique Hotel guests are return visitors and 15% have been referred by past guests. Thus, the quality of stay and customer satisfaction are important factors in the decision process and are based on the following amenities:
1.   Mattress and pillow quality   (88%0
2.   Towels   (84%)

3.	Washcloths	(75%)
4.	Glasses	(62%)
5.	Reading lights	(61%)
6.	Soap	(50%)
7.	Reading Materials	(30%)

The three most popular information sources are:
1. Recommendations from friends and family
2. Boutique Hotel's brochure
3. Guidebooks
4. Online Reservation Service Organizations

_____ (company name) will gear its offerings, marketing, and pricing policies to establish a loyal client base. Our affordable pricing, attractive facility, area guidance, and basic quality services will be welcomed in _____(city) and contribute to our success.

4.5   Market Growth

We will assess the following general factors that affect market growth:

	Current Assessment
1. Interest Rates	_____
2. Government Regulations	_____
3. Perceived Environment Impact	_____
4. Consumer Confidence Level	_____
5. Population Growth Rate	_____
6. Unemployment Rate	_____
7. Political Stability	_____
8. Currency Exchange Rate	_____
9. Innovation Rate	_____
10. Home Sales	_____
11. Overall Economic Health	_____

Thanks to high occupancy levels and cheap interest rates, developers are scrambling to build new properties. At the same time, hotels are trying to lure a new generation of travelers in search of authenticity. They want unique and hip places to sleep, not cookie-cutter facsimiles of hundreds of other hotels. These 'lifestyle hotels' are the hot, new area for growth. They are designed to attract millennials: travelers between the ages of 18 and 34 who hotels say aren't interested in marble bathtubs but might enjoy beanbag chairs.

Sales are expected to grow by ___% for the next few years. This growth can be attributed to a couple of factors. The first factor is an appreciation for personalized services and sense of security that our Boutique Hotel provides. Another factor driving market growth is the increase in airfare that makes non-local vacations less practical and cost effective. People are turning to hotels in unique locations as a vacation spot instead of flying.

Lastly, as the number of work hours Americans perform has increased in the last few years, people are relying on weekend getaways as a way to distance themselves, albeit briefly, from their work week. hotels provide people this option, and this has been a user group that has gotten larger in the last few years.

The _____ area is expected to grow _____ % annually. The _____ zip code area is expected to grow ____% annually. These estimates are based on the most recent US Census Data and the _____ County Chamber of Commerce figures.

The general industry analysis shows that ____ (city) is expected to experience substantial population, housing and commercial business growth. This suggests that as more families continue to move into the _____ area, there will be an increasing demand for quality, uniquely designed, mind and spirit enriching, and personalized lodging services, and this makes it a prime location for a Boutique Hotel business.

4.6   Service Business Analysis

Research indicates that boutique and lifestyle hotels are defined by the following physical attributes:
>   Cultural/Historic/ Authentic
>   Individual hotel / not a Chain
>   Interesting, unique services
>   Many, high-quality in-room features
>   Social spaces, such as living rooms and libraries, with social events
>   Innovative
>   Less about brand; more personal.

There are two branches of Boutique Hotels: Boutique Hotels in city destinations, and Boutique Hotels in resort destinations. The Boutique Hotels in city destinations are not only visited because of their convenience, but also because of the city's fashion. Therefore, the most common locations of the Boutique Hotels are London, New York, Miami, and Los Angeles. Technology is an important attribute of a city Boutique Hotel. It could be technology used to emotionally connect the guest with the Hotel, like music and light, or it could be technology for the guests' convenience, such as computers with high-speed internet, cordless phones, DVD players, and flat-screen televisions.

Of the lodgings in _____ (city), ____ (#) are categorized as boutique hotels, ___ (#) as resort hotels, ____(#) as B&B Inns, , ____(#) as long-term lease facilities (rentals, condos, and houses) and ____ (#) as motels. .

Market conditions have a significant impact on a hotel's profitability. The strength of the business community and tourism activity impacts how many units are rented and the rates that can be charged.

4.7 Barriers to Entry

_____ (company name) will benefit from the following combination of barriers to entry, which cumulatively present a moderate degree of entry difficulty or obstacles in the path of other **Boutique Hotel** businesses wanting to enter our market.

1. Industry Experience.
2. Community Networking
3. Referral Program Set-up
4. People Skills
5. Marketing Skills
6. Licensing/Zoning Variance
7. Operations Management
8. Cash Flow Management
9. Website Design
10. Renovation Design/Management

4.7.1   Porter's Five Forces Analysis

We will use Porter's five forces analysis as a framework for the industry analysis and business strategy development. It will be used to derive the five forces which determine the competitive intensity and therefore attractiveness of our market. Attractiveness in this context refers to the overall industry profitability.

Competitors   The degree of rivalry is high in this segment, but less when compared to the overall category. There are _____ (#) major competitors in the _____ area and they include: _____

Threat of Substitutes

Substitutes are high for this industry. These include other Boutique Hotels, hotels, motels, B&B Inns, etc.

Bargaining Power of Buyers

Buyer power is moderate in the business. Buyers are sensitive to quality and pricing as the segment attempts to capitalize on the pricing and quality advantage.

Bargaining Power of Suppliers

Supplier power is moderate in the industry. Supplies can be obtained from a number of distributors. A high level of operational efficiency for managing supplies can be achieved.

Threat of New Entrants

Relatively high in this segment. The business model can be easily copied.

Conclusions: _____ (company name) is in a competitive field and has to move fast to retain its competitive advantage. The key success factors are to develop operational efficiencies, innovative programs, unique facility design, cost-effective marketing and personalized customer service excellence.

4.8   Competitive Analysis

Competitor analysis in marketing and strategic management is an assessment of the strengths and weaknesses of current and potential competitors. This analysis will provide both an offensive and defensive strategic context through which to identify our business opportunities and threats. We will carry out continual competitive analysis to ensure our market is not being eroded by developments in other firms. This analysis needs to be matched with the target segment needs to ensure that our products and services continue to provide better value than the competitors. The competitive analysis needs to be able to show very clearly why our products and services are preferred in some market segments to other offerings and to be able to offer reasonable proof of that assertion.

Competitor	What We Can Do and They Can't	What They Can Do and We Can't

We will conduct good market intelligence for the following reasons:
1.   To forecast competitors' strategies.
2.   To predict competitor likely reactions to our own strategies.
3.   To consider how competitors' behavior can be influenced in our own favor.
4.   To learn valuable lessons from past competitor strategies.

Competitive analysis conducted by the company owners has shown that there are ____ (# or no other?) companies currently offering the same combination of Boutique Hotel services in the _____ (city) area. However, the existing indirect competitors offer only a limited range of Boutique Hotel services. In fact, of these _____ (#) competitors only _____ (#) offered a range of Boutique Hotel services and packaged options comparable with what _____ (company name) plans to offer to its guests. Some of the demand for boutique hotels has been eaten up by Airbnb (www.airbnb.com) and other sites that allow travelers to rent rooms in other people's homes.

Self-assessment

Competitive Rating Assessment:	1 = Weak ....5 = Strong		
	Our Company	Prime Competitor	Compare
Our Location	_____	_____	_____
Our Facilities	_____	_____	_____
Our Products	_____	_____	_____
Our Services and Amenities	_____	_____	_____
Our Management Skills	_____	_____	_____
Our Training Programs	_____	_____	_____
Our Research & Development	_____	_____	_____
Our Company Culture	_____	_____	_____
Our Business Model	_____	_____	_____
Our Distribution System	_____	_____	_____
Overall Rating	_____	_____	_____

Rationale: _____

The following establishments are considered direct Boutique Hotel competitors in ____ (city):

Competitor	Address	Market Share	Primary Focus	Secondary Prod/Svcs	Strengths	Weaknesses

Indirect Competitors include the following campgrounds, inns, hotels and motels:

_____

_____

Alternative Competitive Matrix

Competitor Name:	Us			
Location	____	____	____	
Distance	____	____	____	

Comparison Items:

Sales Revenue _____

No. of Rooms _____

Occupancy Rate _____

Avg. Daily Room Rate _____

Percent Repeat Guests _____

Minimum Stays (Y/N) _____

Adequate Parking (Y/N) _____

Facility Condition _____

Facility Visibility _____

Facility Accessibility _____

Guest Room Quality _____

Proximity to demand sources _____

Accessibility _____

Visibility _____

Surrounding neighborhood _____

Facility Age _____

Ext. appearance/condition _____

Int. appearance/condition _____

Cleanliness _____

Signage _____

Types of rooms (suites, etc.) _____

Food and beverage outlets _____

Function rooms (Y/N) _____

Recreation/pool, fitness club) _____

Service

Quality of service _____

Extra services offered	_____
Weekday vs. end patterns	_____
Occupancy growth/decline	_____
Monthly occupancy levels	_____
No. of 100% occup.days/month	_____
Average room rate per month	_____
Maj. segments served/month	_____
Major sources of demand	_____
General Information	
Number of rooms	_____
Months open	_____
Published rates	_____
Franchise affiliation	_____
Ratings in travel guides	_____
Private Bathrooms (Y/N)	_____
Amenities	_____
Owner Occupied (Y/N)	_____
Capacities	_____
Profitability	_____
Market Share	_____
Service Extras	_____
Funding Source	_____
Décor	_____
Target Market	_____
Operating Hours	_____
Pricing/Rate Strategy	_____
Yrs in Business	_____
Management	_____
Reputation	_____
Quality Ratings	_____
Food Quality	_____
Marketing Strategy	_____
Alliances	_____
Sales Brochure/Catalog	_____
Website	_____
Sales Revenues	_____
No. of Staff	_____
Competitive Advantages	_____
Credit Card Accept (Y/N)	_____
Special Events	_____
Recreational Activities	_____
Comments	_____

Competitor Profile Matrix

	Our	Competitor 1		Competitor 2		Competitor 3	
Critical Success Factors	Score	Rating	Score	Rating	Score	Rating	Score

Advertisement _____
Product Quality _____
Service Quality _____
Price Competition _____
Management _____
Financial Position _____
Customer Loyalty _____
Brand Identity _____
Market Share _____
Total _____

We will use the following sources of information to conduct our competition analysis:
1. Competitor company websites.
2. Mystery shopper visits.
3. Annual Reports (www.annual reports.com)
4. Thomas Net (www.thomasnet.com)
5. Trade Journals and Associations
6. Local Chamber of Commerce
7. Sales representative interviews
8. Research & Development may come across new patents.
9. Market research surveys can give feedback on the guest's perspective
10. Monitoring services will track a company or industry you select for news.
    Resources: www.portfolionews.com   www.Office.com
11. Hoover's   www.hoovers.com
12. www.zapdata.com   (Dun and Bradstreet) You can buy one-off lists here.
13. www.infousa.com   (The largest, and they resell to many other vendors)
14. www.onesource.com (By subscription, they pull information from many sources)
15. www.capitaliq.com   (Standard and Poors).
16. Obtain industry specific information from First Research
    (www.firstresearch.com) or IBISWorld, although both are by subscription only,
    although you may be able to buy just one report.
17. Get industry financial ratios and industry norms from RMA (www.rmahq.com) or
    by using ProfitCents.com software.
18. Company newsletters
19. Industry and Market Research Consultants
20. Local Suppliers and Distributors
21. guest interviews regarding competitors.
22. Analyze competitors' ads for their target audience, market position, product
    features, benefits, prices, etc.
23. Attend speeches or presentations made by representatives of your competitors.
24. View competitor's trade show display from a potential guest's point of view. 25.
    Search computer databases (available at many public libraries).
26. Review competitor Yellow Book Ads.
27. American Automobile Association Tour Books
28. Mobil Travel Guides

29. State association and local lodging directories
30. www.bls.gov/cex/ (site provides information on consumer expenditures nationally, regionally, and by selected metropolitan areas).
31. www.sizeup.com
32. Business Statistics and Financial Ratios   www.bizstats.com

4.9 Market Revenue Projection

For each of our chosen target markets, we will estimate our market share in number of customers, and based on consumer behavior, how often do they buy per year? What is the average dollar amount of each purchase? We will then multiply these three numbers to project sales volume for each target market.

Target Market	Number of Customers	No. of Purchases per Year	Average Dollar Amount per Purchase	Total Sales Volume
	A x	B x	C =	D

Using the target market number identified in this section, and the local demographics, we have made the following assessments regarding market opportunity and revenue potential in our area:

	# Rooms Sold	Cost/Night	Weeks/Year Occupied	Total
Weekend (Friday & Saturday)				
Sundays				
Weekdays				
Total				

Or

Business Clientele				
Travelers Passing Through				
Attraction Events/Tours				
Family Visits				
Misc.				
Total				

Recap:

Month	Jan Feb Mar Apr May Jun Jul Aug Sep Oct Nov Dec	Total
Products		
Services		

Gross Sales:	_____
(-) Returns	_____
Net Sales	_____

Revenue Assumptions:

1. The sources of information for our revenue projection are:
    _____

2. If the total market demand for our product/service = 100%, our projected sales volume represents ____% of this total market.

3. The following factors might lower our revenue projections:
    _____

Projected Revenue Worksheet

Room Rates	Room Names	Amenities	Peak Season Cost/Night	Off-season Cost/Night
1._____	_____	_____	_____	_____
2._____	_____	_____	_____	_____
3._____	_____	_____	_____	_____
4._____	_____	_____	_____	_____
Totals:			_____	

Divide by Number of Rooms: _____ _____
Average Cost per Room: _____ (D) _____ (E)
Annual Area Occupancy Rate: _____ (A) (Requires Market Research)
Number of Guest Rooms: _____
Nights per year (x) 365
Maximum Occupancy: (=) _____ Room Nights (B)

Year 1 Occupancy

Est. percent of annual area occupancy rate (Yr 1):   50%
Annual Area Occupancy Rate: (x)_____ (A)
Forecasted Year 1 Occupancy Rate   (=)_____ (Z)
Maximum Occupancy Room Nights   _____ (B)
Divide by 2 for Peak & Off-season Breakdown (/)   2   (assumes 6 mos. each)
Peak Season Room Nights   (=)_____ (F)
Average Cost Per Room Peak Season   (x)_____ (D)
Peak Season Income   (=)_____ (G)
Off-season Room Nights (same as Peak Season)   _____ (F)
Average Cost per Room Off-Season   (x)_____ (E)
Off-Season Income   (=)_____ (H)
Total Year 1 Projected Income: _____ (G + H)
Notes: Est. Yr 2 Forecasted Occupancy Rate = 10% + Yr 1 Forecasted Rate (Z)
Est. Yr 3 Forecasted Occupancy Rate = 10% + Yr 2 Forecasted Rate

5.0　　　Industry Analysis

SIC: 7011　　　**NAICS:** 721110

The Boutique Hotel industry in the United States is an extremely fragmented industry that has a number of different operators working in many markets. No player commands more than 20 percent of the market share. Competition in the industry is generally based on the quality of rooms, restaurants, meeting facilities and services, attractiveness of locations, availability of a global distribution system, price and other factors.

There are a few large corporations that offer Boutique Hotel rooms on a national scale. Although these are large businesses, their portion of the overall Boutique Hotel market is very limited According to a US Economic Census report, there are over 43,000 individual Resort Hotel facilities in the United States. It is a $74 billion dollar per year industry that employees approximately 1.7 million people. The Boutique Hotel industry is mature. The future growth rate of the industry is expected to remain in line with the growth of the general economy.

In recent years, the Boutique Hotel industry has been a casualty of subdued economic conditions and international political instability. The average US retail price for diesel and regular gas, which determines how much people travel domestically on vacation or on business, jumped 31.2 percent and 34.5 percent respectively in the week ending September 12, 2017, compared to the same week in 2010.

Boutique Hotel operators are poised for an uptick in room reservations as consumers begin to loosen their travel budgets. The industry will continue to evolve, with internet booking services becoming the norm, investors building in growing tourist zones outside the United States, and large franchises expanding into spas and health resorts.

Segmentation is based mainly on the size of the concern, relative price and level of service provided to the guest. The Boutique Hotel segment can be characterized by the following generalizations:
1.　　Pricing is on the medium to high-end of the scale relative to others.
2.　　Character of the building and personalized ambience are key factors.
3.　　hotels are often the only accommodations available in more rural　areas.
4.　　The quality of the breakfast is a major differentiating factor.
5.　　A well planned and implemented marketing strategy can dramatically increase Boutique Hotel occupancy rates.

The Boutique Hotel industry is a subset of the $130 billion per year US lodging industry. Classification between country hotels and Boutique Hotel hotels isn't always clear, although a Boutique Hotel has 10 or more rooms and operates a restaurant on premises, while B& B Inns average about seven rooms and serve only breakfast.

Demand is driven by personal disposable income. The profitability of individual establishments depends on occupancy rate and operational efficiency. Larger hotels may have advantages in providing a range of offerings and prices to suit a variety of traveler budgets. Small establishments can compete effectively by offering superior guest service to target markets. The industry is highly labor intensive: average annual revenue per worker for hotels with paid employees is about $90,000.

This industry does not include casino hotels or bed and breakfast inns, which are both covered separately. Also not included in the hotel and motel industry are youth hostels, housekeeping cabins and cottages, or tourist homes.

Business and tourist travel drive demand. Both are affected by the strength of the economy. The profitability of individual companies depends on efficient operations, because many costs are fixed, and on effective marketing. Large companies have advantages in economies of scale in operations, can more easily raise capital, and have strong name recognition. Small companies, such as boutique hotels, can compete effectively in favorable locations and by providing specialty services.

Hotels compete for overnight accommodations with other hospitality establishments such as motels, extended-stay motels, country inns, RV parks, and campgrounds. The world's 10 largest hotel chains now offer a combined 113 brands at various price points, 31 of which didn't exist a decade ago. The major offering of hotels is rental of guest rooms (about 85 percent of revenue): other sources of revenue are gift shop sales, food and beverage sales, and spa services. Some hotels also rent their reception, meeting or conference rooms. According to the Professional Association of Innkeepers International (PAII), in 2004, there were 20,000 professionally-run, fully licensed motels/country hotels representing nearly 150,000 guest rooms, plus 10,000 home-stay hotels, collectively serving over 55 million guests annually.

In November 2005, PAII released the *2004 Industry Study of Operations and Finance*. This survey of 285 properties showed occupancy rates averaged 41.4% in 2004 up from 39.9% in 2003. The average daily rate (ADR) paid by Boutique Hotel guests increased from $142.73 to $143.90 over the same period, driving revenue per available room (RevPar) to $59.57, a growth of 4.6%. This drove industry revenue to an estimated $3.2 billion in 2004. The study also noted that "while new hotels continued to open in 2004, the increase was offset by the reversion of some properties to single family homes, particularly in resort areas where real estate prices have escalated."

Leisure travel continues to dominate this sector, with particular interest from cultural and historic travelers who enjoy staying at unique or historic properties. Weddings, family reunions, and special events continue to be regular features at over half of all hotels. Urban hotels that cater to business travelers are seeing continued recovery after 9-11 with as much as 20% of their revenue coming from business.

The study included significant information on in-room amenities. Most hotels now offer luxury beds and linens (80%) and premium toiletries (76%). Similarly, in terms of overall guest services, 88% of hotels surveyed offer assistance with restaurant reservations, and 73% help with event reservations. A total of 60% offer wireless Internet access, a high figure considering many hotels are still in rural locations with no access to high-speed

Internet.

5.1   Key Industry Statistics

1. A 2012 report from PricewaterhouseCoopers(PwC) reveals that almost 4,000 new luxury rooms have opened in London since 2005—an increase of 33 percent—and this growth has been largely driven by new boutique hotels
2. Based on information obtained from industry associations, a new Boutique Hotel can expect a first year occupancy of about 50-55% of the area average, with a minimum annual increase of 10%.
3. The average first year occupancy rate for all non-urban Boutique Hotel establishments was found to be 20%, rising to 60% by the third year.
4. The typical Boutique Hotel has only eight guest rooms, and the vast majority are owned by individuals that take a very active part in the operation.
5. About 83 percent of all Boutique Hotel owners live on the premises, while 88 percent describe themselves as "active" in their operations.
6. On average, 41 percent of all the hours logged by Boutique Hotel employees are those put in by the owners themselves.
7. From 1999 to 2000, the average Boutique Hotel in the United States increased occupancy from 49 percent to 50 percent. This compares to the 69.3 percent and 70.6 percent occupancy levels, respectively, for U.S. hotels in PKF Consulting Annual Trends in the Hotel Industry survey.
8. It is wise to assume that the occupancy rate will start off at half the national average for the first year or two.
9. In 1996, 6 percent of hotels reported increases in business via the Internet, in 2006, that number has risen to 33 percent.
10. In 2017, U.S. hotels are selling 65 percent of their room nights, up from 55 percent five years ago, according to travel-research company STR Inc. Guests are also paying more: $115.72 on average a night, up from $97.31.
11. In 2017, there are 128,874 additional hotel rooms already under construction in the U.S., up 32 percent from last year, according to STR. Another 306,644 rooms are in various planning stages, all of which will be added to the existing supply of 5 million rooms.

5.2   Industry Trends

Industry trends are important because they signal a change in customer needs and behaviors. Studying these trends will help our company to identify opportunities and threats that may influence our operation profitability. Sources of trends include:
1. Other boutique hotel operators
2. State lodging and resort associations
3. Industry Periodicals such as Resort Management, Hotel & Motel Management

and Lodging (AHMA)
4.   Travel Periodicals such as Midwest Living and Country Inns Magazine
5.   Research reports produced by the U.S. Travel Data Center
6.   Local Extension and State Tourism Offices

We will determine the trends that are impacting our consumers and indicate ways in which our guests' needs are changing and any relevant social, technical or other changes that will impact our target market. Keeping up with trends and reports will help management to carve a niche for our business, stay ahead of the competition and deliver products that our customers need and want

Other trends include:
1.   Within the last decade, more people have begun to use the Internet to discover hotels and appreciate the additional services that they offer relative to traditional accommodations.
2.   The industry has seen an increase in occupancy, from out of state or region travelers, as well as and more importantly, local people that are looking for a place to escape from their homes.
3.   Tourism is closely tied to performance in the economy, however, total tourism volume, from foreign and domestic sources, has steadily risen over the past decade.
4.   Many hotels are using value-added services such as free gourmet breakfasts, discounted coupons to local attractions and in-room office set-ups to keep bookings up during recessionary times.
5.   Many hotels are setting up conference room facilities for local businesses and staging special events, such as cooking classes, to diversify their revenue streams.
6.   hotels are also expanding their gift store operations by taking in antiques and crafts from local collectors and artisans on a consignment basis.
7.   Once largely associated with small towns in quaint places like New England, boutique hotels today are appearing in urban areas throughout the United States as alternatives to pricey and impersonal hotels.
8.   WorldRes provides a free connection to the SABRE travel agent system, providing access to over 100,000 agents worldwide, as well as to users of Travelocity, one of the most popular online travel sites.
9.   Due to two income families, people are replacing the traditional two to three week vacation with the taking of three to four day vacations over a weekend, which in the travel industry, is referred to as a "Get-Away-Weekend."
10. The older population, or aging baby boomers, tend to have more disposable income and the time to travel.
11. Boutique hotels have adopted a visual-first mindset across all of their consumer-facing media, including standalone lifestyle blogs with individual URLs and a fashion magazine's zest for compelling imagery.
12. There are now boutiques owned by big chains (such as Edition by Marriott and W by Starwood);
13. There is an explosion of new health and happiness, and wellness or lifestyle boutique hotel chains and environments becoming more mainstream. Fitness

gyms and spas are mere amenities, and established hotel chains are re-branding around wellness and it's not just about fitness. Customized food and beverage offerings (gluten-free and vegan menus) are becoming standard fare, and hotels are jumping into the detox -themed vacation frenzy.

Source: www.boutiquehotelnews.com/home/blog/2012/12/18/boutique-hotel-future-trends-2017/

14. Operators of boutique hotels were mainly independent operators in the 1980's, but faced with growing demand, dedicated boutique hotel chains emerged, such as Malmaison and Joie De Vivre Hospitality in Europe.

15. Guests can now walk into any property belonging to a chain hotel organization and the staff at the property will know their name, preferences and other personal information thanks to a computer database.

16. The incorporation of members' clubs with special member-only privileges, is expected to become more popular.

17. There is a greater focus on a more environmentally friendly stay, which includes the use of larger recycling bins and sourcing locally produced and in season ingredients for on-site food and beverage operations.

18. Increasing popularity of budget boutique hotels with smaller rooms, limited on-site food and beverage services, usually only vending machines will be available, and creating and promoting common living spaces, such as the lobby, that encourages guest to guest social interactions.

19. Major developers are working through the process of "repurposing" historic buildings as boutique hotels while maintaining their original look and feel.

Ex: www.pasadenastarnews.com/news/ci_23439688/historic-ywca-building-become-boutique-hotel

20. Local sensitivity both to the local community's needs and economy and to travelers' desires for authentic local experiences is increasingly demanded as companies adopt global and multi-domestic expansion strategies.

21. The hospitality industry is not only fragmenting into price-driven, usage-driven or demographics-driven niches but into psychographic niches based on shared tastes, interest sharing and experience preferences.

22. The new trend for "no frills chic" has emerged and has now led to an alternative solution for hoteliers to be different and attractive in turning to budget boutique hotels

Source: https://tourismsierre.wordpress.com/2012/11/11/budget-boutique-hotels-a-new-kind-of-boutique-hotels/

5.3   Key Industry Terms

We will use the following term definitions to help our company to understand and speak the common language of our industry, and aid efficient communication.

Ambiance
A feeling about or an identity for an establishment created by the combination of decor, lighting, furnishings, and other factors. Applied to environments, a feeling or mood

associated with a particular place, person, or thing; an atmosphere.

Amenity

Service or item offered to guests or placed in guestrooms for the comfort and convenience of guests, and at no extra cost. Examples are various guest services (such as in-room entertainment systems, automatic check-out, free parking, concierge services, and multilingual staff) in addition to an array of personal bathroom items offered by most hotels and hotels. Amenities are designed to increase a hotel's appeal, enhance a guest's stay, and encourage guests to return.

Average Daily Room Rate

Equals the Total Room Revenue divided by the Number of Rooms Sold

Boutique Hotel

A small hotel (less than 100 rooms) that express its singularity in light-hearted, mildly rebellious room details and personalized guest programs. They have a clear theme for the design and furnishings, as well as an ambiance of comfortable luxury. Their source of differentiation is commonly associated with the design, artistic, cultural or historic appeal, the halo effect of celebrity patronage, and the prestige and exclusivity of a property.
Resource:
https://mbrowndotwordpressdotcom.files.wordpress.com/2012/05/blla-white-paper.pdf

Continental Breakfast

Typically, anything served cold and often prepackaged, including sweet rolls, bagels, individually packaged cold cereals, juice and coffee or tea.

Country Resort Hotel

Owner-operated establishments providing lodging and meals (generally breakfast and dinner). Some provide dinners to overnight guests only, others have full-service restaurants open to the public. Typically 10 or more guest rooms.

Homestay or Host Home

A private residence where paying guests are sometimes accommodated in 1-3 guest rooms. Breakfast is usually the only meal served. Guests and owners may share the same common areas. Typically posts no front sign, but relies on reservation services.

Lifestyle Hotel

Represent the next generation of boutique hotels. Driven by the chains, they borrow the best elements of boutiques – small, intimate and modern – and throw in advantages only a chain can offer, like loyalty perks, consistency and economies of scale. As a result, lifestyle hotels are generally more affordable and accessible than boutiques – and soon to be ubiquitous. Several hotel companies tested this segment by putting their toes in the waters of the category, with brands such as Aloft by Starwood, Hyatt Place by Hyatt and Cambria by Choice defining themselves as boutique offerings, yet having every hotel exactly the same in every location.
Resource: https://boutiquelodging.wordpress.com/2010/10/15/what-is-a-lifestyle-hotel/

Rack Rate

A term used in the hotel industry to describe the cost to a customer that requests accommodations for the same day without prior booking arrangements . The rack rate price tends to be more expensive than the rate that the customer could have received if he/she used a travel agency or third-party service. Rack rates can vary based on the day that the room is requested. For instance, the rack rate may be more expensive on weekends, which are usually high travel days.

Resort Hotel
Enterprises formed around multiunit buildings that provide temporary lodging to the general public.
Retina Display
A brand name used by Apple for screens that have a pixel density high enough that the human eye is unable to discern individual pixels at a typical viewing distance. The term is used for several Apple products, including the iPhone, iPod Touch, iPad, MacBook Pro, iPad Mini, and iPad Air. Because the typical viewing distance is different, depending on each device's use, the pixels per inch claimed to be of *Retina* quality can differ, depending on the size of the display, with higher PPI for smaller displays and lower PPI for larger displays: 326 PPI for the smallest devices (iPhone, iPod Touch, and iPad Mini (2nd generation)), 264 PPI for mid-sized devices (iPad (3rd & 4th generations), iPad Air), and 220 PPI for larger devices (MacBook Pro).
Occupancy Percent
Equals the Number of Rooms Sold divided by the Number of Rooms Available
Reservation Service Organization (RSO)
Owners list their properties with the RSO and they require an inspection to determine the property meets their standards and criteria. The listings are published on the RSO website, in magazines and/or guidebooks. The RSO performs a guest screening and host matching function, makes the reservation, processes the deposit and payment, confirms the reservation, and sends the payment less a commission of about 20% to the host Boutique Hotel.
Room Night
One guestroom occupied for one night.
Unhosted Facility
A city apartment or freestanding cottage or carriage house on the host family's property, but self-contained.

5.4   Industry Leaders

We plan to study the best practices of industry leaders and adapt certain selected practices to our business model concept. Best practices are those methods or techniques resulting in increased customer satisfaction when incorporated into the operation.

Library Hotel Collection
The current members of the Library Hotel Collection include the Library Hotel, Hotel Giraffe, Hotel Elysée, and Casablanca Hotel.
1.   Casablanca Hotel, now ranked as #1 on TripAdvisor, has a Moroccan motif inspired by the romance of the movie, "Casablanca" and is situated at Broadway on West 43rd Street, just steps from Times Square.
2.   Library Hotel, currently ranked #2 on TripAdvisor, features 6,000 books organized throughout the hotel based on the Dewey Decimal System, and is located at Madison and East 41st Street.
3.   Hotel Elysée, currently ranked #4 on TripAdvisor, features the romantic ambiance of a private country inn and is located on East 54th Street, between Park and

Madison Avenues.

4.   Hotel Giraffe, currently ranked #8 on TripAdvisor, offers an urban oasis of sophisticated style and is situated at Park Avenue South and East 26th Street.

Morgans Hotel Group

Evolved from a single property, Ian Schrager's Morgan Hotel in New York, to a chain of six boutique properties (Mintel, 2011). Sold ownership of their properties to increase the organization's liquidity and meet debt payments in face of financial duress. The group's flagship Morgan Hotel, which introduced the boutique hotel concept to the United Sates, along with the chain's second most prominent property, the Royalton Hotel, were placed on the market and sold for $140 million US (Mintel, 2011).

Studio Boutique Hotel

A new five star boutique hotel, provides guests with lodging in a unique, modern and comfortable environment, one located in the heart of the city. Less than one mile south of the Forum I business center, Studio Boutique Hotel lies in one of the fastest growing areas of the city and is a 20 minute drive from the Juan Santamaria International Airport. The preferential rate includes amenities such as a buffet style breakfast, a safety box, access to the business center and an airport shuttle which consistently comes in under schedule. Inspiration for the hotel came from the "Art Studio" concept and the atmosphere is both comfortable and welcoming. New ideas are sure to be born here thanks to the luxurious surroundings and the company of other guests. Boasting 82 rooms, this environmentally friendly hotel offers a charming getaway, one where you will be able to admire the works of great artists, such as Guillermo Conte and Valerio Triguero.

The Chocolate Boutique Hotel

Founded in 2004 by the Wilton family, Chocolate Delight was one of the first companies to have a commercial chocolate fountain in the UK and quickly established itself as the leading chocolate fountain hire company. It was soon called on by corporates, event companies and celebrities to provide fountains for functions such as film premieres and weddings, including Peter and Jordan's. In 2006, the Wilton family saw the opportunity to expand and bought a beautiful but outdated 19th century grade II listed hotel in Bournemouth. Christmas 2007 saw the renovation of the building and it became The Chocolate Boutique Hotel, the world's first chocolate themed hotel. Today, Chocolate Delight is one of the most successful UK chocolate companies in its field and holds Chocolate Workshops at venues nationwide. Its Corporate Chocolate Teambuilding events commenced late in 2005 and are now run all over the UK and more recently in Europe. In the 2017 Michelin Guide, the Chocolate Boutique Hotel is described as a unique chocolate themed hotel owned by a chocolatier who runs regular workshops. Contemporary bedrooms come in browns and creams. The small lounge-bar features an automatic cocktail machine, which even serves 'choctails'. The Hotel has also been named one of the six best novelty hotels in the world by The Sunday Times Travel magazine.

Kimpton Hotels   www.kimptonhotels.com

Based in San Francisco, Kimpton Hotels is the first and leading collection of boutique style hotels throughout the U.S. Founded in 1981 by the enigmatic Bill Kimpton, this exceptional group of hotels provides true personal attention, thoughtful amenities, beautifully appointed accommodations and culinary experiences, while each telling their own story. The Kimpton Group opened the first rock n' roll and wine themed hotel property, propelling them into a highly recognized boutique chain brand.

Loews Hotels Holding Corporation
The company operates about 20 upscale hotels located in prime business and travel locations in the US and Canada. In addition to offering amenities such as fine dining options, spas, and golf courses, the properties also feature facilities for weddings, meetings, and other events. Loews' hotels include Lowes Regency Hotel in New York City, Loews Santa Monica Beach Hotel in California, and Loews Le Concorde in Quebec City. The company also has resort locations and hotels operated in conjunction with such tourist destination brands as Hard Rock Cafe and Universal Studios' theme parks. It is a subsidiary of diversified holding company Loews Corporation.

Starwood Hotels & Resorts Worldwide
One of the world's largest hotel companies, it has some 1,000 properties in about 100 countries. Starwood's hotel empire consists of upscale brands such as Sheraton and Westin. It operates about 100 luxury resorts and hotels through its St. Regis and Luxury Collection, while its chain of about 40 W Hotels offers ultra-modern style. Other brands include Four Points (value-oriented), Le Méridien (European-inspired), Aloft (select-service), and Element (extended stay). Its Starwood Vacation Ownership operates about 15 time-share resorts. Notable Starwood hotels include the St. Regis in New York and the Hotel Gritti Palace in Venice. In 1998, the opening of the first W Hotel in New York marked the entrance of a third type of operator into the boutique hotel subsector: major chain operators (Mintel, 2011). Major chain hotels developing boutique hotels include the key international lodging brands with diversified lodging operations, Starwood with their W Hotels.

Marriott International, Inc.
A worldwide operator and franchiser of hotels and related lodging facilities. The company has around 3,500 hotels spread across almost 70 countries. Marriott generates around 90% of its earnings from hotel operations and a nominal amount from timeshares. The company's largest geographic segment is the United States. Marriott operates reservation centers, many of which are located in the United States, and has a distinct multi-brand, multi-channel central reservation system, which enables a customer to choose the rooms as per his/her preference. For example, the system will enable the customer to find and book the cheapest room available in all the Marriott hotels in a city. Marriott is subject to declines and rapid recoveries from declines as dictated by the global business cycle. This recovery is due to an increase in personal income. Since decrease in personal disposable income brought forth the reduction in demand for hospitality and transportation industries, increasing incomes put upward pressure on demand for hotels and transport. This upward pressure has resulted in increased prices. Increased prices may bring Marriott more profits. During recessions, new orders for rooms have come to a standstill, thus reducing the available number of rooms present for an ever-increasing

global travel and hotel population. For example, in 2010, the smaller increase in supply and higher demand lead to a rise in occupancy. Higher occupancy rate is typically followed by increased daily rates. This increase in occupancy rate may continue beyond the first year since hotels are delaying or have delayed construction orders for more rooms until market has shown stability. In general, the hotel industry faces a threat from Internet reservation channels, which represent a growing share of hotel room bookings. These intermediate channels charge higher commissions and demand lower room rates from hotels, which puts tremendous pressure on the revenues as well as margins of hotels. Marriott has built its own central reservation system to counter this threat from third parties. Marriott is the leader with respect to its online reservation usage in the industry, with 75% of all Marriott room reservations booked online on Marriott's website. In 2014, Marriott International Inc. launched Moxy, Hilton Worldwide Holdings Inc. created Canopy, Best Western International Inc. came up with Vib and InterContinental Hotels Group PLC — the parent company of Holiday Inn — purchased Kimpton, adding its boutique hotels to the larger chain.

The Raphael Hotel, Autograph Collection
  www.marriott.com/hotels/travel/mciak-the-raphael-hotel-autograph-collection
A one-of-a-kind boutique hotel that combines the charm and intimacy of a locally significant landmark with highly individualized service. It is the original boutique concept among historic Kansas City Plaza hotels. The nine-story, Italian Renaissance Revival structure is a member of National Trust Historic Hotels of America and is listed on the National Register of Historic Places. The Raphael is noted for distinctive luxury Kansas City hotel deals and packages within its portfolio of romantic getaway, destination-rich and special affinity packages that can be booked online.

The Dylan Hotel   **www.dylansfo.com**
A newly renovated 58 room boutique hotel, located one mile south of the San Francisco International Airport (SFO), has received a TripAdvisor® Certificate of Excellence award. The accolade, which honors hospitality excellence, is given only to establishments that consistently achieve outstanding traveler reviews on TripAdvisor, and is extended to qualifying businesses worldwide. Only the top-performing 10 percent of businesses listed on TripAdvisor receive this prestigious award. The owners at The Dylan Hotel are also committed to improving the community. They are proud sponsors of a little league team, and just recently sponsored a local street fair for families to come together and enjoy outdoor activities and meet face to face with community leaders. The owner is currently chairman of the Millbrae Tourism Committee.

The Cromwell   **www.thecromwell.com**
A boutique hotel in the Las Vegas Strip,, only houses 40,000-square-feet of casino space and 188 rooms. The boutique hotel features lush décor, upscale amenities and staff instructed to make guests feel like royalty. All guests receive personalized service. Dripping with casual elegance, the casino floor is filled with velvet sofas, dark woods and intimate lighting. The goal is to make guests feel at home rather than at a hotel. Team members work to ensure guests' arrival is smooth, contacting patrons ahead of time to gather information about their visit, learn preferences and take special requests.

Discouraging guests from checking in at their traditional reception area, The Cromwell offers curbside room key delivery. For guests wishing to be out of the public eye, there is a private check-in behind a hidden door in the lobby. Concierge members will even meet guests at the airport or in their limo to ensure safe and comfortable transportation.

Atlas Hotels   **http://www.atlas.co.il/about-us-hotels-israel**
Based in Tel Aviv, Atlas Hotels is the leading boutique-hotel management company in Israel. They set ourselves apart by taking a conceptual approach to the creation of their hotels: from the movies-inspired Cinema Hotel to the sophisticated Melody Hotel; each property presents its own dynamic personality. Established 40 years ago, Atlas Hotels became the largest boutique hotel operator in Israel with hotels in Tel Aviv, Jerusalem and Eilat. Their group currently accommodates over 500,000 room-nights per year. Their sales and marketing department, which reaches more than 4,500 companies in Israel, and over 500 travel agencies around the world, is one of the most successful in the country. The Atlas Call Center and their internet - based reservations system generate a substantial portion of their room-nights demand.

Hyatt
This group is comprised of Hyatt Regency, Park Hyatt, Grand Hyatt, Hyatt House, Hyatt Place and, coming soon, Hyatt Centric.

5.5   Industry News and New Business Concepts

Boutique Hotel for Cyclists
George Hincapie, a Tour de France cyclist, announced the August 2017 opening of the Hotel Domestique, in Travelers Rest, SC. The 13-room boutique getaway is high on a hilltop and immediately evocative of the Tuscan countryside, blending contemporary flair with French and Mediterranean influences. All guest rooms have stylish bathrooms, flat screen TVs and fireplaces, and all overlook the 29-acre grounds, full of gardens, courtyards, fountains and vineyards. Specifically appealing to guests seeking an active getaway, the site is surrounded by countless miles of country roads well suited for cycling and running. The hotel will have a small bike shop with onsite mechanic, preset suggested ride routes, and high-end rental road and mountain bikes from Hincapie's last team sponsor. Besides the self-guided suggestions, there will be several scheduled rides each week led by staffers, including women's rides, beginner rides, and general rides. Hincapie himself will lead a weekly ride, usually midweek, based on his schedule and availability. There will also be a specially designed storage room for those bringing their own bikes, and a 25-meter pool catering to aspiring triathletes.

Great Northern Hotel   **www.gnhlondon.com**
This is in an ideal location between King's Cross and St Pancras stations in London. It's a luxury boutique hotel, called the world's first great railway hotel, which feels like a train inside. When it opened its doors in 1854, it stood at the centre of London's revolutionary new age of steam. It was designed, like King's Cross, by Lewis Cubbit. It has been restored to its former grandeur, complete with wide curved corridors.

The couchette room feels like a luxury first class sleeper carriage, only with a more comfortable bed, TV, luxurious bathroom and soundproofing to ensure a great night's sleep. A nice touch is the pantry at the end of each corridor where guests can help themselves to goodies like tea, coffee, fresh cake, Wagon Wheels and Jelly Babies.

Pop-up Hotels

Edgy Copenhagen-based group Pink Cloud has designed an genius hotel concept to convert New York's empty office spaces into hip pop-up hotels, Gizmag reports. The design, winner of Hospitality Magazine's 2017 Radical Innovations in Hospitality competition, is a win win. It would provide tenants for some of the 17 million square feet of empty office space in New York while serving the city's booming tourism sector. The modular hotel would be flat-packed into boxes designed to fit through an elevator door and be unfolded to form partitions, beds, sofas, chairs, toilets, tubs and other items. Parties, fashion shows and other events would launch the four-week pop-ups, which would include funky extras like lounges with playground slides and giant rubber duckies. Source: http://blog.zagat.com/2017/06/new-pop-up-could-turn-office-buildings.html

Boutique Hotel for Business Travelers

In Melbourne, a boutique hotel called the Bray Hotel will open in October of 2017. With 16 floors and 146 rooms, there will be four executive, two-bedroom apartments, along with two, two-bedroom penthouse apartments. On the top two levels, all two-bedroom apartments enjoy views over Melbourne and pack in two bathrooms, full kitchen facilities and a dining and living area. On the lower floors are 84 standard and executive rooms, along with 56 studio apartments. As with the two-bedroom apartments, these also offer private guest balconies. A separate working space makes executive rooms the best fit for business travelers, and for longer stays, studio rooms also come with a kitchenette. Wireless Internet is available throughout the hotel at a cost of $15 per day, with Foxtel and in-room Smart TVs. Rooms feature Scandinavian-inspired timbers, blue stone floors, copper fittings, Japanese tiles and custom-designed furniture, along with flexible-configuration Sealy 'Posturepedic' mattresses. Also for work, hunger and recreation are a business centre, an on-site restaurant and bar, and a gymnasium. Conference facilities for up to 80 people are available, which come with an LED display and teleconferencing capabilities.

Boutique Hotel for Wedding Destinations

Liostasi Ios Hotel & Spa is a leading boutique hotel of Ios and the only member of Small Luxury Hotels of the World on the island. There is a total of 30 stylishly appointed rooms including the six brand-new Liostasi Suites with a strikingly minimal Cycladic design. Valued features of the hotel are the high quality of its cuisine, the playful signature cocktails created by Liostasi's bartender, the selection of treatments offered at the boutique spa and, most importantly, the sensational vistas from the hotel's pool terrace complete with sweeping views of nearby islands and one of the Mediterranean's most dramatic sunsets. Due to its utterly romantic atmosphere, Liostasi has established itself as a hip wedding venue for couples from all over the world.

Small Luxury Hotels of the World™   **www.SLH.com**

A brand with an unrivalled portfolio of some of the world's finest small luxury independent hotels. Comprising over 520 hotels in more than 70 countries, the diversity of the individual hotels, and the experiences that they offer, is exceptional. From cutting-edge design hotels to palatial 17th century mansions, the breadth and depth of the brand is far reaching. While a hotel undoubtedly enjoys the benefits of being part of a global brand, SLH places enormous emphasis on celebrating the individuality of each hotel. This remains one of their core values and is central to the continued success of the brand. They strongly believe that the strength and credibility of the Small Luxury Hotels of the World™ brand is dependent on the quality of its individual hotels. Strict controls are applied to ensure that only the very best hotels with the highest standards are accepted into the brand, thus ensuring that the quality of the experience that guests receive is consistent across all SLH properties. To ensure that these exceptional standards of excellence are maintained, SLH has a carefully monitored 'mystery guest' program which relies on valuable reviews from inspectors who importantly are also consumers.

Citizen M   **www.citizen.com**
One of the new budget boutique hotels, call that "affordable luxury". Their hotels are located in Amesterdam, Glasgow and London and soon in New York and Paris. Their offer includes smaller rooms than most of the usual hotels but with a unique design and possibilities of customizing the rooms in choosing the light mood, for instance. They also offer a 24h food & beverage service, 24h assistance service, self check-in service option, free WiFi, free movies on demand, and common living spaces, to cite a few of their offers. All these add-on services allow them to differentiate themselves and be competitive. Other examples of budget boutique hotels are the low-scale W boutique hotel from Starwoods or the different hotels Yotel with their "cabins", located in three European airports, Hotel Indigo created by Intercontinental, the 25-Hours hotels in Germany, and Qbic an original concept that allows space maximization thanks to its cubic design (http://veilletourisme.ca).

The National Geographic Society
It has launched National Geographic Unique Lodges of the World, which it describes as "a collection of boutique hotels in extraordinary places around the world with a demonstrated commitment to sustainability, authenticity, and excellence."
Source: www.successfulmeetings.com/News/Hotel-Updates/National-Geographic-
                Launches-Collection-of-Boutique-Hotels/

Virgin Hotels   **www.virginhotels.com**
In October 2011 Virgin Hotels bought the 27-story Old Dearborn Bank Building in the Loop area of Chicago for $14.8 million from Urban Street Group LLC. On January 16, 2017 the first Virgin Hotel opened. Other hotels are being planned in New York and Nashville. The 300 room New York site is due to open in 2018 and will be located on the corner of 29th Street and Broadway. The 240 room Nashville property is to be located at One Music Row and is also due to open in 2018. Branson has stated that the brand is geared toward the female business traveler.
Resource: http://virginhotels.com/about-the-app/

6.0   Strategy and Implementation Summary

_____ (company name) will aggressively market to both winter and summer visitors of the _____ area. The _____ area has activities occurring year round. During the winter there is _____ (skiing/hunting/ice fishing/snowmobiling/?) but in the summer months, the resort has hot-air balloon trips, white water adventures, day hikes into ____ State Park, and other recreational activities that take advantage of area's spectacular beauty.

There are only ___ (#) lodges and inns in the _____ resort area. These facilities represent only ____ (#) room units of the total of _____ (#) room units in the resort area. The majority of room units in the area are condos.

Our customers are looking for a different lodging experience that cannot be found in any of the area's condo complexes or hotels. We will offer our customers a comfortable, congenial environment that will assure return visits to the _____ (company name). The lodge will cost a little more but we will offer our customers all the services they need to make their stay memorable. We will offer a foodservice store that will be able to take special orders daily. There will be a ____ (ski/gun?) rental shop where customers can outfit themselves and purchase ____ (ski/hunting) passes/licenses. Each evening, guests can gather in the Boutique Hotel's main room, where guests can experience a large stone fireplace, exotic drinks and/or vibrant dance music.

Our sales strategy is based on serving our niche markets better than the competition and leveraging our competitive advantages. These advantages include superior attention to understanding and satisfying guest needs and wants, creating a one-stop lodging experience, and value pricing.

The objectives of our marketing strategy will be to recruit new customers, retain existing customers, get good customers to spend more and return more frequently. Establishing a loyal guest base is very important because such core customers will not only generate the most lifetime sales, but also provide valuable referrals.

We will generate word-of-mouth buzz through direct-mail campaigns, exceeding guest expectations, developing a Web site and getting involved in community events and with local businesses, and donating our services at charity functions, in exchange for press release coverage. Our sales strategy will seek to convert potential and first-time customers into long-term relationships and referral agents. The combination of our competitive advantages, targeted marketing campaign and networking activities, will enable _____ (company name) to continue increasing our market share.

Our Marketing Objectives include:
1.   Place the Boutique Hotel's name within online travel sites such as Expedia, Travelocity, and Orbitz.
2.   Establish relationships with travel agents within the targeted market.

3.   Develop an online presence by developing a website and placing the Company's name and contact information with online directories.

6.1.0   Promotion Strategy

Our promotional strategy is targeted to create maximum awareness and repeat business with the most cost-effective use of funds.

There are several Boutique Hotel associations that we intend to join. They offer a relatively inexpensive, effective advertising media. Ranging from very local to international in coverage, most include yearly fees and some require certain inspection standards to be met to qualify for membership. Inclusion in travel guides and Boutique Hotel directories is indicated as the most effective advertising tool for this industry. Consequently, we plan to be included in AAA materials and the Mobil Travel Guide, Chamber of Commerce directories in this region and every guidebook we can resource.

Return guests and referrals constitute a valuable source of revenue in this industry, and we will encourage this by offering exceptional service, a unique assortment of amenities, gourmet breakfasts and incentives for referrals by prior business guests. We will also build a guest database to issue online special occasion reminder invitations and special rates to past guests . We plan to use the off-season as an opportunity to develop retreat/conference business from the local urban _____ (colleges/businesses).

Our promotional strategies will also make use of the following tools:
- **Advertising**
  - o   Yearly anniversary parties to celebrate the success of each year.
  - o   Multiple Yellow Pages ads in the book and online.
  - o   Flyers promoting our special events.
  - 0   Doorknob hangers, if not prohibited by neighborhood associations.
- **Local Marketing / Public Relations**
  - o   Client raffle for gift certificates or discount coupons
  - 0   Participation in local civic groups.
  - 0   Press release coverage of our sponsoring of events at the local community center for families and residents.
  - 0   Article submissions to travel magazines describing the benefits of staying at a Boutique Hotel.
  - O   Sales Brochure to convey our packages to prospective guests.
- **Local Media**
  - o   Direct Mail - We will send quarterly direct mailings to residents with a ___ (20?) mile radius of our center. It will contain an explanation of our services, packages and a newsletter with a listing of house events.
  - o   Radio Campaign - We will make "live on the air" presentations of our trial coupons to the disk jockeys, hoping to get the promotions broadcasted to the listening audience.
  - o   Newspaper Campaign - We will place several ads in the getaway weekend

section of the local community newspaper. We will include a trial coupon in the ad to track the return on investment.

o   Website – We will collect email addresses for a monthly newsletter.

6.1.1   Grand Opening

Our Grand Opening celebration will be a very important promotion opportunity to create word-of-mouth advertising results.

We will do the following things to make the open house a successful event:
1. Enlist local business support to contribute a large number of door prizes.
2. Use a sign-in sheet to create an email/mailing list.
3. Create free children ID cards.
4. Schedule appearance by local celebrities.
5. Create a festive atmosphere with balloons, beverages and music.
6. Get the local radio station to broadcast live from the event and handout fun gifts.
7. Offer an application fee waiver.
8. Giveaway our logo imprinted T-shirts as a contest prize.
9. Allow potential customers to view your facility and ask questions.
10. Print promotional flyers and pay a few kids to distribute them locally.
11. Arrange for face painting, storytelling, clowns, and snacks for everyone.
12. Arrange for local politician to do the official opening ceremony so all the local newspapers came to take pictures and do a feature story.
13. Arrange that people can tour our facility on the open day in order to see our facilities, collect sales brochures and find out more about our services.
14. Organize a drawing with everyone writing their name and phone numbers on the back of business cards and give a voucher as a prize to start a marketing list.
15. Organize tours of the hotel led by knowledgeable staff at various intervals during the event.
16. Create eye-catching signage or a hotel map that will guide attendees to the areas you want to highlight, such as meeting rooms, guest rooms, fitness center, pool deck, etc.

Resource:
http://www.eventmanagerblog.com/5-tips-planning-successful-hotel-grand-opening/

6.1.2   Value Proposition

Our value proposition will summarize why a consumer should use our Boutique Hotel services. We will offer uniquely designed rooms, local flavors and personalized experiences.

Our proposition will convince prospects that our services will add more value or better solve their need for a convenient, personalized, secure, one-stop lodging service. We will use this value proposition statement to target customers who will benefit most from using our Boutique Hotel services. These are romantic getaway couples who are concerned about maintaining their lifestyle and partaking in stress-free escapism. Our value proposition will be concise and appeal to the guest's strongest decision-making drivers, which are convenience, safety, availability, convenience and quality of personal relationships.

Recap of Our Value Proposition:

Trust – We are known as a trusted business partner with strong customer and vendor endorsements. We have earned a reputation for quality, integrity, exotic room design, and the delivery of personalized hotel experiences.

Quality – We offer _____ experience and extensive professional backgrounds at competitive salary rates.

Experience – Our ability to bring people with ___ (#) years of _____ experience with deep technical knowledge of _____ is at the core of our success.

True Vendor Partnerships – Our true vendor partnerships with _____ and _____ enable us to offer the resources of much larger organizations with greater flexibility.

Customer Satisfaction and Commitment to Success – Through partnering with our customers and delivering quality solutions, we have been able to achieve an impressive degree of repeat and referral business. Since ____ (year), more than ____% of our business activity is generated by existing customers. Our philosophy is that "our customer's satisfaction is our success." Our success will be measured in terms of our customer's satisfaction survey scores and testimonials.

6.1.3   Positioning Statement

Our first step will be to understand our boutique hotel's position in the market place. This will determine which segments of the market we will attract; what rates to charge, per segment, per season; and what services and amenities to offer. A firm understanding of who we are, where we want to be in the marketplace, and what we offer relative to our competition and general market conditions, will determine all strategic plans and will influence any decisions to be made with changing market conditions. A clear focus and understanding of our chosen market position, will avert costly sales and marketing mistakes for both the short term and the long term.

Resource:
https://blog.udemy.com/positioning-strategy/

It is the objective of _____ (company name) to become the local leader in quality Boutique Hotel lodging services in the _____ area. The one-stop convenience of our personalized Boutique Hotel services will allow us to pursue a differentiation business strategy and not have to focus intently on low cost leadership.

We also plan to develop specialized services that will enable us to pursue a niche focus on specific interest based groups, such as women business travelers. These objectives will position us at the _____ (mid-level/high-end) of the market and will allow the company to realize a healthy profit margin in relation to its low-end, no-frills, discount rivals and achieve long-term growth.

_____ (company name) will position itself as an upscale Boutique Hotel with a gorgeous facility and unmatched guest attention. We will leverage our competitive edge:

1. **Attention to Personalized Service**
    This will be done through the unrelenting pursuit of personal attention. At _____ (company name) all interactions with the guest will be with the owners, who sees it as his/her duty to do whatever it takes to make the guest feel at home. The feeling of personal attention, or more accurately defined as a sense of personal concern, not just mere personal attention, will really add a very positive dimension to the Boutique Hotel experience.

2. **Uniqueness and Beauty of the Facility**
    The ____ Boutique Hotel has been recently renovated to accommodate our new guests. We have added ____ (#) more bedrooms with private baths, a patio, and enlarged the common area. One unique aspect of _____ (company name) is the setting within the _____ region, known for its outstanding _____. To compliment this setting, we will have a large outside patio allowing guests to spend time relaxing outside with a nice view of the valley. The guests also have the option to wander through our own magnificent garden. Basically, every room in the Boutique Hotel has a breathtaking view.

Market Positioning Recap

Price: The strategy is to offer competitive prices that are lower that the market leader, yet set to indicate value and worth. .

Quality: The Boutique Hotel's quality of guest services will have to be very good as the finished service results will be showcased in highly visible situations and be spread by word-of-mouth.

Service: Highly individualized and personalized service will be the key to success in this type of business. Personal attention to the customers will result in higher sales and word of mouth advertising.

Design: Every room will be creatively designed around a _____ theme.

6.1.4   Unique Selling Proposition (USP)

Our unique selling proposition will answer the question why a guest should choose to do business with our company versus any and every other option available to them in the marketplace. Our USP will be a description of a unique important benefit that our Boutique Hotel offers to customers, so that price is no longer the key to our sales.

Our USP will include the following:

Who our target audience is: _____

What we will do for them: _____

What qualities, skills, talents, traits do we possess that others do not: _____
What are the benefits we provide that no one else offers: _____
Why that is different from what others are offering: _____
Why that solution matters to our target audience: _____

Our unique selling proposition will include the following factors: (select)

1. **Our location**
   We will keep our website updated with special events, activities and attractions happening within walking or close driving distance to our boutique hotel.

2. **Our restaurant/bar**
   We will keep foodies at our hotel by organizing regular culinary events and packages, such as gourmet weekends, cooking classes with our executive chef, whisky and wine tastings, etc. We will create videos of our chef sharing cooking tips.

3. **Our (medical) spa**
   We will promote wellness and healthy living by creating wellness packages and specials, and become a source of health and wellness tips for spa lovers.

4. **Our architecture/design/art collection**
   We will engage local artists and musicians, and invite arts and culture bloggers and writers to our hotel. We will promote our hotel as a photography and videography venue.

5. **Our guest-focused staff**
   We will ask our staff to leave travel tips on social media and to share with guests. We will become a thought leader in the industry and offer structured training programs for new hospitality employees.

6. **Our gift boutique**
   We will feature apparel and artwork made by local artisans.

6.1.5   Distribution Strategy

We will enable the booking of our rooms by the following reservation methods:

1.	Telephone	2.	In person
3.	Through agents.	4.	Via our website.
5.	Fax.	6.	Mail

Note: We will provide a commission to travel agents that is comparable to that provided by other accommodation facilities in the area.

Our customers will have the following access points:

1. **Order by Phone**
   Customers can contact us 24 hours a day, 7days a week at _____.
   Our Customer Service Representatives will be available to assist customers Monday through Friday from ___ a.m. to ____ p.m. EST.

2. **Order by Fax**
   Customers may fax their orders to _____ anytime.
   They must provide: Account number, Billing and shipping address, Purchase

order number, if applicable, Name and telephone number, Product number/description, Unit of measure and quantity ordered and Applicable sales promotion source codes.

3.   **Order Online**
Customers can order online at www._____.com.Once the account is activated, customers will be able to place orders, browse the catalog, check stock availability and pricing, check order status and view both order and transaction history.

4.   **In-person**
All customers can be serviced in person at our facilities Monday through Friday from ___ a.m. to ____ p.m. EST.

5.   **Order by EDI (Electronic Data Interchange)**
Wholesale customers can enter the order once directly into our dealer management system and it is transmitted to us. We will provide customers with electronic notification of expected ship-date, prices, tracking numbers, order status and distribution center from which the order will be shipped. Orders may be reviewed right from the dealer management system.

6.   **Travel Consultants/Distributors**

We plan to pursue the following distribution channels: **(select)**

	Number	Reason Chosen	Sales Costs
1. Our own retail outlets			
2. Independent retail outlets			
3. Chain store retail outlets			
4. Wholesale outlets			
5. Independent distributors			
6. Independent commissioned sales reps			
7. In-house sales reps			
8. Direct mail using own catalog or flyers			
9. Catalog broker agreement			
10. In-house telemarketing			
11. Contracted telemarketing call center			
12. Cybermarketing via own website			
13. Online sales via Expedia, Priceline, etc.			
14. TV and Cable Direct Marketing			
15. TV Home Shopping Channels			
16. Mobile Units			
17. Franchised Business Units			
18. Trade Shows			
19. Home Party Sales Plans			
20. Fundraisers			
21. Kiosks			
22. Sublet Retail Boutique Space			

6.1.6   Sales Rep Plan

The following parameters will help to define our sales rep plan:
1.   In-house or Independent   _____
2.   Salaried or Commissioned   _____
3.   Salary or Commission Rate   _____
4.   Salary Plus Commission Rate   _____
5.   Special Performance Incentives   _____
6.   Negotiating Parameters   Price Breaks/Added Services/
                                       _____
7.   Performance Evaluation Criteria No. of New Customers/Sales Volume/
                                       _____
8.   Number of Reps   _____
9.   Sales Territory Determinants   Geography/Demographics/
                                       _____
10.   Sales Territories Covered   _____
11.   Training Program Overview   _____
12.   Training Program Cost   _____
13.   Sales Kit Contents   _____
14.   Primary Target Market   _____
15.   Secondary Target Market   _____

Rep Name	Compensation Plan	Assigned Territory

We will locate sales reps using the following techniques:
1.   Place classified ads in trade magazines that serve the Boutique Hotel industry.
2.   Seek other operator recommendations.
3.   Attend travel trade shows where the reps are showing similar product lines.

6.2   Competitive Advantages

A **competitive advantage** is the thing that differentiates a business from its competitors. It is what separates our business from everyone else. It answers the questions: "Why do customers buy from us versus a competitor?", and "What do we offer customers that is unique?". We will make certain to include our key competitive advantages into our marketing materials. We will use the following competitive advantages to set us apart from our competitors. The distinctive competitive advantages which _____ (company name) brings to the marketplace are as follows:
(Note: Select only those you can support)

The competitive edge of _____ (company name) will be the exceptional service. The owners of the Boutique Hotel have over ___ (#) years experience in managing ___ lodging facilities. Another significant advantage for the _____ (company name) is its location. Being located in the recently opened _____ area, _____ (company name) is uniquely positioned to be centrally located to both _____ Village (__ (#) away miles) and the _____Resort Area (___ (#) miles away).

We have a depth of experience in day-to-day hotel operations management, and an exceptional knowledge of, and immediate access to, systems, manpower sourcing, skills training, material resources, operating supplies, and industry networking, which could all be called upon according to the needs of our Boutique Hotel.

Other Competitive Advantages include:
1. We offer a unique experience in a climate of unrivaled luxury.
2. Our facility is handicapped accessible.
3. We clearly publish our 'Boutique Hotel Rules'.
4. Gourmet breakfast menu is available.
5. In-room wood-burning/gas fireplaces.
6. Satellite and cable TV access with _____ movie channels.
7. DVD players in all rooms.
8. Public computer with internet access and printer
9. In-ground swimming pool and hot tub.
10. Gazebo
11. Gift basket and floral arrangement rush deliveries.
12. Discounted access to local fitness center.
13. On-premises fully equipped fitness center.
14. Professional massage service available in room.
15. Expanded gift and antique shops on premises.
16. Discounted tickets available to local attractions and events.
17. The guest rooms have walls that are ___% glass providing a breathtaking view of the spectacular landscape.
18. Offers a huge patio and _____ (?) for the guests to explore.
19. Our relentless attention to personal service and the pampering of our guests.
20. The facilities are handcrafted and the architectural detail is simply beautiful.
21. We will assemble a walking guidebook with brochures from local attractions and restaurant menus, along with flyers on special events and local maps.
22. Our guests will be within walking distance of restaurants, shopping, _____.
23. Besides our great location, guests will get great hospitality with special amenities of homemade knit slippers, a fireplace and home-style breakfast.
24. The overwhelming advantage of our Boutique Hotel is its personalized service, individualized decor, and delivery of a unique multi-sensory "experience".
25. Our Boutique Hotel will appeal to the aesthetic tastes and expectations of the discerning, affluent traveler looking for a higher standard of attentive, personalized service and amenities.
26. In comparison with other hotels in the area, we will stand out in our unparalleled delivery of amenities and features.

27. Using information obtained through extensive market research, including independently conducted surveys and the owner's own travel experiences, those amenities that guests most desire are being provided.

28. _____ (company name) is also above average in its added features, such as in-room whirlpool baths, fireplaces, etc.

29. The location in a quiet and safe neighborhood surrounded by fine examples of Victorian architecture, it's secluded backyard and deck, and the spacious common room areas will also compare well to other hotels.

30. The Boutique Hotel will also have handicap accessibility, which is not available in most other hotels in the area.

31. The Boutique Hotel will be positioned as a "full service" Boutique Hotel, offering a variety of services for its guests. This will range from assisting guests with restaurant reservations to providing food trays, wine, and flowers for special occasions.

32. Amenities that go beyond the typical Boutique Hotel will include:
Pralines on pillows.
A complimentary music CD for each room that the guest may keep.
An extensive video and audio library for guest use.
CD stereo systems and VCRs in each room.
Gourmet coffee.
A variety of herbal teas.
Daily fresh-baked muffins and fresh fruit.
Links to other businesses and services.
Each room is individually decorated with a country setting that is tasteful and comfortable. You feel as if you have stepped back in time.

33. Customer service is our number one priority.

34. Uniquely positioned, centrally located to _____ (cycling trails/ hunting) areas, a national park, and historical places.

35. Celebrity chefs showcase the local culture, heritage and specialties, delivering different and authentic culinary experiences.

6.2.1   Branding Strategy

Our branding strategy involves what we do to shape what the guest immediately thinks our business offers and stands for. The purpose of our branding strategy is to reduce guest perceived purchase risk and improve our profit margins by allowing use to charge a premium for our Boutique Hotel accommodations and services.

We will invest $_____ every year in maintaining our brand name image, which will differentiate our boutique hotel business from other companies. The amount of money spent on creating and maintaining a brand name will not convey any specific information about our products, but it will convey, indirectly, that we are in this market for the long haul, that we have a reputation to protect, and that we will interact repeatedly with our customers. In this sense, the amount of money spent on maintaining our brand name will signal to consumers that we will provide products and services of consistent quality.

We will use the following ways to build trust and establish our personal brand:
1. Build a consistently published blog and e-newsletter with informational content.
2. Create comprehensive social media profiles.
3. Contribute articles to related online publications.
4. Earn Career and Business Certifications

Resources:
https://www.abetterlemonadestand.com/branding-guide/

Our key to marketing success will be to effectively manage the building of our brand platform in the marketplace, which will consist of the following elements:

Brand Vision - our envisioned future of the brand is to be the source for ultimate Boutique Hotel experiences and to manage the complications of vacation planning

Brand Attributes - Partners, problem solvers, responsive, travel and lodging experts, comprehensive, reliable, flexible and easy to work with.

Brand Essence - the shared soul of the brand, the spark of which is present in every experience a customer has with our products, will be "Problem Solving" and "Responsive" This will be the core of our organization, driving the type of people we hire and the type of behavior we expect.

Brand Image - the outside world's overall perception of our organization will be that we are the 'Boutique Hotel' pros who are alleviating the complications of selecting the right hotel for the right occasion.

Brand Promise - our concise statement of what we do, why we do it, and why customers should do business with us will be, "To experience the ultimate in comfort at solid value-driven prices with the help of our knowledgeable staff"

We will use the following methodologies to implement our branding strategy:
1. Develop processes, systems and quality assurance procedures to assure the consistent adherence to our quality standards and mission statement objectives.
2. Develop business processes to consistently deliver upon our value proposition.
3. Develop training programs to assure the consistent professionalism and responsiveness of our employees.
4. Develop marketing communications with consistent, reinforcing message content.
5. Incorporate testimonials into our marketing materials that support our promises.
6. Develop marketing communications with a consistent presentation style.
   (Logo design, company colors, slogan, labels, packaging, stationery, etc.)
7. Exceed our brand promises to achieve consistent guest loyalty.
8. Use surveys, focus groups and interviews to consistently monitor what our brand means to our guests.
9. Consistently match our brand values or performance benchmarks to our guest requirements.
10. Focus on the maintenance of a consistent number of key brand values that are tied

to our company strengths.
11. Continuously research Boutique Hotel industry trends in our markets to stay relevant to guest needs and wants.
12. Attach a logo-imprinted product label and business card to all products, marketing communications and invoices.
13. Develop a memorable and meaningful tagline that captures the essence of our Boutique Hotel brand.
14. Prepare a one page company overview and make it a key component of our sales presentation folder.
15. Hire and train employees to put the interests of guests first.
16. Develop a professional website that is updated with fresh content on a regular basis.
17. Use our blog to circulate content that establishes our Boutique Hotel niche expertise and opens a two-way dialogue with our guests.
18. Tell a unique story behind the location or history of the boutique hotel.

The communications strategy we will use to build our brand platform will include the following items:

Website - featuring product line information, research, testimonials, cost benefit analysis, frequently asked questions, and policy information. This website will be used as a tool for both our sales team and our customers.

Presentations, brochures and mailers geared to the consumer, explaining the benefits of our product line as part of a comprehensive vacation servicing plan.

Presentations and brochures geared to the family decision maker explaining the benefits of our club programs in terms of positive outcomes, reduced cost from complications, and reduced risk of negative survey results.

A presentation and recruiting brochure geared to prospective sales people that emphasizes the benefits of joining our organization.

Training materials that help every employee deliver our brand message in a consistent manner.

6.2.2   Brand Positioning Statement

We will use the following brand positioning statement to summarize what our brand means to our targeted market:

To _____ (target market)
_____ (company name) is the brand of _____ (product/service frame of reference) that enables the customer to _____ (primary performance benefit) because _____ (company name) _____ (products/services) _____ (are made with/offer/provide) the best _____ (key attributes)

6.3   Business SWOT Analysis

Definition: SWOT Analysis is a powerful technique for understanding your Strengths and Weaknesses, and for looking at the Opportunities and Threats faced.

Strategy: We will use this SWOT Analysis to uncover exploitable opportunities and carve a sustainable niche in our market. And by understanding the weaknesses of our business, we can manage and eliminate threats that would otherwise catch us by surprise. By using the SWOT framework, we will be able to craft a strategy that distinguishes our business from our competitors, so that we can compete successfully in the market.

Strengths

What lodging services are we best at providing?
What unique resources can we draw upon?

1. Experienced management team from the _____ (lodging) industry.
2. Strong networking relationships with many different organizations, including _____.
3. Excellent sales staff who are experienced, highly trained and very guest attentive.
4. Wide diversity of product/service bundled/packaged offerings.
5. High guest loyalty.
6. Remarkable introduction of creativity into the learning process.
7. Great location.
8. Fantastic facilities.
9. Owners who are passionate about their work.
10. A strong differentiation strategy.
11. Maintained the integrity of our historical building.
12. Property has an authentic fit with its destination location.
13. _____

Weaknesses

In what areas could we improve?
Where do we have fewer resources than others?

1. New comer to the area.
2. Lack of marketing experience.
3. The struggle to build brand equity.
4. A limited marketing budget to develop brand awareness.
5. Finding dependable and people oriented staff.
6. We need to develop the information systems that will improve our productivity.
7. Don't know the health needs of the local population.
8. Few shared care guidelines developed.
9. Limited number of rooms means limited amount of sales.
10. The struggle with taking care of everything with low labor overhead.
11. High employee turnover rate.
12. Management expertise gaps.
13. Inadequate monitoring of competitor strategies, reviews and responses.
14. _____

Opportunities

What opportunities are there for new and/or improved services?
What trends could we take advantage of?

1.   Could take market share away from existing competitors.
2.   Greater need for mobile home services by time starved dual income families.
3.   Growing market with a significant percentage of the target market still not aware that _____ (company name) exists.
4.   The ability to develop many long-term guest relationships.
5.   Expanding the range of product/service packaged offerings.
6.   Greater use of direct advertising to promote our services.
7.   Establish referral relationships with local businesses serving the same target market segment.
8.   Networking with non-profit organizations.
9.   The aging population will need and expect a greater range of home services.
10.   Increase public awareness of the importance of health and nutrition matters.
11.   Increase in sales from university-related events.
12.   The ability to become more efficient as the learning curve steepens over time.
13.   Greater attention to environmental sustainability.
14.   Incorporation of technology into the property
15.   Introduction of budget boutique hotels and growth within the Asian markets.
16.   Forming partnerships with fashion houses.
17.   _____

Threats

What trends or competitor actions could hurt us?
What threats do our weaknesses expose us to?

1.   Another Boutique Hotel business could move into this area.
2.   Resistance to awarding zoning variances to Boutique Hotel businesses in residential communities.
3.   Inflation affecting operations for gas, labor, and other operating costs.
4.   Keeping trained efficient staff and key personnel from moving on or starting their own business venture.
5.   Imitation competition from similar indirect service providers.
6.   Price differentiation is a significant competition factor.
7.   The government could enact legislation that could effect reimbursements.
8.   We need to do a better job of assessing the strengths and weaknesses of all of our competitors.
9.   The introduction of a Boutique Hotel-style hotel that understands the basic market need.
10.   A slump in the economy, decreasing people's discretionary income.
11.   Increasing competition for real estate and financing opportunities.

12. Concept copying
13. Human resource issues related to finding highly service oriented people.
14. The lack of available sites, including culturally vibrant areas, buildings with heritage or historical value, and exotic resort destinations.
15. Availability of funding to develop new properties.
16. Association with bargain price websites can undermine the reputation of the boutique brand.
17. _____

Recap:

We will use the following strengths to capitalize on recognized opportunities:
1. _____
2. _____

We will take the following actions to turn our weaknesses into strengths and prepare to defend against known threats.
1. _____
2. _____

6.4.0   Marketing Strategy

Marketing Objectives
1. Engage a broad based public relations firm targeted towards high end travel publications.
2. Establish relationships with travel agents both domestically and internationally.
3. Develop an online presence by developing a website and placing the Company's name and contact information with online directories.

The _____ area has its own website and advertising/promotion program that promotes the area's lodging. Currently, _____% of the area's visitors use the website to identify lodging and service options.

_____ (company name) will be positioned as a new upscale facility that is focused on the _____ (middle/high) -income visitors to _____ area. The area's lodges and inns receive approximately _____% of their guests from the area's central booking system. Since the total number of room units are few with the area's lodges and inns, these lodging units fill up quickly. In addition, the _____ (company name) will be highlighted in a promotional piece for _____ area in the _____ (month) issue of _____ Magazine.

Marketing in the Boutique Hotel industry primarily depends on reputation and referral. We will seek to build our reputation by having an involved commitment to those we serve. The company will rely heavily on word-of-mouth referrals for business.

Our marketing strategy will also revolve around two different types of media, sales brochures and a website. These two tools will be used to make customers aware of our broad range of service offerings. One focus of our marketing strategy will be to drive customers to our website for information about our packages.

Our marketing strategy will utilize prime time radio spots, print ads, press releases, yellow page ads, flyers, reservation service organizations, facility tours and newsletter distribution. We will make effective use of direct response advertising, and include coupons in all print ads.

We will use comment cards, newsletter sign-up forms and surveys to collect guest email addresses and feed our client relationship management (CRM) software system. This system will automatically send out, on a predetermined schedule, follow-up materials, such as article reprints, postcard reminder invitations, email messages, surveys and e-newsletters. We will offset some of our advertising costs by asking our suppliers and other local merchants to place ads in our newsletter.

Resource:
Insightly   https://accounts.insightly.com/?plan=trial
CRM software that empowers the user to serve the guests well by storing all their information in one place, allowing the operator to personalize their guest's experience and ensure a return visit.

Current Situation
We will study the current marketing situation on a weekly basis to analyze trends and identify sources of business growth. As onsite owners, we will be on hand daily to insure guest service. Our services include products of the highest quality and a prompt response to feedback from customers. Our extensive and highly detailed financial statements, produced monthly, will enable us to stay competitive and exploit presented opportunities.

Marketing Budget
Our marketing budget will be a flexible $_____ per quarter. The marketing budget can be allocated in any way that best suits the time of year.

Marketing budget per quarter:

Newspaper Ads	$_____	Radio advertisement	$_____
Web Page	$_____	Guest contest	$_____
Direct Mail	$_____	Sales Brochure	$_____
Trade Shows	$_____	Seminars	$_____
Superpages	$_____	Google Adwords	$_____
Giveaways	$_____	Vehicle Signs	$_____
Business Cards	$_____	Flyers	$_____
Labels/Stickers	$_____	Videos/DVDs	$_____
Samples	$_____	Newsletter	$_____
Bandit Signs	$_____	Email Campaigns	$_____
Sales Reps Comm.	$_____	Restaurant Placemats	$_____
Press Releases	$_____	Billboards	$_____

Movie Theater Ads	$ _____	Fund Raisers	$ _____
Infomercials	$ _____	Speeches	$ _____
Postcards	$ _____	Proof Books	$ _____
Social Networking	$ _____	Charitable Donations	$ _____
Other	$ _____		
Total:			$ _____

Our objective in setting a marketing budget has been to keep it between _____ (6?) and _____ (9?) percent of our estimated annual gross sales in the early years.

The following represents a recap of our marketing programs:
  Promotion expenses (free gifts for coming in the shop)
  Printed materials (sales brochures, pamphlets, fliers, postcards)
  Media advertisements (radio, newspapers, outdoor billboards)
  Facility Tours
  Donations (door prizes, charities)
  Referral Program Brochure
  Website Development

Marketing Mix
Clients will primarily come from word-of-mouth and our referral program. The overall market approach involves creating brand awareness through targeted advertising, public relations, co-marketing efforts with select alliance partners, direct mail, email campaigns (with constant contact.com), and a website.

Advertising
_____ (company name) will rely on the recommendations of satisfied customers as a means of attracting customers away from the competition. Past experience has proven that many customers come on the recommendations of others. Although word-of-mouth is an effective way of increasing market share, it is also extremely slow. To accelerate the process of expanding the guest base, the business will maintain an advertising budget of $___ for the first year. The bulk of this budget will be spent on listings in the __ (city) yellow pages, complimentary trial coupons, and direct mailings to ad respondents.

Video Marketing
We will use video marketing to bring travelers into the unique experience they can enjoy at our boutique hotel. We will try formatting our videos as travel shows, with a guide to walk guests through all we have to offer. We will also link to our website a series of YouTube.com based video clips that talk about our range of Boutique Hotel services and amenities. We will utilize tour videos to show guests the inside of the rooms, the pool area and any other amenities that may boost reservations. We will create business marketing videos that are both entertaining and informational, and improve our search engine rankings. For each video, we will be sure to include our business keyword in the title and at least once in the description section.

The video will include:

Client testimonials - We will let our best customers become our instant sales force because people will believe what others say about us more readily than what we say about ourselves.

Product Demonstrations - We will train and pre-sell our potential clients on our most popular Boutique Hotel services just by talking about and showing them. Often, our potential clients don't know the full range and depth of our Boutique Hotel services because we haven't taken the adequate time to show and tell them.

Include Business Website Address

Post commercial created for Cable TV or DVD Sales Presentation.

Owner Interview: Discussion of company mission statement and competitive advantages.

Video tour of our Boutique Hotel and local attractions.

Record Frequently Asked Questions Session - We will answer questions that we often get, and anticipate objections we might get and give great reasons to convince potential clients that we are the best Boutique Hotel in the area.

Include a Call to Action - We have the experience and the know-how to host your next family or business event. So call us, right now, and let's get started.

Seminar - Include a portion of a seminar on how to maximize the benefits of staying at a Boutique Hotel.

Comment on industry trends and product news - We will appear more in-tune and knowledgeable in our market if we can talk about what's happening in our hospitality industry and marketplace.

Resources: www.businessvideomarketing.tv
                www.hotpluto.com
                www.hubspot.com/video-marketing-kit
                www.youtube.com/user/mybusinessstory

Analytics Report
http://support.google.com/youtube/bin/static.py?hl=en&topic=1728599&guide=1
    714169&page=guide.cs

Note: Refer to Video Marketing Tips in rear marketing worksheets section.

Example:
www.youtube.com/watch?v=2KQVWGB7Qbk

Top 11 places where we will share our videos online:

YouTube   **www.youtube.com**
This very popular website allows you to log-in and leave comments and ratings on the videos. You can also save your favorite videos and allows you to tag posted videos. This makes it easier for your videos to come up in search engines.

Google Video   **http://video.google.com/**
A video hosting site. Google Video is not just focused on sharing videos online, but this is also a market place where you can buy the videos you find on this site using Google search engine.

Yahoo! Video   **http://video.yahoo.com/**
Uploading and sharing videos is possible with Yahoo Video!. You can find several types of videos on their site and you can also post comments and ratings for the videos.

Revver   **http://www.revver.com/**
This website lets you earn money through ads on your videos and you will have a 50/50 profit split with the website. Another great deal with Revver is that your fans who posted your videos on their site can also earn money.

Blip.tv   **http://blip.tv/**
Allows viewers to stream and download the videos posted on their website. You can also use Creative Commons licenses on your videos posted on the website. This allows you to decide if your videos should be attributed, restricted for commercial use and be used under specific terms.

Vimeo   **http://www.vimeo.com/**
This website is family safe and focuses on sharing private videos. The interface of the website is similar to some social networking sites that allow you to customize your profile page with photos from Flickr and embeddable player. This site allows users to socialize through their videos.

Metacafe   **http://www.metacafe.com/**
This video sharing site is community based. You can upload short-form videos and share it to the other users of the website. Metacafe has its own system called VideoRank that ranks videos according to the viewer reactions and features the most popular among the viewers.

ClipShack   **http://www.clipshack.com/**
Like most video sharing websites you can post comments on the videos and even tag some as your favorite. You can also share the videos on other websites through the html code from ClipShack and even sending it through your email.

Veoh   **http://www.veoh.com/**
You can rent or sell your videos and keep the 70% of the sales price. You can upload a range of different video formats on Veoh and there is no limit on the size and length of the file. However when your video is over 45 minutes it has to be downloaded before the viewer can watch it.

Jumpcut   **http://download.cnet.com/JumpCut/3000-18515_4-10546353.html**
Jumpcut allows its users to upload videos using their mobile phones. You will have to attach the video captured from your mobile phone to an email. It has its own movie making wizard that helps you familiarize with the interface of the site.

DailyMotion   **www.dailymotion.com**
As one of the leading sites for sharing videos, Dailymotion attracts over 114 million unique monthly visitors (source: comScore, May 2017) 1.2 billion videos views worldwide (source: internal). Offers the best content from users, independent content creators and premium partners. Using the most advanced technology for both users and content creators, provides high-quality and HD video in a fast, easy-to-use online service that also automatically filters infringing material as notified by content owners.
Offering 32 localized versions, their mission is to provide the best possible entertainment experience for users and the best marketing opportunities for advertisers, while respecting content protection.

Networking

Networking will be a key to success because referrals and alliances formed can help to improve our community image and keep our business growing. We will strive to build

long-term mutually beneficial relationships with our networking contacts and join the following types of organizations:
1. We will form a LeTip Chapter to exchange business leads.
2. We will join the local BNI.com referral exchange group.
3. We will join the Chamber of Commerce to further corporate relationships.
4. We will join the Rotary Club, Kiwanis Club, Church Groups, etc.
5. We will do volunteer work for the American Heart Association and Habitat for Humanity.
6. We will join Boutique Hotel trade associations.
7. We will join local women's clubs and clubs centered around the hobby or interests featured at our boutique hotel, such as cycling or cooking.

We will use our metropolitan _____ (city) Chamber of Commerce to target prospective business contacts. We will mail letters to each prospect describing our personalized services. We will follow-up with phone calls.

Newsletter
We will develop a monthly e-newsletter to stay in touch with our clients and use it to market to local businesses. Sending out a monthly email newsletter will be a highly effective boutique hotel marketing strategy. It will give us a way to remind guests of their wonderful experience at our hotel, while providing them with an incentive to indulge in repeat stays. Because our boutique hotel can provide a personalized experience, we will create unique promotions to encourage return visits. Segmenting our email list and creating several different promotions designed specifically for each set of travelers will make this hotel marketing strategy much more effective. We will offer discount coupons for adventure excursions to the Millennial guests, and create romantic getaway packages to entice the couples to return.

We will include the following types of information:
1. Special Promotions
2. New Service/Package Introductions
3. Featured employee/guest of the month.
4. Boutique Hotel industry trends.
5. Client endorsements/testimonials.
6. New renovations/décor.
7. Nutrition / Breakfast Recipes.
8. Upcoming local and on-site events and attractions.
9. Gift Certificate Application
Resource: Microsoft Publisher

We will adhere to the following newsletter writing guidelines:
1. We will provide content that is of real value to our subscribers.
2. We will provide solutions to our subscriber's problems or questions.
3. We will communicate regularly on a weekly basis.
4. We will create HTML Messages that look professional and allow us to track how many people click on our links and/or open our emails.

5.　　We will not pitch our business opportunity in our Ezine very often.
6.　　We will focus our marketing dollars on building our Ezine subscriber list.
7.　　We will focus on relationship building and not the conveying of a sales message.
8.　　We will vary our message format with videos, articles, checklists, quotes, pictures and charts.
9.　　We will recommend occasionally affiliate products in some of our messages to help cover our marketing costs.
10.　 We will consistently follow the above steps to build a database of qualified prospects and customers.

Resources:
www.mailchimp.com
www.constantcontact.com/email-templates/newsletter-templates
http://lmssuccess.com/10-reasons-online-business-send-regular-newsletter-customers/
www.smallbusinessmiracles.com/how/newsletters/
www.fuelingnewbusiness.com/2010/06/01/combine-email-marketing-and-social-media-for-ad-agency-new-business/

Vehicle Signs

We will place magnetic and vinyl signs on our vehicles and include our company name, phone number, company slogan and website address, if possible. We will create a cost-effective moving billboard with high-quality, high-resolution vehicle wraps. We will wrap a portion of the vehicle or van to deliver excellent marketing exposure.
Resource:　http://www.fastsigns.com/

Design Tips:
1.　　Avoid mixing letter styles and too many different letter sizes.
2.　　Use the easiest to recognize form of your logo.
3.　　The standard background is white.
4.　　Do not use a background color that is the same as or close to your vehicle color.
5.　　Choose colors that complement your logo colors.
6.　　Avoid the use too many colors.
7.　　Use dark letter colors on a light background or the reverse.
8.　　Use easy to read block letters in caps and lower case.
9.　　Limit content to your business name, slogan, logo, phone number and website-address.
10.　 Include your license number if required by law.
11.　 Magnetic signs are ideal for door panels (material comes on 24" wide rolls).
12.　 Graphic vehicle window wraps allow the driver to still see out.
13.　 Keep your message short so people driving by can read it at a glance.
14.　 Do not use all capital letters.
15.　 Be sure to include your business name, phone number, slogan and web address.

Vehicle Wraps

Vehicle wrapping will be one of our preferred marketing methods. According to company research, wrapped vehicles have more impact than billboards, create a positive image for the company and prompt the public to remember the words and images featured in the company's branding. Vehicle wrapping is also an inexpensive marketing strategy. A typical truck wrap costs about $2,500, and is a one-time payment for an ad that spans the life of a truck's lease.

Direct Mailings

The key to the success of our direct mail campaign will be the quality of our mailing list. Our best list will be our house list, which will be compiled from past guest stays and response to our advertisements, including yellow page ads and discounted trial coupons. We will also intend to rent lists from matching lifestyle magazine subscribers and qualified list brokers, and use the following criteria:

1.   College educated
2.   Annual household income > $60,000
3.   Zip code range
4.   Age range: 25 to 69
5.   Lifestyle Interests; Cycling/Hunting/Reading/Painting/Fashion/Tourism?

We will increase our group meetings with direct mail that speaks to our target audience of corporations, and motivates them to host their events at our Boutique Hotel. Direct mail that is high-end and elegant will be read by our customer and our message or offer will be conveyed. Our marketing expertise, clean design style, and knowledge of our target audience needs and wants will allow us to create direct mail that is cost-effective and will help to build and retain loyal customers.

DVD Presentation

We plan to create a DVD that will provide a tour of our facility, an educational seminar, and present testimonials from some our satisfied guests. We will include this DVD in our sales presentation folder and direct mail package.

Advertising Wearables

We will give all preferred club members an eye-catching T-shirt or sweatshirt with our company name and logo printed across the garment to wear about town. We will also give them away as a thank you for guest referral activities. We will also ask all employees to wear our logo-imprinted shirts at sponsored events. We will also sell the logo garments in our facility.

Charitable Donations

We will use these coupon donation opportunities to meet and greet many new potential clients and distribute lots of sales brochures and business cards to event sponsors and attendees.

Corporate Sales Promotion/Information Package Kit

Intelligently designed Boutique Hotel print collateral has the power to reach our new or existing customer and prompt more reservations in both the leisure and business traveler segment. Print collateral will be a tangible means of conveying our Boutique Hotel brand and showcasing our amenities and offerings. We will engage our target audience with vibrant photography and insightful copy and will create print collateral that is memorable and effective. Our promotional sales presentation kit will contain the following items:

- Owner/Key Staff Resumes
- Rate Sheet
- DVD Presentation
- FAQs
- Press Release Clippings
- Testimonials
- Referral Program Form
- Boutique Hotel Photography
- Policies
- Article Reprints
- Sales Brochure
- Business Card
- Community Service Awards
- House Rules
- Client Satisfaction Survey

Trade Shows

We will exhibit at as many local trade shows per year as possible. These include Home and Garden Shows, travel trade shows, resort/real estate development trade shows, County Fairs, Business Expos, open exhibits in shopping malls, business spot-lights with our local Chamber of Commerce, and more. The objective is to get our company name and service out to as many people as possible. We will do our homework and ask other stores where they exhibit their products and services. When exhibiting at a trade show, we will put our best foot forward and represent ourselves as professionals. We will be open, enthusiastic, informative and courteous. We will exhibit our products and services with sales brochures, logo-imprinted giveaways, sample products to taste, a photo book for people to browse through and a computer to run our video presentation through. We will use a 'free drawing' for a gift basket prize and a sign-in sheet to collect names and email addresses. We will also develop a questionnaire or survey that helps us to assemble an ideal customer profile and qualify the leads we receive. We will train our booth attendants to answer all type of questions and to handle objections. We will also seek to present educational seminars at the show to gain increased publicity, and name and expertise recognition. Most importantly, we will develop and implement a follow-up program to stay-in-touch with prospects.

Resources:

www.tsnn.com
www.acshomeshow.com/
www.hospitalityexpos.com/
www.biztradeshows.com/trade-events/
www.biztradeshows.com/travel-tourism/

www.expocentral.com
www.EventsInAmerica.com
www.spaandresortexpo.com/whoops

Stage Events

We will host events at our Boutique Hotel to become known in our community. This is essential to attracting referrals. We will schedule regular events, such as seminar talks, catered open house events, art exhibits, cooking classes, tournaments, contests, Bingo and fundraisers. We will use event registration forms, our website and an event sign-in sheet to collect the names and email addresses of all attendees. This database will be used to feed our automatic guest relationship follow-up program and newsletter service.

Resource: www.eventbrite.com

Host Events

We will host an occasional event for a charity or a special group that we would like to be associated with. It will be a great way to get the right people in our hotel so they can keep it in mind in the future. These hosted events will help Word of Mouth a great deal. We will also seek out sponsors and throw a party that will have an impact and supply content for a press release.

Association membership and advertising

A large number of visitors will look to regional Boutique Hotel associations for information about the different Boutique Hotel's in the area. Most associations publish a guide to the local Boutique Hotel's and we plan to be in this guide. One of the other perks of membership is visibility on the associations website with a link to ours. Additionally, we will be a member of the Chamber of Commerce because people typically inquire with the local Chamber when planning a vacation.

Travel Guidebooks

These are specialized Boutique Hotel guide books. These are normally purchased at a book store. There is a charge to be included in the guide book. These may be local, regional or national. To be in some guide books the Boutique Hotel must meet certain standards. We will send the following guidebook publishers a package that will include a descriptive cover letter, a free stay comp coupon and our sales brochure.

AAA Tourbook   Features inspection rating system.   www.aaa.biz
Annual Directory of hotels   http://www.bnb-directory.com/
Boutique Hotel USA   http://www.usabedandbreakfast.com/
Country hotels Magazine
Fodor's   www.fodors.com
Frommer's Travel Guide   http://www.frommers.com/
Mobil Travel Guide   Star Ratings   //mobiltravelguide.howstuffworks.com/
Complete Guide to hotels, hotels and Guesthouses
National Trust
Official Airline Guide
Mr. and Mrs. Smith   www.mrandmrssmith.com/us/
I Escape   www.i-escape.com/travel-guides
Welcome Beyond   www.welcomebeyond.com/small-boutique-hotels/guide/#location
Secret Places   www.secretplaces.com/
Tablet Hotels   www.tablethotels.com/

Fodor's Travel
Presents resources that users will want to read as well as reference. Includes guide books and website, which offer current and discerning shopping, dining, hotel, and culture recommendations, as well as compelling features and articles that convey the essence of each destination
Example: http://www.fodors.com/news/boutique-hotel-opens-nantucket-6903.html

About.com
With more than 900 topic sites (Guide sites), About.com offers expert, quality content that helps users find solutions to a wide range of daily needs – from parenting, health care and technology to cooking, travel and many others. Since 1996, About.com has continually maintained its relevance to users by routinely providing expert information on a large range of topics. About.com covers more than 88,000 topics and adds more than 1,600 pieces of new content each week.
Ex: http://gocaribbean.about.com/b/2017/06/28/five-summer-deals-from-anguillas-anacaona-hotel.htm

HotelChatter.com
Dedicated to covering everything related to hotels and lodging around the world. Covers hotel deals and reviews, which celebrities are staying where, hotel industry news, tips for booking online, the hotels you should stay away from, the hotels you should book, and more.
Ex: www.hotelchatter.com/story/2017/6/27/113510/771/hotels/What_You_Should_Know_About_The_Mykonos_Hotel_Scene

Curbed.com
Focuses on all-things design, decor, and shelter, from Malibu dream houses to Wyoming ranches to Maine cabins, and all residences in between.
Ex: http://curbed.com/archives/2017/06/24/the-definitive-guide-to-opening-a-hipster-boutique-hotel.php

Tourism Agencies.
There are state, regional and local travel and tourism organizations. These are all in the business of promoting travel and tourism. There may be a membership fee to belong to these organizations. We will do research to determine if our states has a travel and tourism hot line where people can call in for travel and tourism information.
Resources:
Tourism Offices Worldwide Directory   www.towd.com/
Travel and Tourism Sites for U.S. States and Territories
                    www.usa.gov/Citizen/Topics/Travel_Tourism/State_Tourism.shtml
U.S. Travel Association   www.ustravel.org/

Reservation Service Organization (RSOs).
This is a private business that handles making the reservation for Boutique Hotel businesses. The RSO will charge a fee for each reservation it makes. There may be an annual or one time membership fee charged to belong to the RSO. The RSO generally is involved in marketing all of its hotels. Some RSOs have standards that we as a Boutique Hotel will have to meet.
Resources:
1.   www.go-lodging.com/Media.html
2.   www.cenres.org/
3.   www.everythinginn.com/ApplicationsMembershipFees/rsoapplication.htm
4.   www.guestserve.com/

5.   www.worldres.com

Local Travel Agents

We will list our services with all the travel agencies in our area. A brochure or a short synopsis of what we offer and our amenities will give the travel agents an idea for steering visitors to our Boutique Hotel.

Travel Magazine Directories

We will list our services in the directories of a number of national travel magazines, particularly those that cater to women, because they make 75 percent of all family travel decisions.

Ex: http://adventure.nationalgeographic.com/adventure/
.   http://www.travelmagazineusa.com/   http://www.travelgirlinc.com/

Sales Brochures

Research indicates that brochures are the number one way hotels advertise. Our sales brochure will include the following contents and become a key part of our direct mail package:

- Reservation Contact Information
- Guest Testimonials/Endorsements
- Competitive Advantages
- Trial Coupon
- Photo of Boutique Hotel Exterior
- Include separate rate sheet by room.
- Area Map
- Area sights and attractions.
- Business Logo

- Hotel Ambiance Description
- List of Services/Benefits
- Owner Resume/Bio
- Panoramic Room Views
- Policies (kids, smoking, pets)
- Policies (cancel, deposits, refunds)
- Special Package Options
- Complimentary Amenities

We will also make arrangements to display our sales brochures at the local tourist office and at tourist attractions near our Boutique Hotel. In return, we will take some of their brochures to hand to our guests. This will create a win, win situation.

Sales Brochure Design

1.   Speak in Terms of Our Guests Wants and Interests.
2.   Focus on all the Benefits, not Just Features.
3.   Put the company logo and Unique Selling Proposition together to reinforce the fact that your company is different and better than the competition.
4.   Include a special offer, such as a discount, a free report, a sample, or a free trial to increase the chances that the brochure will generate sales.

We will incorporate the following Brochure Design Guidelines:

1.   Design the brochure to achieve a focused set of objectives (marketing of programs) with a target market segment (residential vs. commercial).
2.   Tie the brochure design to our other marketing materials with colors, logo, fonts and formatting.
3.   List capabilities and how they benefit clients.

4. Demonstrate what we do and how we do it differently.
5. Define the value proposition of our engineering installing services
6. Use a design template that reflects your market positioning strategy.
7. Identify your key message (unique selling proposition)
8. List our competitive advantages.
9. Express our understanding of client needs and wants.
10. Use easy to read (scan) headlines, subheadings, bullet points, pictures, etc.
11. Use a logo to create a visual branded identity.
12. The most common and accepted format for a brochure is a folded A3 (= 2 x A4), which gives 4 pages of information.
13. Use a quality of paper that reflects the image we want to project.
14. Consistently stick to the colors of our corporate style.
15. Consider that colors have associations, such as green colors are associated with the environment and enhance an environmental image.
16. Illustrations will be appropriate and of top quality and directly visualize the product assortment, product application and production facility.
17. The front page will contain the company name, logo, the main application of your product or service and positioning message or Unique Selling Proposition.
18. The back page will be used for testimonials or references, and contact details.

Employee Personal Marketing

We will develop a training program and business cards to help employees to market themselves as sales agents and get new people interested in our boutique hotel business. Employee personal marketing is the ability to showcase employee talents and present them in a fashion that our customers and prospects will recognize them. We will need to be able to back up and actually do what we say we can do. This type of marketing will also be very important for the customers we already have. We will develop an employee certification program to make sure our customers are aware of all the ways our products and services can benefit them, and that every guest gets served properly.

Coupons

We will use coupons with limited time expirations to get prospects to try our service programs. We will also accept the coupons of our competitors to help establish new client relationships. We will run ads directing people to our Web site for a $___ coupon certificate. This will help to draw in new clients and collect e-mail addresses for the distribution of a monthly newsletter. We will use "dollars off" and not "discount" percentages, as customers are not impressed with "10 to 20 percent off" coupons today. Research indicates that we can use our coupons to spark online searches of our website and drive sales. This will help to draw in new clients and collect e-mail addresses for the distribution of a monthly newsletter. We will include a coupon with each sale, or send them by mail to our mailing list.

Examples:
www.retailmenot.com/view/rumorvegas.com
http://freehotelcoupons.com/hotels/FL/St-Petersburg/hollander-boutique-hotel/
www.dontpayfull.com/at/sundialhotel.com

www.hotelcoupons.com/hotels/florida/miami-beach/crowne-plaza-south-beach-z-ocean-
hotel/MIASB/

We will use coupons selectively to accomplish the following:
1.   To introduce a new product or service.
2.   To attract loyal customers away from the competition
3.   To prevent customer defection to a new competitor.
4.   To help celebrate a special event at our boutique hotel.
5.   To thank customers for a large order and ensure a repeat order within a certain
       limited time frame.

Types of Coupons:
1.   Courtesy Coupons   Rewards for repeat business
2.   Cross-Marketing Coupons   Incentive to try other products/services.
3.   Companion Coupon   Bring a friend incentive.
Resources:
www.google.com/offers/business/how-it-works.html

Websites like Groupon.com, LivingSocial, Eversave, and BuyWithMe sell discount
vouchers for services ranging from custom _____ to _____ consultations. Best known is
Chicago-based Groupon. To consumers, discount vouchers promise substantial savings
— often 50% or more. To merchants, discount vouchers offer possible opportunities for
price discrimination, exposure to new customers, online marketing, and "buzz." Vouchers
are more likely to be profitable for merchants with low marginal costs, who can better
accommodate a large discount and for patient merchants, who place higher value on
consumers' possible future return visits.
Examples:
https://www.groupon.com/hotels/new-york-ny-us/room-mate-hotel-grace

Yipit.com
Gathers over 30,000 offers per month from 809 daily deal sites like Groupon,
LivingSocial, Gilt City, Google Offers and filters them based on where subscribers are
located and what types of deals they want to be notified of. Yipit is a simple way to
access them all - via web, a personalized email or iPhone - in 118 cities in North
America.
Examples:
http://yipit.com/business/the-one-boutique-hotel-spa-castle/

Cross-Promotions
We will develop and maintain partnerships with local professionals that cater to the needs
of business travelers and seniors, and conduct cross-promotional marketing campaigns.
We will develop and maintain partnerships with local businesses that cater to the needs of
our customers, such as beauty salons, fitness clubs and senior daycare centers, and
conduct cross-promotional marketing campaigns. These cross-promotions will require the
exchanging of poster displays, flyers, business card holders, discount coupons, guest
mailing lists and endorsements. We will host weekly free wine tastings in a kitchen area

that encourages local restaurants to bring in popular dishes so customers can sample wines with food.

Premium Giveaways
We will distribute logo-imprinted promotional products at events, also known as giveaway premiums, to foster top-of-mind awareness (www.promoideas.org). These items include logo-imprinted T-shirts, business cards with magnetic backs, mugs with contact phone number, recipe cards and calendars that feature important date reminders.

Local Newspaper Ads
We will use these ads to announce the opening of our Boutique Hotel and get our name established. We will include info about our romantic getaway weekends and uniquely themed rooms. We will include a coupon to track results in zoned editions.

Our newspaper ads will utilize the following design tips:
1. We will start by getting a media kit from the publisher to analyze their demographic information as well as their reach and distribution.
2. Don't let the newspaper people have total control of our ad design, as we know how we want our company portrayed to the market.
3. Make sure to have 1st class graphics since this will be the only visual distinction we can provide the reader about our business.
4. Buy the biggest ad we can afford, with full-page ads being the best.
5. Go with color if affordable, because consumers pick color ads over black 82% of the time.
6. Ask the paper if they have specific days that more of our type of buyer reads their paper.
7. If we have a hit ad on our hands, we will make it into a circular or door-hanger to extend the life of the offer.
8. Don't change an ad because we are getting tired of looking at it.
9. We will start our headline by telling our story to pull the reader into the ad.
10. We will use "Act Now" to convey a sense of urgency to the reader.
11. We will use our headline to tell the reader what to do.
12. The headline is a great place to announce a free offer.
13. We will write our headline as if we were speaking to one person, and make it personal.
14. We will use our headline to either relay a benefit or intrigue the reader into wanting more information.
15. Use coupons giving a dollar amount off, not a percentage, as people hate doing the math.

Publication Type	Ad Size	Timing	Circulation	Section	Fee

Journal Display Ads
We will consider placing display ads in business and trade journals read by professionals,

and possibly rent a list of their local subscribers for a planned direct mailing. The mailing will describe our spa facilities and in-room computer workstations.

Resource:
The Business Journals   http://www.bizjournals.com/
The premier media solutions platform for companies strategically targeting business decision makers. Delivers a total business audience of over 10 million people via their 42 websites, 62 publications and over 700 annual industry leading events. Their media products provide comprehensive coverage of business news from a local, regional and national perspective.

Examples:
www.bizjournals.com/tampabay/blog/2017/05/boutique-hotel-opens-on-st-
     petersburg.html
www.bizjournals.com/albuquerque/news/2017/06/05/heritage-acquires-taos-
     boutique-hotel.html
www.bizjournals.com/seattle/news/2017/06/07/penrose-walla-walla-hotel-and-spa-wine-
     tourism.html

Publication Type	Ad Size	Timing	Circulation	Section	Fee

Local Publications

We will place low-cost classified ads in neighborhood publications to advertise our organic wines. We will also submit public relations and informative articles to improve our visibility and establish our expertise and trustworthiness. These publications include the following:
1.   Neighborhood Newsletters
2.   Local Restaurant Association Newsletter
3.   Local Chamber of Commerce Newsletter
4.   Realtor Magazines
5.   Homeowner Association Newsletters
Resources:
Hometown News   www.hometownnews.com
Pennysaver   www.pennysaverusa.com

Publication Type	Ad Size	Timing	Circulation	Section	Fee

Doorhangers

Our doorhangers will feature a calendar of special events at our Boutique Hotel. The doorhanger will include a list of all our service categories and info about our Preferred Club Membership Program. We will also attach our business card to the doorhanger and distribute the doorhangers multiple times to the same subdivision.

Article Submissions

We will pitch articles to consumer magazines, local newspapers, business magazines and internet articles directories to help establish our specialized expertise and improve our visibility. Hyperlinks will be placed within written articles and can be clicked on to take the guest to another webpage within our website or to a totally different website. These clickable links or hyperlinks will be keywords or relevant words that have meaning to our Boutique Hotel. In fact, we will create a position whose primary function is to link our Boutique Hotel with opportunities to be published in local publications.

We will write a 1,000 word piece on a topic that reflects our Boutique Hotel consulting expertise, and submit it for publication in the Sunday opinion section of our local newspaper and the _____ (*New York Times?*). We will also submit articles or post to blogs or email newsletters that were created around a boutique hotel theme. We will do extensive research to find the blogger or other "thought leaders" out there who have a sway over discussion in our specific field of hospitality and their own audience. We will reach out to these influential bloggers, because they will provide a very powerful way to promote our Boutique Hotel. Their audience may be smaller, but it is much more concentrated and passionate about luxury accommodations, and will thus take action in much higher numbers. Our objective will be to locate a single-author blog with a large audience that is highly focused, and the author favors or endorses our approach to hotel design and management style. We will then seek to build a long-term, mutually beneficial relationship with the author. We will attempt to make friends with them and show them that our methodology is sound and relevant to their audience, so that they will confidently and actively promote our methods and _____ to their followers. In fact, we will take the following approach:

1. We will focus on a relevant idea to the unique vacation theme of the blog and endeavor to add value to the selected blog over time.
2. We will leave some thoughtful comments on their blog, highlighting certain helpful ideas from our Boutique Hotel guest discovery approach.
3. We will forward interesting articles with a different perspective on the blogger's position or focus, to add content value from the blogger's perspective.
4. We will pose questions in our cover letter like; "do you think maybe this might be interesting to your audience?."

Publishing requires an understanding of the following publisher needs:
1. Review of good work.   2. Editor story needs.
3. Article submission process rules 4. Quality photo portfolio
5. Exclusivity requirements.   6. Target market interests

Our Article Submission Package will include the following:
1. Well-written materials   2. Good Drawings
3. High-quality Photographs   4. Well-organized outline.

Examples of General Publishing Opportunities:
1. Document a new solution to old problem 2. Publish a research study
3. Mistake prevention advice   4. Present a different viewpoint
5. Introduce a local angle on a hot topic. 6. Reveal a new trend.

7.	Share specialty niche expertise.	8.	Share wine health benefits

Examples of Specific Article Titles:
1. "Everything You Ever Wanted to Know About Boutique Hotel Policies"
2. "How to Evaluate and Compare Boutique Hotel Establishments"
3. " New Trends in Boutique Hotel Accommodations"
5. "Using Boutique Hotel Vacations to Relieve Stress".
6. "The Six Things You Must Ask Before Booking a Boutique Hotel Reservation".
7. "Why Stay at a Boutique Hotel…rather than just a Hotel?"
8. "Just Who Is the Boutique Hotel Target Audience?"

Write Articles With a Closing Author Resource Box or Byline

1.	Author Name with credential titles.	2.	Explanation of area of expertise.
3.	Mention of a special offer.	4.	A specific call to action
5.	A Call to Action Motivator	6.	All possible contact information
7.	Helpful Links	8.	Link to Boutique Hotel Website.

Article Objectives:

Article Topic	Target Audience	Target Date

Article Tracking Form

SubjectPublication	Target Audience	Business Development	Resources Needed	Target Date

Possible Print and Online Magazines to submit articles include:

1.	Gourmet Magazine	2.	Food and Wine Magazine
3.	Luxury Life & Style Magazine	4.	Press Democrat
5.	San Diego Magazine	6.	Passport Magazine
7.	Wine Enthusiast Magazine	8.	Robb Report
9.	Sunset Magazine	10.	Appellation Magazine
11.	Country Home Magazine	12.	Conde Nast Traveler
13.	Travelgirl Magazine	14.	*Travel + Leisure* magazine
15.	Zagat Survey	16.	Color Magazine
17.	Yahoo Travel	18.	Boutique Hotel News
19.	Masquerade (Dubai)	20.	Global Citizen (GCC)
21.	Hautetime.ae		

Examples:
http://www.cntraveler.com/story/best-boutique-hotels-in-bangkok
www.usatoday.com/story/experience/las-vegas/2017/05/21/boutique-hotels-artisan-
 rumor-royal-house/2346125/
www.colormagazineusa.com/index.php?option=com_content&view=article&id=8
 65:upscale-chic-at-chandler-studios&catid=46:business&Itemid=80
http://travel.yahoo.com/blogs/compass/boutique-hotel-boom-bohemian-valparaiso-

chile-221425567.html

Resources: Writer's Market   www.writersmarket.com
              Directory of Trade Magazines   www.techexpo.com/tech_mag.html

Internet article directories include:

http://ezinearticles.com/
http://www.wahm-articles.com
http://www.articlecity.com
http://www.articledashboard.com
http://www.webarticles.com
http://www.article-buzz.com
www.articletogo.com
http://article-niche.com
www.internethomebusinessarticles.com
http://www.articlenexus.com
http://www.articlefinders.com
http://www.articlewarehouse.com
http://www.easyarticles.com
http://ideamarketers.com/
http://clearviewpublications.com/
http://www.goarticles.com/
http://www.webmasterslibrary.com/
http://www.connectionteam.com
http://www.MarketingArticleLibrary.com
http://www.dime-co.com
http://www.allwomencentral.com
http://www.reprintarticles.com
http://www.articlestreet.com
http://www.articlepeak.com
http://www.simplysearch4it.com
http://www.zongoo.com
http://www.mainstreetmom.com
http://www.valuablecontent.com
http://www.article99.com

http://www.mommyshelpercommunity.com
http://www.ladypens.com/
http://www.amazines.com
http://www.submityourarticle.com/articles
http://www.articlecube.com
http://www.free-articles-zone.com
http://www.content-articles.com
http://superpublisher.com
http://www.site-reference.com
www.articlebin.com
www.articlesfactory.com
www.buzzle.com
www.isnare.com
//groups.yahoo.com/group/article_announce
www.ebusiness-articles.com
www.authorconnection.com/
www.businesstoolchest.com
www.digital-women.com/submitarticle.htm
www.searchwarp.com
www.articleshaven.com
www.marketing-seek.com
www.articles411.com
www.articleshelf.com
www.articlesbase.com
www.articlealley.com
www.selfgrowth.com
www.LinkGeneral.com
www.articleavenue.com
www.virtual-professionals.com

Online Classified Ad Placement Opportunities

The following free classified ad sites, will enable our Boutique Hotel to thoroughly describe the benefits of our using our services:

1.	**Craigslist.org**	2.	Ebay Classifieds
3.	Classifieds.myspace.com	4.	KIJIJI.com
5.	//Lycos.oodle.com	6.	Webclassifieds.us
7.	USFreeAds.com	8.	www.oodle.com
9.	Backpage.com	10.	stumblehere.com
11.	Classifiedads.com	12.	gumtree.com
13.	Inetgiant.com	14.	www.sell.com

15.	Freeadvertisingforum.com	16.	Classifiedsforfree.com
17.	www.olx.com	18.	www.isell.com
19.	Base.google.com	20.	www.epage.com
21.	Chooseyouritem.com	22.	www.adpost.com
23.	Adjingo.com	24.	Kugli.com
Ex:	www.classifiedsadsworld.com/ad-category/hotels-resorts/		

Sample Classified Ad#1:

Looking for a Conveniently Located Boutique Hotel in the _____ Area that Offers a Truly Unique Guest Experience? Want to Get Away for a Few Days and Still be Close to Home? _____ (company name) is a full-service Boutique Hotel that has been serving the _____ area since _____ (year). Give us a call at _____, or visit us at _____ (Website) for our seasonal rate specials and event schedule.

Sample Classified Ad#2:

_____ (company name), _____ (city), ____ (state)
_____ (company name) invites you to a holiday in the best of environment. _____ Boutique Hotel is one place that promises to make you feel one with nature. The Boutique Hotel organizes entertaining cultural programs, besides offering recreational facilities like Swimming pool, Japanese garden, Shopping arcade, Travel and Car rental services, 24 hours rooms and restaurant services, Car parking, and Indoor and outdoor games. Each room has been decorated in a different _____ theme. Call _____, or visit us at _____ (Website) for our seasonal rate specials and special event schedule.

Sample Classified Ad#3:

The _____ (company name) has a unique and desirable mix of the look of boutique hotel but with the warm and friendly feel of a B&B, where our staff takes the time to really get to know our guests. With ___ (#) rooms, a bar, a restaurant and conference facilities all lying in stunning grounds, the _____ (company name) on _____ (location) offers guests the perfect sense of peace and tranquility. Each room has been decorated in a different ____ theme. Call _____, or visit us at _____ (Website) for our seasonal rates.

Two-Step Direct Response Classified Advertising

We will use 'two-step direct response advertising' to motivate readers to take a step or action that signals that we have their permission to begin marketing to them in step two. Our objective is to build a trusting relationship with our prospects by offering a free unbiased, educational report in exchange for permission to continue the marketing process. This method of advertising has the following benefits:

1.	Shorter sales cycle.	2.	Eliminates need for cold calling.
3.	Establishes expert reputation.	4.	Better qualifies prospects
5.	Process is very trackable.	6.	Able to run smaller ads.

Sample Two Step Lead Generating Classified Ad:

FREE Report Reveals "The Health Benefits of De-stressing Weekend Getaways"
Or….. "How to Plan the Perfect Weekend Getaway".
Or…. "What's So Special About the Experience at a Boutique Hotel?"
Call 24 hour recorded message and leave your name and address.

Your report will be sent out immediately.
Note: The respondent has shown they have an interest in our service specialty. We will also include a section in the report on our catering service and our complete contact information, along with a time limited discount coupon.

Yellow Page Ads

Research indicates that the use of the traditional Yellow Page Book is declining, but that new residents or people who don't have many personal acquaintances will look to the Yellow Pages to establish a list of potential businesses to call upon. Even a small 2" x 2" boxed ad can create awareness and attract the desired target client, above and beyond the ability of a simple listing. We will use the following design concepts:

1. We will use a headline to sell people on what is unique about our Boutique Hotel amenities.
2. We will include a service guarantee to improve our credibility.
3. We will include a coupon offer and a tracking code to monitor the response rate and decide whether to increase or decrease our ad size in subsequent years.
4. We will choose an ad size equal to that of our competitors, and evaluate the response rate for future insertion commitments.
5. We will include our hours of operation, motto or slogan and logo.
6. We will include our competitive advantages.
7. We will list under the same categories as our competitors.
8. We will use some bold lettering to make our ad standout.
9. We will utilize yellow books that also offer an online dimension.

Resource: www.superpages.com   www.yellowpages.com
Example: www.yellowpages.com/philadelphia-pa/mip/rittenhouse-1715-a-boutique-
              hotel-371426?lid=371426

Ad Information:

Book Title: _____   Coverage Area: _____
Yearly Fee: $_____   Ad Size: _____ page
Renewal date: _____   Contact: _____

Cable Television Advertising

Cable television will offer us more ability to target certain market niches or demographics with specialty programming. We will use our marketing research survey to determine which cable TV channels our customers are watching. It is expected that many watch the Home & Garden TV channel, and that people with surplus money watch the Golf Channel and the Food Network. Our plan is to choose the audience we want, and to hit them often enough to entice them to take action. We will also take advantage of the fact that we will be able to pick the specific areas we want our commercial to air. Ad pricing will be dependent upon the number of households the network reaches, the ratings the particular show has earned, contract length and the supply and demand for a particular network.
Resource:
Spot Runner   www.spotrunner.com
Television Advertising   http://televisionadvertising.com/faq.htm
Ad Information:

Length of ad "spot": ___ seconds   Development costs: $____ (onetime fee)
Length of campaign: __ (#) mos.   Runs per month: Three times per day
Cost per month.: $_____   Total campaign cost: $_____.

Radio Advertising

We will use non-event based radio advertising. This style of campaign is best suited for non-retail businesses, such as our Boutique Hotel. We will utilize a much smaller schedule of ads on a consistent long-range basis (48 to 52 weeks a year) with the objective of continuously maintaining top-of-mind-awareness. This will mean maintaining a sufficient level of awareness to be either the number one or number two choice when a triggering-event, such as a vacation plan, moves the consumer into the market for services and forces "a consumer choice" about which Boutique Hotel company in the consumer's perception might help them the most. This consistent approach will utilize only one ad each week day (260 days per year) and allow our company to cost-effectively keep our message in front of consumers once every week day. The ad copy for this non-event campaign, called a positioning message, will not be time-sensitive. It will define and differentiate our business' "unique market position" , and will be repeated for a year.

Note: On the average, listeners spend over 3.5 hours per day with radio.

Radio will give us the ability to target our audience, based on radio formats, such as news-talk, classic rock and the oldies. Radio will also be a good way to get repetition into our message, as listeners tend to be loyal to stations and parts of the day. The Company may also use a number of radio personalities to visit and experience the location so that they may "plug" the facility in lifestyle and travel columns during their respective interviews.

1.   We will use radio advertising to direct prospects to our Web site, advertise a limited time promotion or call for an informational brochure.
2.   We will try to barter our services for radio ad spots.
3.   We will use a limited-time offer to entice first-time customers to use our services.
4.   We will explore the use of on-air community bulletin boards to play our public announcements about community sponsored events.
5.   We will also make the radio station aware of our expertise in the hospitality field and our availability for interviews.
6.   Our choice of stations will be driven by the market research information we collect via our surveys.
7.   We will capitalize on the fact that many stations now stream their programming on the internet and reach additional local and even national audiences, and if online listeners like what they hear in our streaming radio spot, they can click over to our website.
8.   Our radio ads will use humor, sounds, compelling music or unusual voices to grab attention.
9.   Our spots will tell stories or present situations our target audience can relate to.
10.   We will make our call to action, a website address or vanity phone number, easy to remember and tie it in with our company name or message.
11.   We will approach radio stations about buying their unsold advertising space for

deep discounts. (Commonly known at radio stations' as "Run of Station")
On radio, this might mean very early in the morning or late at night. We will talk
to our advertising representatives and see what discounts they can offer when
one of those empty spaces comes open.

Resources: Radio Advertising Bureau   www.RAB.com

                Radio Locator   www.radio-locator.com

                Radio Directory   www.radiodirectory.com

Ad Information:

Length of ad "spot": ___ seconds	Development costs: $____ (onetime fee)
Length of campaign: __ (#) mos.	Runs per month: Three times per day
Cost per month.: $_____	Total campaign cost: $_____.

Blog Talk Radio

National Public Radio (www.NPR.org) plays host to a radio program called _____.
The program features Boutique Hotel experts who talk and blog about travel tips. This
will help to establish our Boutique Hotel expertise and build the trust factor with potential
clients. Even if we can't get our own nationally syndicated talk show, we will try to make
guest appearances and try our hand with podcasting by using apps like Spreaker or
joining podcasting communities like BlogTalkRadio.

Resources:

National Public Radio   www.npr.org

Spreaker   http://www.spreaker.com/

Blog Talk Radio   http://www.blogtalkradio.com/

With BlogTalkRadio, people can either host their own live talk radio show with any
phone and a computer or listen to thousands of new shows created daily.
Ex: http://boutiquelodging.wordpress.com/tag/travel-talk-radio/

Press Release Overview:

We will use market research surveys to determine the media outlets that our demographic
customers read and then target them with press releases. We will draft a cover letter for
our media kit that explains that we would like to have the newspaper print a story about
the start-up of our new local business or a milestone that we have accomplished. And,
because news releases may be delivered by feeds or on news services and various
websites, we will create links from our news releases to content on our website. These
links which will point to more information or a special offer, will drive our clients into
the sales process. They will also increase search engine ranking on our site. We will
follow-up each faxed package to the media outlet with a phone call to the lifestyle section
editor.

Media Kit

We will compile a media kit with the following items:

1.   A pitch letter introducing our company and relevant impact newsworthiness for
their readership.
2.   A press release with helpful newsworthy story facts.
3.   Biographical fact sheet or sketches of key personnel.
4.   Listing of product and service features and benefits to customers.

5.   Photos and digital logo graphics
6.   Copies of media coverage already received.
7.   FAQ
8.   Customer testimonials
9.   Sales brochure
10.   Media contact information
11.   URL links to these online documents instead of email attachments.
12.   Our blog URL address.

Public Relations Opportunities
The following represents a partial list of some of the reasons we will issue a free press release on a regular basis:
1.   Announce Grand Opening Event.
2.   Planned Open House Event after a completed renovation project.
3   Introduction of a new package offering.
4.   Support for a Non-profit Cause or other local event.
5.   Presentation of a cooking workshop on gourmet breakfasts.
6.   Report Survey Results
7.   Publication of an article on Boutique Hotel industry trends or a new cookbook.
8.   Seminar on how-to restore historic homes with related tour.
9.   Speech on historic home decorating.
10.   Publication of our own cookbook.
11.   Announcement of half price for kids to coincide with a big local event.
Examples:
       www.sbwire.com/press-releases/studio-boutique-hotel-named-one-of-the-top-25-
          hotels-in-costa-rica-by-tripadvisor-253911.htm
       www.bizjournals.com/tampabay/news/2017/06/11/groundbreaking-signals-
          hotel-project.html

Green Public Relations
We will create a positive image for our _____ by creating newsworthy stories that tout our green qualities and 'green' mission using the following tactics:
1.   We will host an environmental film screening or a tasting featuring organic and locally-grown foods. We will also hold a fundraiser or a community gathering that focuses on the environment.
2.   We will ask other business to join in initiating a recycling or composting program.
      We will also partner with another eco-friendly business by offering our customers coupons for that business and asking them to do the same for our _____.
3.   We will help with community programs, such as the hosting of school field trips or environmental educational classes for kids. This kind of community involvement will not only encourage environmentally responsible behavior in the next generation, but it will also get the community interested in our business as an established green leader in the community.
4.   Our green mission is to support a sustainable world, and reflect the values of our employees, guests, and investors, by using non-intrusive, high quality, eco-

friendly products and services at our boutique hotel.

Ex: http://www.kimptonhotels.com/kimpton-cares/earthcare.aspx

We will use the following techniques to get our press releases into print:
1. Find the right contact editor at a publication, that is, the editor who specializes in lifestyle issues.
2. Understand the target publication's format, flavor and style and learn to think like its readers to better tailor our pitch.
3. Ask up front if the journalist is on deadline.
4. Request a copy of the editorial calendar--a listing of targeted articles or subjects broken down by month or issue date, to determine the issue best suited for the content of our news release or article.
5. Make certain the press release appeals to a large audience by reading a couple of back issues of the publication we are targeting to familiarize ourselves with its various sections and departments.
6. Customize the PR story to meet the magazine's particular style.
7. Avoid creating releases that look like advertising or self-promotion.
8. Make certain the release contains all the pertinent and accurate information the journalist will need to write the article and accurately answer the questions "who, what, when, why and where".
9. Include a contact name and telephone number for the reporter to call for more information.

PR Distribution Checklist
We will send copies of our press releases to the following entities:
1. Send it to clients to show accomplishments.
2. Send to prospects to help prospects better know who you are and what you do.
3. Send it to vendors to strengthen the relationship and to influence referrals.
4. Send it to strategic partners to strengthen and enhance the commitment and support to our firm.
5. Send it to employees to keep them in the loop.
6. Send it to Employees' contacts to increase the firm's visibility exponentially.
7. Send it to elected officials who often provide direction for their constituents.
8. Send it to trade associations for maximum exposure.
9. Put copies in the lobby and waiting areas.
10. Put it on our Web site, to enable visitors to find out who we are and what our firm is doing, with the appropriate links to more detailed information.
11. Register the Web page with search engines to increase search engine optimization.
12. Put it in our press kit to provide members of the media background information about our firm.
13. Include it in our newsletter to enable easy access to details about company activities.
14. Include it in our brochure to provide information that compels the reader to contact our firm when in need of legal counsel.
15. Hand it out at trade shows and job fairs to share news with attendees and establish

credibility.

Media List

Journalist	Interests	Organization	Contact Info

Distribution:
- www.1888PressRelease.com
- www.prweb.com
- www.PR.com
- www.24-7PressRelease.com
- www.PRnewswire.com
- www.digitaljournal.com
- www.businesswire.com
- www.primezone.com
- www.xpresspress.com/
- www.Mediapost.com

- www.ecomwire.com
- www.WiredPRnews.com
- www.eReleases.com
- www.NewsWireToday.com
- www.onlinePRnews.com
- www.PRLog.org
- www.marketwire.com
- www.primewswire.com
- www.ereleases.com/index.html

Journalist Lists:
- www.mastheads.org
- www.helpareporter.com
- www.easymedialist.com

Media Directories
- Bacon's – www.bacons.com/
- Newspapers – www.newspapers.com/
- AScribe – www.ascribe.org/
- Gebbie Press – www.gebbieinc.com/

Support Services
- PR Web - http://www.prweb.com
- Yahoo News – http://news.yahoo.com/
- Google News – http://news.google.com/

HARO ("Help A Reporter Out")   www.helpareporter.com/
An online platform that provides journalists with a robust database of sources for upcoming stories. It also provides business owners and marketers with opportunities to serve as sources and secure valuable media coverage.

Area Convention, Tourism and Visitors Bureau
We will register with the local tourism board and ask for their help in promoting our Boutique Hotel.

Postcards
1. We will use personalized postcards to stay-in-touch with prior guests.
2. Postcards will offer cheaper mailing rates, staying power and attention grabbing graphics, but require repetition, like most other advertising methods.
3. We will develop an in-house list of potential clients for routine communications from open house events, seminar registrations, direct response ads, etc.
4. We will use postcards to encourage users to visit our website, and take advantage of a special offer.
5. We will utilize a "wish you were here" theme and include a season appropriate photo of our Boutique Hotel, featuring the local landscape.

6.   We will grab attention and communicate a single-focus message in just a few words.
7.   The visual elements of our postcard (color, picture, symbol) will be strong to help get attention and be directly supportive of the message.
8.   We will facilitate a call to immediate action by prominently displaying our phone number and website address.
9.   We will include a clear deadline, expiration date, limited quantity, or consequence of inaction that is connected to the offer to communicate immediacy and increase response.

Resource: www.Postcardmania.com

Reminder Service

We will use our Guest Registration Form to capture important guest dates and occasion visits reasons, such as Mother's Day, anniversaries and birthdays, and email a special invitation in advance of the date, event or holiday. We will also use the key date information to mail stay-in-touch greeting cards.

Resource: www.yourmailinglistprovider.com/
             www.easyivr.com/reminder-service.htm

Flyers

1.   We will seek permission to post flyers on the bulletin boards in local businesses, community centers, doctor and clinic waiting rooms, housing development offices and local schools.
2.   We will also insert flyers into our direct mailings.
3.   We will use our flyers as part of a handout package at open house events.
4.   The flyers will feature a discount coupon.
5.   We will circulate flyers to the following local agencies and organizations:

      - YWCA   - YMCA
      - Churches and Synagogues   - Parent Support Groups
      - Nat'l Council of Jewish Women   - National Org. for Women
      - Junior League   - United Way

Flyer Design:
1.   The Headline must draw attention and motivate a reader to take action.
     Example: Looking for Best Hotel Experience Money Can Buy?   Call Us!
2.   Do not simply list services, but show people how they solve problems.
     Example: Got Party Planning Problems? Our Consultants have the contacts and
              expertise to cure your vacation planning headaches!
3.   Take the opportunity to personalize your ad.
     Example: Our family-owned business has proudly served the _____ area for
              _____ years from the same location.
4.   Include high-quality images of the boutique hotel that sell!
     Example: High-resolution photos of successful projects and delighted clients.
5.   Strike a balance of text on one clear selling point, relevant images, white space, bullet points, sub-headlines and branding with full contact information to make it easy to read.

Referral Program

We understand the importance of setting up a formal referral program with the following characteristics:

1.   Give a premium reward based simply on people giving referral names.
2.   Send an endorsed testimonial letter from a loyal client to the referred prospect.
3.   Include a separate referral form as a direct response device.
4.   Provide a space on the response form for leaving positive comments that can be used to build a testimonial letter, that will be sent to each referral.
5.   We will clearly state our incentive rewards, and terms and conditions.
6.   We will distribute a newsletter to stay in touch with our clients and include articles about our referral program success stories.

Sources:

1.   Referrals from other retailers, particularly those of other niche specialties.
2.   Give speeches on a complicated niche area that other practitioners may feel is too narrow for them to handle, thus triggering referrals.
3.   Structured Client Referral Program.
4.   Newsletter Coupons.

Methods:

1.   Always have ready a 30-second elevator speech that describes what you do and who you do it for.
2.   Use a newsletter to keep our name in front of referrals sources.
3.   Repeatedly demonstrate to referral sources that we are also thinking about their practice or business.
4.   Regularly send referrals sources articles on unique yet important topics that might affect their businesses.
5.   Use Microsoft Outlook to flag our contacts to remind us it is time to give them some form of personal attention.
6.   Ask referral sources for referrals.
7.   Get more work from a referral source by sending them work.
8.   Immediately thank a referral source, even for the mere act of giving his name to a third party for consideration.
9.   Remember referral sources with generous gift baskets and gift certificates.
10.   Schedule regular lunches with former school classmates and new contacts.

Examples:
https://siouxfalls.clubhouseinn.com/meetings-and-events/business-meetings/customer-
        referral-program

We will offer an additional donation of $ _____ to any organization whose member use a referral coupon to become a client. The coupon will be paid for and printed in the organization's newsletter.

Referral Tracking Form

Referral Source	Presently	No. of Clients	Anticipated	Actions to	Target

Name	Referring Yes/No	Referred	Revenue	be Taken	Date

Sample Referral Program

We want to show our appreciation to established customers and business network partners for their kind referrals to our business. ____ (company name) wants to reward our valued and loyal customers who support our _____ Programs by implementing a new referral program. Ask any of our team members for referral cards to share with your family and friends to begin saving towards your next ____ (product/service) purchase. We will credit your account $___ (?) for each new customer you refer to us as well as give them 10% off their first visit. When they come for their first visit, they should present the card upon arrival. We will automatically set you up a referral account.

Resources:
https://hotelemarketer.com/2008/11/11/hotel-referral-marketing-hotel-guests-are-a-key-distribution-channel-of-the-future/

The Referral Details Are As Follows:

1. You will receive a $__ (?) credit for every customer that you refer for _____ (products/services). Credit will be applied to your referral account on their initial visit.
2. We will keep track of your accumulated reward dollars and at any time we can let you know the amount you have available for use in your reward account.
3. Each time you visit ____ (company name), you can use your referral dollars to pay up to 50% of your total charge that day
4. Referral dollars are not applicable towards the purchase of _____ products.
5. All referral rewards are for _____ services and cannot be used towards _____ services.

Referral Coupon Template

Company Name: _____
Address: _____
Phone: _____ Website: _____
Print and present this coupon with your first order and the existing customer who referred you will receive a credit for $_____ towards _____.

Current customer   **Referred customer**
Name: _____   Name: _____
Address: _____   Address: _____
Phone: _____   Phone: _____
Email: _____   Email: _____
Date referred:

Office use only
Credit memo number:_____

Credit issued date: _____   Credit applied by: _____

Invite-A-Friend

We will setup an aggressive invite-a-friend referral program. We will encourage new members or newsletter subscribers, during their initial registration process, to upload and send an invitation to multiple contacts in their email address books. We will reward our guests whenever they recommend our boutique hotel to their friends and family. We will do this and track it with a service like Flip.to (www.flip.to/), which will automatically generate whatever incentive we are offering in exchange for guests sharing their stay via social media. Incentives will include offering a free drink at the bar, free dessert, or a discount off of spa services.

Examples:
http://www.maximizingmoney.com/hotel-discounts/stayful/
www.extole.com/blog/an-epic-list-of-50-referral-program-examples/#Travel

Portable Sales Tents

We will set-up temporary sales tents and tables at local festivals and fairs to handout our business cards and sales brochures.

Co-Publish a Book

We will publish a book of local attraction photos and recipes through our state's Boutique Hotel Association to share the most requested recipes and cultural events, improve the visibility of our business and generate another stream of income.

Testimonial Marketing

We will either always ask for testimonials immediately after a completed project or contact our clients once a quarter for them. We will also have something prepared that we would like the client to say that is specific to a service we offer, or anything relevant to advertising claims that we have put together. For the convenience of the client we will assemble a testimonial letter that they can either modify or just sign off on. Additionally, testimonials can also be in the form of audio or video and put on our website or mailed to potential clients in the form of a DVD or Audio CD. A picture with a testimonial is also excellent. We will put testimonials directly on a magazine ad, slick sheet, brochure, or website, or assemble a complete page of testimonials for our sales presentation folder.

Examples:
http://urbanboutiquehotel.com/about/testimonials/
http://mboutiquehotel.com/en/testimonials/

We will collect customer testimonials in the following ways:
1.   Our website – A page dedicated to testimonials (written and/or video).
2.   Social media accounts – Facebook fan pages offer a review tab, which makes it easy to receive and display customer testimonials.
3.   Google+ also offers a similar feature with Google+ Local.

4.   Local search directories – Ask customers to post more reviews on Yelp and Yahoo Local.
5.   Customer Satisfaction Survey Forms

We will pose the following questions to our customers to help them frame their testimonials:
1. What was the obstacle that would have prevented you from buying this service?
2. "What was your main concern about buying this hospitality service?"
3. What did you find as a result of buying this service?
4. What specific feature did you like most about this product?
5. What would be three other benefits about this experience?
6. Would you recommend our boutique hotel? If so, why?
7. Is there anything you'd like to add?

Business Logo

Our logo will graphically represent who we are and what we do, and it will serve to help brand our image. It will also convey a sense of uniqueness and professionalism. The logo will represent our company image and the message we are trying to convey. Our business logo will reflect the philosophy and objective of the Boutique Hotel business. Our logo will incorporate the following design guidelines:
1.   It will relate to our industry, our name, a defining characteristic of our company or a competitive advantage we offer.
2.   It will be a simple logo that can be recognized faster.
3.   It will contain strong lines and letters which show up better than thin ones.
4.   It will feature something unexpected or unique without being overdrawn.
5.   It will work well in black and white (one-color printing).
6.   It will be scalable and look pleasing in both small and large sizes.
7.   It will be artistically balanced and make effective use of color, line density and shape.
8.   It will be unique when compared to competitors.
9.   It will use original, professionally rendered artwork.
10. It can be replicated across any media mix without losing quality.
11. It appeals to our target audience.
12. It will be easily recognizable from a distance if utilized in outdoor advertising.

Resources: www.freelogoservices.com/   www.hatchwise.com
                www.logosnap.com   www.99designs.com
                www.fiverr.com   www.freelancer.com
                www.upwork.com
Logo Design Guide:
www.bestfreewebresources.com/logo-design-professional-guide
www.creativebloq.com/graphic-design/pro-guide-logo-design-21221

Fundraisers

Community outreach programs involving charitable fundraising and showing a strong interest in the local school system will serve to elevate our status in the community as a "good corporate citizen" while simultaneously increasing store traffic. We will execute a successful fundraising program for our convenience store and build goodwill in the community, by adhering to the following guidelines:

1.   Keep It Local
      When looking for a worthy cause, we will make sure it is local so the whole neighborhood will support it.
2.   Plan It
      We will make sure that we are organized and outline everything we want to accomplish before planning the fundraiser.
3.   Contact Local Media
      We will contact the suburban newspapers to do stories on the event and send out press releases to the local TV and radio stations.
4.   Contact Area Businesses
      We will contact other businesses and have them put up posters in their stores and pass out flyers to promote the event.
5.   Get Recipient Support
      We will make sure the recipients of the fundraiser are really willing to participate and get out in the neighborhood to invite everyone into our store for the event, plus help pass out flyers and getting other businesses to put up the posters.
6.   Give Out Bounce Backs
      We will give a "bounce-back" coupon that allows for both a discount and an additional donation in exchange for guest next purchase. (It will have an expiration date of two weeks to give a sense of urgency.)
7.   Be Ready with plenty of product and labor on hand for the event.

Fundraiser Action Plan Checklist:
1.   Choose a good local cause for your fundraiser.
2.   Calculate donations as a percentage for normal sales.
3.   Require the group to promote and support the event.
4.   Contact local media to get exposure before and after the event.
5.   Ask area businesses to put up flyers and donate printing of materials.
6.   Use a bounce-back coupon to get new customers back.
7.   Be prepared with sufficient labor and product.
Resource:
www.thefundraisingauthority.com/fundraising-basics/fundraising-event/

Online Directory Listings

The following directory listings use proprietary technology to match customers with industry professionals in their geographical area. The local search capabilities for specific niche markets offer an invaluable tool for the guest. These directories help member businesses connect with purchase-ready buyers, convert leads to sales, and maximize the value of guest relationships. Their online and offline communities provide a quick and easy low or no-cost solution for customers to find a hotel quickly. We intend to sign-up with all no cost directories and evaluate the ones that charge a fee.

1. www.kayak.com/
2. www.hotels.com
3. http://www.hotelmotelaccomodation.com/
4. http://www.resortsandlodges.com/
5. http://boutiquelodgingassociation-hotel.guestcentric.net/home.html
6. http://www.realboutiquehotels.com/home.html
7. http://www.blla.org/blla-directory.htm
8. www.cvent.com/rfp/boutique-hotels-directory-
   5ba2bfefa8946cb9c54cd866267efa0.aspx
9. http://www.greatsmallhotels.com/
10. http://www.miamiboutiquehotels.com/guide.aspx
11. www. tablethotels.com
12. www.roomkey.com

Resource:
https://synup.com/?utm_source=fitsmallbusiness&utm_medium=fsb_domain_ref&utm_
   campaign=fitsmallbusiness

TabletHotels.ocm
Founded in the year 2000 by Laurent Vernhes and Michael Davis, a pair of new-media veterans in search of a cure for boring travel and an antidote to the internet's most common affliction: an overdose of options. They do the hard work of selecting only the world's most extraordinary hotels, and they make booking them as painless as it can be. Tablet's purpose is to put the ease, the romance, the glamour back in travel, from inspiration to confirmation. Hotels are anonymously visited and evaluated by their team of experts, and they will only keep them on the site if they're making their users happy. Only real Tablet guests are allowed to submit reviews, and they will remove any hotel with a less-than-stellar rating

Stayful.com
This website offers discounts at hundreds of boutique hotels around the country. The site promises a chance to try hotels and inns with more local character and to save a few bucks along the way. Stayful only lets customers book up to 30 days in advance and once a room is booked it is non-refundable. Some of the better-known properties include the Gansevoort Park Avenue in New York, The Standard Downtown in Los Angeles, Hotel Monteleone in New Orleans and the Viceroy Miami. There are also plenty of lesser-known lodging options. The site is currently limited to 10 cities: Boston, Chicago, Los Angeles, Miami, New Orleans, New York, Phoenix, San Diego, San Francisco and Seattle. Stayful asks customers to bid on a hotel price. Some provide instant answers. Others can take up to a day to reply and once the hotel responds, the customers has just three hours to complete the booking. But this isn't like Priceline or Hotwire where you are locked into a hotel without knowing all the details. Stayful gives you the specific hotel name and tells the customer, before a credit card is required, if their bid has been accepted. Room types, however, are assigned at check-in. The site requires a one-day wait before another bid can be offered after a rejection. Since Stayful is designed as a

way for hotels to unload their unsold rooms, there tend to be more properties listed for a city the closer to the stay booked.

Theidealhotels.com
A worldwide online hotels reservation system sponsored by Kewmont Investments Inc, a fast growing company that has developed several online resources to book local and worldwide hotels. The use of this system, will allow individual customers and travel agents to book worldwide hotels online as well as to receive detailed information about each destination. Before you travel our efficient staff will find the perfect way to combine the different travel styles to make a unique product for you. All operations are under the supervision of our staff that monitors reservations, requests and assistance services from one of their offices based in Havana. Customized services and the best Central Reservations System available in the market for online bookings characterizes this site.

Roomkey
The creation of a new distribution push under direct hotel members' control. The goal seems to be to assure a greater control of their distribution channels and associated margins. Room Key is an experience-tailored hotel search engine created by six of the world's leading hotel companies. The personalized service enables travelers to quickly and easily compare value for their stay – based on specific attributes and preferences most important to individual guests – and book directly with more than 100 leading hotel brands in 159 countries around the world.

Other General Directories Include:

Listings.local.yahoo.com	Switchboard Super Pages
YellowPages.com	MerchantCircle.com
Bing.com/businessportal	Local.com
Yelp.com	BrownBook.com
InfoUSA.com	iBegin.com
Localeze.com	Bestoftheweb.com
YellowBot.com	HotFrog.com
InsiderPages.com	MatchPoint.com
CitySearch.com	YellowUSA.com
Profiles.google.com/me	Manta.com
Jigsaw.com	LinkedIn.com
Whitepages.com	PowerProfiles.com
Judysbook.com	Company.com

Get Listed	http://getlisted.org/enhanced-business-listings.aspx
Universal Business Listing	https://www.ubl.org/index.aspx
	www.UniversalBusinessListing.org

Universal Business Listing (UBL) is a local search industry service dedicated to acting as a central collection and distribution point for business information online. UBL provides business owners and their marketing representatives with a one-stop location for broad distribution of complete, accurate, and detailed listing information.

Billboards

We will use billboard advertising to create brand awareness and strong name recognition. We will design Billboards that are eye-catching and informative. We will include our business name, location, a graphic, and no more than eight words. In designing the billboard we will consider the fact that the eye typically moves from the upper left corner to the lower right corner of a billboard. We will use colors and pictures to contrast with the sky and other surroundings. We will keep the layout uncluttered and the message simple, and include a direct call to action. Depending on the billboards size and location, the cost will range from $1,000 to $5,000 per month. We will try to negotiate a discount on a long-term contract.

Ex: Ready to Experience the Boutique Hotel Difference?
Resources: Outdoor Advertising Association of America   www.oaaa.org
             EMC Outdoor, Inc.   www.emcoutdoor.com

Theater Advertising

Theater advertising is the method of promoting our business through in-theatre promotions. The objective of theater advertising is to expose the movie patron to our advertising message in various ways throughout the theater. Benefits include; an engaged audience that can't change the channel, an audience that is in a quiet environment, an audience that is in a good mood and receptive, advertising that is targeted to our local geographic area, full color video advertising on a 40 foot screen, and a moving and interactive ad with music and voiceover.

Resources: Velocity Cinema Advertising   www.movieadvertising.com/index.html
             NCM   www.nationalcinemedia.com/intheatreadvertising/
             ScreenVision   www.screenvision.com
             AMC Theaters   www.amctheatres.com
             Regal Entertainment Group www.regmovies.com

Mobile Marketing

We will create a new mobile marketing strategy that spotlights our new flagship product, And the importance of targeting a younger segment to expand our guest base.
We will use mobile advertising to tap into a younger tech-savvy segment of the market to grow our brand in the coming years.

First, consumers will opt-in by sending a text to our SMS platform and in return they will receive an offer for a free burrito via their mobile phones. Once a guest redeems the text message offer, the software will provide us with a report that details what radio station that guest was listening to, the daypart, and which program they were listening to, that prompted the guest to respond to the offer. Our trained staff will be the key in assisting customers with the promotion and up-selling. We will work with Opt It, Inc. to execute its first text messaging campaign. We want the portion of our guest base that does not typically clip coupons out of the Sunday paper to have easy access to the great deals we offer. We believe there will be a large number of people who opted-in on our Web site to receive mobile offers even before the promotion begins. Now, instead of promoting what's happening in a few weeks, we can have managers text local people to let them know about an event that's happening in a few hours.

In a texting component, customers will be able to text "____" to _____ (#) and receive mobile coupons. The second part of the message asks customers if they would like to register their e-mail addresses to receive weekly communications from _____ (company name). The first mobile coupon will reward customers with $___ off any family cheese 8platter/wine package. Customers will continue to receive additional offers, including special offers on holiday gift items. This will purely be an opt in campaign, and will let us create an ongoing conversation with our customers.

Resource: Mobile Marketing Association   www.mmaglobal.com

               BxP Marketing visit   www.bxpmarketing.com.

Customer Reward / Loyalty Program

As a means of building business by word-of-mouth, customers will be encouraged and rewarded as repeat customers. This will be accomplished by offering a discounted bottle of _____ (wine?) to those customers who sign-up for our frequent buyer card and purchase $___ of products and services within a ___ (#) month period.

We will create a loyalty program for our specific type of hotel and target customer, because implementing a loyalty program will influence guests' booking decisions, encourage repeat customers, provide word of mouth marketing and keep our property's highest-earning guests satisfied. We will include instant gratification rewards, as well as accrual benefits. We will enact a loyalty program for our guests with carefully chosen rewards that work with our particular boutique hotel brand, then showcase our rewards through social media. Since we are a boutique hotel, we will shift the focus onto rewards that enhance our guests' experiences rather than money-saving discounts, as experiential rewards make for great social media posts. We will intersperse mentions of our rewards with our regular posts, making sure to include links that take visitors to a custom landing page exclusively for our loyalty program.

The Top 10 Global Hotel Loyalty Programs (as of December 31, 2010)
1. InterContinental Hotels Priority Club ® Rewards: 52 million members (currently, 56 million)
2. Marriott Rewards ®: 33 million members
3. Hilton HHonors: 26 million members
4. Starwood Hotels Preferred Guest ®: 25 million members
5. Hyatt Gold Passport ®: 10.2 million members
6. Best Western Rewards ®: 11 million members
7. Choice Hotels Choice Privileges ®: 10 million members
8. Wyndham Rewards ®: 8 million active members
9. Carlson Hotels Goldpoints Plus ®: 5.5 million members
10. Accor A-Club ®: 5 million members in 2 years

Frequent Buyer Program Types:

1.	Punch Cards	Receive something for free after ? Purchases.
2.	Dollar-for-point Systems	Accrue points toward a free product.
3.	Percentage of Purchase	Accrue points toward future purchases.

Resources:
http://www.refinery29.com/best-store-loyalty-programs
http://blog.fivestars.com/5-companies-loyalty-programs/
www.americanexpress.com/us/small-business/openforum/articles/10-cool-mobile-apps-
        that-increase-customer-loyalty/
https://squareup.com/loyalty

Sample: Loyalty Program

As an loyalty program member, our guests will enjoy the following benefits:
1. Exclusive offers just for our members; all year long
2. "Raid the Mini Bar" in your guest room at every stay, up to $10
3. Free WiFi in guest room and throughout the hotel
4. Free nights earned by making a reservation directly with us
5. Invitations to member only parties and dinners.
6. Honor guest personal preferences: type of pillow, want a yoga mat in room and which newspaper to deliver at doorstep in the morning. W

Sample Loyalty Program: Hyatt's Gold Passport Rewards Program.

The program is free to join. Guests earn five points per eligible stay and they can redeem free nights without blackout dates. After five eligible stays or 15 eligible nights, the guests can reach Platinum status which gets them automatic upgrades, 2pm late check outs and free in-room internet. Diamond membership requires 25 eligible stays or 50 eligible nights and gets them even more perks like 4pm checkouts and welcome point bonuses. Like most hotel loyalty programs, Hyatt also offers many promotions throughout the year to loyalty program members.

Ex: The Trump Loyalty Card

The card offers members a Personalized Preference Program which will keep their room preferences on file "so no request needs repeating"; the best available room rates; early check-in and late check-out (based on availability), 24-hour access to signature Trump Attaché service and a welcome amenity upon arrival. Once the guest meets a certain amount of bookings they can then start to "experience" some of Trump Hotel suites. They can also earn complimentary stays with no blackout dates.

Source: www.hotelchatter.com/story/2013/4/25/111651/960/hotels/A_Quick_Reference_
        Guide_to_Boutique_Hotel_Loyalty_Programs

E-mail Marketing

Direct Email marketing will be an inexpensive and effective way to reach our customers and prospects. We will design, deliver, and track our email campaigns. Email marketing will be used successfully as a branding tool, for notification of our hotel's news and events, and as a lead generation method to acquire client email profiles. We will use the following email marketing tips to build our mailing list database, improve communications, boost guest loyalty and attract new and repeat business.
1. Define our objectives as the most effective email strategies are those that offer

value to our subscribers: either in the form of educational content or promotions. To drive sales, a promotional campaign is the best format. To create brand recognition and reinforce our expertise in our industry we will use educational newsletters.

2. A quality, permission-based email list will be a vital component of our email marketing campaign. We will ask customers and prospects for permission to add them to our list at every touch-point or use a sign-in sheet.
3. We will listen to our customers by using easy-to-use online surveys to ask specific questions about customers' preferences, interests and satisfaction.
4. We will send only relevant and targeted communications.
5. We will reinforce our brand to ensure recognition of our brand by using a recognizable name in the "from" line of our emails and including our company name, logo and a consistent design and color scheme in every email.

Resource:
www.udemy.com/email-marketing-crash-course/

Every ___ (five?) to ____ (six?) weeks, we will send graphically-rich, permission-based, personalized, email marketing messages to our list of clients who registered on our website or responded to an ad or attended a sponsored event. The emails will alert customers in a ___ mile radius to promotions as well as other local events sponsored by our Boutique Hotel. This service will be provided by VerticalResponse.com, ExactTarget.com or ConstantContact.com. The email will announce a special event and contain a short sales letter. The message will invite recipients to click on a link to our website to checkout more information about the event, then print out the page and bring it with them to the event. The software offered by these companies will automatically personalize each email with the guest's name. The software also provides detailed click-through behavior reports that will enable us to evaluate the success of each message. The software will also allow us to dramatically scale back our direct mail efforts and associated costs. Our company will send a promotional e-mail about a promotion that the guest indicated was important to them in their registration application. Each identified market segment will get notified of new products, services, specials and offers based on past buying patterns and what they've clicked on in our previous e-newsletters or indicated on their surveys. The objective is to tap the right guest's need at the right time, with a targeted subject line and targeted content. Our general e-newsletter may appeal to most customers, but targeted mailings that reach out to our various audience segments will build even deeper relationships, and drive higher sales.

We will use our email marketing campaign to convey the following types of information about our boutique hotel:

1. Include high resolution photos of the interior and menu items from the onsite restaurant.
2. Bio profiles of the in residence service providers, such as the tattoo artist and the hair stylists.
3. Artists interviews of the creators of the original art that covers the walls, some of which is for sale.
4. A listing of the planned current events at the hotel and in the area.

5. Links to submit hotel reviews and become a member of the hotel loyalty club.
Resources:
www.myemma.com
www.constantcontact.com/pricing/email-marketing.jsp
www.ipost.com

Voice Broadcasting

A web-based voice broadcast system will provide a powerful platform to generate thousands of calls to clients and customers or create customizable messages to be delivered to specific individuals. Voice broadcasting and voice mail broadcast will allow our company to instantly send interactive phone calls with ease while managing the entire process right from the Web. We will instantly send alerts, notifications, reminders, GOTV - messages, and interactive surveys with ease right from the Web. The free VoiceShot account will guide us through the process of recording and storing our messages, managing our call lists, scheduling delivery as well as viewing and downloading real-time call and caller key press results. The voice broadcasting interface will guide us through the entire process with a Campaign Checklist as well as tips from the Campaign Expert. Other advanced features include recipient targeting, call monitoring, scheduling, controlling the rate of call delivery and customized text to speech (TTS). Resource: http://www.voiceshot.com/public/outboundcalls.asp

Facebook.com

We will use Facebook to move our businesses forward and stay connected to our customers in this fast-paced world. Content will be the key to staying in touch with our customers and keeping them informed. The content will be a rich mix of information, before and after photos, interactive questions, current trends and events, industry facts, education, promotions and specials, humor and fun. We will create a Facebook page for our boutique hotel and connect with all of our customers directly. We will recommend destinations, activities, and special deals on social media to generate direct sales and valuable feedback from our audience.

We will use the following step system to get customers from Facebook.com:
1. We will open a free Facebook account at Facebook.com.
2. We will begin by adding Facebook friends. The fastest way to do this is to allow Facebook to import our email addresses and send an invite out to all our customers.
3. We will post a video to get our customers involved with our Facebook page. We will post a video called "How to Plan a Successful Weekend Getaway." The video will be first uploaded to YouTube.com and then simply be linked to our Facebook page. Video will be a great way to get people active and involved with our Facebook page.
4. We will send an email to our customers base that encourages them to check out the new video and to post their feedback about it on our Facebook page. Then we will provide a link driving customers to our Facebook page.
5. We will respond quickly to feedback, engage in the dialogue and add links to our response that direct the author to a structured mini-survey.

6.   We will optimize our Facebook profile with our business keyword to make it an invaluable marketing tool and become the "go-to" expert in our industry
7.   On a monthly basis, we will send out a message to all Facebook fans with a special offer, as Fan pages are the best way to interact with customers and potential customers on Facebook,
8.   We will use Facebook as a tool for sharing success stories and relate the ways in which we have helped our customers.
9.   We will use Facebook Connect to integrate our Facebook efforts with our regular website to share our Facebook Page activity. This will also give us statistics about our website visitors, and add social interaction to our site.
10. We will use a company called Payvment (www.payvment.com) that has a storefront application for Facebook, that requires a Facebook fan page set up for our dealership. We will install the application on our page, set up the look and feel of the storefront using the tools that Payvment provides, enter information about our dealership, and then start loading products.
11. We will use this Facebook to not only broadcast relevant information but to also interact with guests and prospects.

Examples:
https://www.facebook.com/OliveBoutiqueHotel

Resources:
http://www.facebook.com/advertising/
http://www.guestcentric.com/5-tips-for-a-strong-hotel-facebook-page/
http://www.socialmediaexaminer.com/how-to-set-up-a-facebook-page-for-business/
http://smallbizsurvival.com/2009/11/6-big-facebook-tips-for-small-business.html

Facebook Profiles represent individual users and are held under a person's name. Each profile should only be controlled by that person. Each user has a wall, information tab, likes, interests, photos, videos and each individual can create events.

Facebook Groups are pretty similar to Fan Pages but are usually created for a group of people with a similar interest and they are wanting to keep their discussions private. The members are not usually looking to find out more about a business - they want to discuss a certain topic.

Facebook Fan Pages are the most viral of your three options. When someone becomes a fan of your page or comments on one of your posts, photos or videos, that is spread to all of their personal friends. This can be a great way to get your information out to lots of people...and quickly! In addition, one of the most valuable features of a business page is that you can send "updates" about new products and content to fans and your home building brand becomes more visible.

Facebook Live lets people, public figures and Pages share live video with their followers and friends on Facebook.
Source:
https://live.fb.com/about/
Resources:

https://www.facebook.com/business/a/Facebook-video-ads
http://smartphones.wonderhowto.com/news/facebook-is-going-all-live-video-streaming-your-phone-0170132/

Small Business Promotions
This group allows members to post about their products and services and is a public group designated as a Buy and Sell Facebook group.
Source: https://www.facebook.com/groups/smallbusinesspronotions/
Resource:
https://www.facebook.com/business/a/local-business-promotion-ads
https://www.facebook.com/business/learn/facebook-create-ad-local-awareness
www.socialmediaexaminer.com/how-to-use-facebook-local-awareness-ads-to-target-customers/

Facebook Ad Builder
https://waymark.com/signup/db869ac4-7202-4e3b-93c3-80acc5988df9/?partner=fitsmallbusiness

Best social media marketing practices:
1. Assign daily responsibility for Facebook to a single person on your staff with an affinity for dialoguing .
2. Set expectations for how often they should post new content and how quickly they should respond to comments – usually within a couple hours.
3. Follow and like your followers when they seem to have a genuine interest in your area of health and wellness expertise.
4. Post on the walls of not only your own Facebook site, but also on your most active, influential posters with the largest networks.
5. Periodically post a request for your followers to "like" your page.
6. Monitor Facebook posts to your wall and respond every two hours throughout your business day.

We will use Facebook in the following ways to market our Boutique Hotel:
1. Promote our blog posts on our Facebook page
2. Post a video of our service people in action.
3. Make time-sensitive offers during slow periods
4. Create a special landing page for coupons or promotional giveaways
5. Create a Welcome tab to display a video message from our owner.
   Resource: Pagemodo.
6. Support a local charity by posting a link to their website.
7. Thank our customers while promoting their businesses at the same time.
8. Describe milestone accomplishments and thank customers for their role.
9. Give thanks to corporate accounts.
10. Ask customers to contribute stories about _____ occurrences.
11. Use the built-in Facebook polling application to solicit feedback.
12. Use the Facebook reviews page to feature positive comments from customers, and to respond to negative reviews.
13. Introduce customers to our staff with resume and video profiles.

14.   Create a photo gallery of unusual _____ (requests/jobs?) to showcase our expertise.

We will also explore location-based platforms like the following:
- FourSquare   - GoWalla
- Facebook Places   - Google Latitude

As a Boutique Hotel serving a local community, we will appreciate the potential for hyper-local platforms like these. Location-based applications are increasingly attracting young, urban influencers with disposable income, which is precisely the audience we are trying to attract. People connect to geo-location apps primarily to "get informed" about local happenings.

Foursquare.com

A web and mobile application that allows registered users to post their location at a venue ("check-in") and connect with friends. Check-in requires active user selection and points are awarded at check-in. Users can choose to have their check-ins posted on their accounts on Twitter, Facebook, or both. In version 1.3 of their iPhone application, foursquare enabled push-notification of friend updates, which they call "Pings". Users can also earn badges by checking in at locations with certain tags, for check-in frequency, or for other patterns such as time of check-in.]
Resource: https://foursquare.com/business/
Examples:
https://foursquare.com/v/carat-boutique-hotel/4cd1e6417f56a143eb4dd7a6

Instagram

Instagram.com is an online photo-sharing, video-sharing and social networking service that enables its users to take pictures and videos, apply digital filters to them, and share them on a variety of social networking services, such as
Facebook, Twitter, Tumblr and Flickr. A distinctive feature is that it confines photos to a square shape, similar to Kodak Instamatic and Polaroid images, in contrast to the 16:9 aspect ratio now typically used by mobile device cameras. Users are also able to record and share short videos lasting for up to 15 seconds.

We will establish an Instagram account because consumers are using it as a primary method of research to decide which boutique hotels feel like the best fit for their needs. There's an assumption that hotel-generated web content can be misleading, so consumers have turned to social media to peruse user-generated content of the property to see what the resort "actually" looks like. Their first impression is often the hotel's own Instagram page, so it will be important that we maintain a well-groomed account that greets these researchers with authenticity and professionalism. We will use Instagram in the following ways to help amplify the story of our brand, get people to engage with our content when not at our boutique hotel, and get people to visit our hotel or website:
1.   Let our customers and fans know about specific room availability.
2.   Tie into trends, events or holidays to drive awareness.
3.   Let people know we are open and our ambiance is spectacular.
4.   Run a monthly contest and pick the winning hashtagged photograph
       to activate our customer base and increase our exposure.

5. Encourage the posting and collection of happy onsite or offsite customer photos.

Examples:
http://fathomaway.com/postcards/scenery/boutique-hotels-for-your-instagram-feed/
https://www.instagram.com/watsonsbayboutiquehotel/?hl=en

Note: Commonly found in tweets, a hashtag is a word or connected phrase (no spaces) that begins with a hash symbol (#). They're so popular that other social media platforms including Facebook, Instagram and Google+ now support them. Using a hashtag turns a word or phrase into a clickable link that displays a feed (list) of other posts with that same hashtag. For example, if you click on #_____ in a tweet, or enter #_____ in the search box, you'll see a list of tweets all about _____.

MySpace Advertising

MySpace.com offers a self-service, graphical "display" advertising platform that will enable our company to target our marketing message to our audience by demographic characteristics. With the new MySpace service, we will be able to upload our own ads or make them quickly with an online tool, and set a budget of $25 to $10,000 for the campaigns. We can choose to target a specific gender, age group and geographic area. We will then pay MySpace each time someone clicks on our ad. Ads can link to other MySpace pages, or external websites. MyAds will let us target our ads to specific groups of people using the public data on MySpace users' profiles, blogs and comments. MySpace will enable our company to target potential customers with similar interests to our existing guest base, as revealed via our marketing research surveys. Also the bulletin function on MySpace will allow us to update customers on company milestone achievements and coming events. We will also post a short video to our home page and encourage the sharing of the video with other MySpace users.

LinkedIn.com

LinkedIn groups will be a fantastic source of information and a great source of leads for our Boutique Hotel business. LinkedIn ranks high in search engines and will provide a great platform for sending event updates to business associates. To optimize our LinkedIn profile, we will select one core keyword. We will use it frequently, without sacrificing consumer experience, to get our profile to skyrocket in the search engines. Linkedin provides options that will allow our detailed profile to be indexed by search engines, like Google. We will make use of these options so our business will achieve greater visibility on the Web. We will use widgets to integrate other tools, such as importing your blog entries or Twitter stream into your profile, and go market research and gain knowledge with Polls. We will answer questions in Questions and Answers to show our expertise, and ask questions in Questions and Answers to get a feel for what customers and prospects want or think. We will publish our LinkedIn URL on all our marketing collateral, including business cards, email signature, newsletters, and web site. We will grow our network by joining industry and alumni groups related to our business. We will update our status examples of recent work, and link our status updates with our other social media accounts. We will start and manage a group or fan page for our product,

brand or business. We will share useful articles that will be of interest to customers, and request LinkedIn recommendations from customers willing to provide testimonials. We will post our presentations on our profile using a presentation application. We will ask our first-level contacts for introductions to their contacts and interact with LinkedIn on a regular basis to reach those who may not see us on other social media sites. We will link to articles posted elsewhere, with a summary of why it's valuable to add to our credibility and list our newsletter subscription information and archives. We will post discounts and package deals. We will buy a LinkedIn <u>direct ad</u> that our target market will see. We will find vendors and contractors through <u>connections.</u>
Examples:
http://www.linkedin.com/company/bass-boutique-hotel

Podcasting
Podcasting is a way of publishing audio broadcasts via the internet through MP3 files, which users can listen to using PCs and i-Pods. Our podcasts will provide both information and advertising. Our podcasts will allow us to pull in a lot of customers. Our monthly podcasts will be heard by ___ (#) eventual subscribers. Podcasts can now be downloaded for mobile devices, such as an iPod. Podcasts will give our company a new way to provide information and an additional way to advertise. Podcasting will give our business another connection point with customers. We will use this medium to communicate on important issues, what is going on with a planned event, and other things of interest to our health conscious customers. The programs will last about 10 minutes and can be downloaded for free on iTunes. The purpose is not to be a mass medium. It is directed at a niche market with an above-average educational background and very special interests. It will provide a very direct and a reasonably inexpensive way of reaching our targeted audience with relevant information about our Boutique Hotel services.
Resources:
www.apple.com/itunes/download/.
www.cbc.ca/podcasting/gettingstarted.html
Examples:
https://itunes.apple.com/us/podcast/the-hotel-marketing-podcast/id287820404?mt=2

Blogging
We will use our blog to keep customers and prospects informed about products, events and services that relate to our Boutique Hotel business, new releases, contests, and specials. Our blog will show readers that we are a good source of expert information that they can count on. With our blog, we can quickly update our customers anytime our company releases a new product, the holding of a contest or are placing items on special pricing. We will use our blog to share guest testimonials and meaningful product usage stories. We will use the blog to supply advice on creative recipes for our breakfast menu. Our visitors will be able to subscribe to our RSS feeds and be instantly updated without any spam filters interfering. We will also use the blog to solicit product usage recommendations and future product addition suggestions. Additionally, blogs are free and allow for constant ease of updating.

Our blog will give our company the following benefits:
1. An cost-effective marketing tool.
2. An expanded network.
3. A promotional platform for new _____ services.
4. An introduction to people with similar interests.
5. Builds credibility and expertise recognition.

We will use our blog for the following purposes:
1. To share customer testimonials, experiences and meaningful success stories.
2. Update our clients anytime our company releases a new service.
3. Supply advice on _____ options.
4. Discuss research findings.
5. To publish helpful content.
6, To welcome feedback in multiple formats.
7. Link together other social networking sites, including Twitter.
8. To improve Google rankings.
9. Make use of automatic RSS feeds.

We will adhere to the following blog writing guidelines:
1. We will blog at least 2 or 3 times per week to maintain interest.
2. We will integrate our blog into the design of our website.
3. We will use our blog to convey useful information and not our advertisements.
4. We will make the content easy to understand.
5. We will focus our content on the needs of our targeted audience.

Our blog will feature the following on a regular basis:
1. Useful articles and assessment coupons.
2. Give away of a helpful free report in exchange for email addresses
3. Helpful information for our professional referral sources, as well as clients, and online and offline community members.
5. Use of a few social media outposts to educate, inform, engage and drive people back to our blog for more information and our free report.

To get visitors to our blog to take the next action step and contact our firm we will do the following:
1. Put a contact form on the upper-left hand corner of our blog, right below the header.
2. Put our complete contact information in the header itself.
3. Add a page to our blog and title it, "Become Our Guest.", giving the reader somewhere to go for the next sign-up steps.
4. At the end of each blog post, we will clearly tell the reader what to do next; such as subscribe to our RSS feed, or to sign up for our newsletter mailing list.

Resources: www.blogger.com   www.blogspot.com
                www.wordpress.com   www.tumblr.com
                www.typepad.com

Examples:

Twitter

We will use our hotel's Twitter feed as a virtual concierge. This will offer dual marketing benefits for our boutique hotel: first, we will provide our guests with better service because when we will answer guest concerns virtually. This means that we can provide instant assistance without delays. Also, anyone checking out our Twitter account will see the care we devote to taking care of our guests' needs. This instant attention to guest concerns will be a huge selling feature that will help to set our boutique hotel apart from the large hotel chains. We will also use 'Twitter.com' as a way to produce new business from existing clients and generate prospective clients online. Twitter is a free social networking and micro-blogging service that allows its users to send and read other users' updates (otherwise known as tweets), which are text-based posts of up to 140 characters in length. Updates will be displayed on the user's profile page and delivered to other users who have signed up to receive them. The sender can restrict delivery to those in his or her circle of friends, with delivery to everyone being the default. Users can receive updates via the Twitter website, SMS text messaging, RSS feeds, or email. We will use our Twitter account to respond directly to questions, distribute news, solve problems, post updates, and offer special discounts on our Boutique Hotel Weekend Getaways.

We will provide the following instructions to register as a 'Follower' of _____ (company name) on Twitter:
1. In your Twitter account, click on 'Find People' in the top right navigation bar, which will redirect to a new page.
2. Click on 'Find on Twitter' which will open a search box that says 'Who are you looking for?'
3. Type '_____ (company name) / _____ (owner name)' and click 'search'. This will bring up the results page.
4. Click the blue '_____' name to read the bio or select the 'Follow' button.
Examples:
https://twitter.com/IVYHotelChicago

Business Cards

Our business card will include our company logo, complete contact information, name and title, association logos, slogan or markets serviced, licenses and certifications. The center of our bi-fold card will contain a listing of the brands and services we offer. We will give out multiple business cards to friends, family members, and to each guest, upon the completion of the service. We will also distribute business cards in the following ways:
1. Attached to invoices, surveys, flyers and door hangers.
2. Included in guest product packages.
3. We will leave a stack of business cards in a Lucite holder with the local Chamber of Commerce and any other businesses offering free counter placement.
4. Put a couple of business cards in guest rooms for them to pass onto friends,

family and associates.

We will use fold-over cards because they will enable us to list all of our services and complete contact instructions on the inside of the card. We will also give magnetic business cards to new clients for posting on the refrigerator door.

We will place the following referral discount message on the back of our business cards:
- Our business is very dependent upon referrals. If you have associates who could benefit from our quality services, please write your name at the bottom of this card and give it to them. When your friend presents this card upon their first visit, he or she will be entitled to 10% off discount. And, on your next invoice, you will also get a 10% discount as a thank you for your referral.
Resource: www.vistaprint.com

Google Maps
We will first make certain that our business is listed in Google Maps. We will do a search for our business in Google Maps. If we don't see our business listed, then we will add our business to Google Maps. Even if our business is listed in Google Maps, we will create a Local Business Center account and take control of our listing, by adding more relevant information. Consumers generally go to Google Maps for two reasons: Driving Directions and to Find a Business.
Resource: http://maps.google.com/

Bing Maps   www.bingplaces.com/
This will make it easy for customers to find our business.

Apple Maps
A web mapping service developed by Apple Inc. It is the default map system of iOS, macOS, and watchOS. It provides directions and estimated times of arrival for automobile, pedestrian, and public transportation navigation.
Resources:
 http://www.stallcupgroup.com/2012/09/19/three-ways-to-make-your-pawn-business-more-profitable-and-sellable/
http://www.apple.com/ios/maps/
https://en.wikipedia.org/wiki/Apple_Maps

Google Places
Google Places helps people make more informed decisions about where to go for a quality Boutique Hotel. Place Pages connect people to information from the best sources across the web, displaying photos, reviews and essential facts, as well as real-time updates and offers from business owners. We will make sure that our Google Places listing is up to date to increase our online visibility. Google Places is linked to our Google Maps listing, and will help to get on the first page of Google search page results when people search for a Boutique Hotel in our area.
Resource: www.google/com/places

Yelp.com

We will use Yelp.com to help people find our local business. Visitors to Yelp write local reviews, over 85% of them rating a business 3 stars or higher In addition to reviews, visitors can use Yelp to find events, special offers, lists and to talk with other Yelpers. As business owners, we will setup a free account to post offers, photos and message our customers. We will also buy ads on Yelp, which will be clearly labeled "Sponsored Results". We will also use the Weekly Yelp, which is available in 42 city editions to bring news about the latest business openings and other happenings.
Examples:
http://www.yelp.com/biz/urban-boutique-hotel-san-diego
www.yelp.com/search?find_desc=boutique+hotel&find_loc=San+Francisco%2C+CA

Manta.com

Manta is the largest free source of information on small companies, with profiles of more than 64 million businesses and organizations. Business owners and sales professionals use Manta's vast database and custom search capabilities to quickly find companies, easily connect with prospective customers and promote their own services. Manta.com, founded in 2005, is based in Columbus, Ohio.
Resource: http://www.manta.com/getlisted/

Urbanspoon.com

Urbanspoon is a leading provider of time-critical dining data, and a major player in the multi-billion dollar restaurant information industry.
Ex: www.urbanspoon.com/r/18/1552213/restaurant/East-Side/Addiction-at-Rumor-
        Boutique-Hotel-Las-Vegas

Tripadvisor.com

This site will be of critical marketing importance because 60% of American travelers consult TripAdvisor before booking their hotel. TripAdvisor® features reviews and advice on hotels, resorts, flights, vacation rentals, vacation packages, travel guides, and lots more. We will seek to enhance the services and facilities at our boutique hotel based upon feedback from guests on TripAdvisor. We will read each review carefully, and implement changes whenever possible. If a guest at checkout tells the Front Desk Manager s/he had a great stay and can't wait to come back, we will empower our managers to encourage the guest to write a review on TripAdvisor and other such web outlets that are widely read by future guests. Since the reviews tend to be candid, they are seriously read by others and the input can be a decision making factor when booking a hotel.
Examples:
www.tripadvisor.ie/Hotel_Review-g186621-d456039-Reviews-The_Boutique_Hotel-
        Limerick_County_Limerick.html
www.tripadvisor.com/ShowUserReviews-g187892-d656715-r213926562-Hotel_
        Taodomus-Taormina_Province_of_Messina_Sicily.html
www.tripadvisor.com/ShowUserReviews-g49022-d301309-r264932347-

Pay-Per-Click Advertising

Google AdWords, Yahoo! Search Marketing, and Microsoft adCenter are the three largest network operators, and all three operate under a bid-based model. Cost per click (CPC) varies depending on the search engine and the level of competition for a particular keyword. Google AdWords are small text ads that appear next to the search results on Google. In addition, these ads appear on many partner web sites, including NYTimes.com (The New York Times), Business.com, Weather.com, About.com, and many more. Google's text advertisements are short, consisting of one title line and two content text lines. Image ads can be one of several different Interactive Advertising Bureau (IAB) standard sizes. Through Google AdWords, we plan to buy placements (ads) for specific search terms through this "Pay-Per-Click" advertising program. This PPC advertising campaign will allow our ad to appear when someone searches for a keyword related to our business, organization, or subject matter. More importantly, we will only pay when a potential guest clicks on our ad to visit our website. For instance, since we operate a Boutique Hotel in ___ (city), _____ (state), we will target people using search terms such as "Boutique Hotel, unique room themes, weekend getaway, unique experience, hearty breakfast, private bathrooms, scenic tours, festivals and craft fairs, lifestyle hotel, hospitality in ____ (city), ____ (state)". With an effective PPC campaign our ads will only be displayed when a user searches for one of these keywords. In short, PPC advertising will be the most cost-effective and measurable form of advertising for our Boutique Hotel.
Resources:
http://adwords.google.com/support/aw/?hl=en
www.wordtracker.com

Yahoo Local Listings

We will create our own local listing on Yahoo. To create our free listing, we will use our web browser and navigate to http://local.yahoo.com. We will first register for free with Yahoo, and create a member ID and password to list our business. Once we have accessed http://local.yahoo.com, we will scroll down to the bottom and click on "Add/Edit a Business" to get onto the Yahoo Search Marketing Local Listings page. In the lower right of the screen we will see "Local Basic Listings FREE". We will click on the Get Started button and log in again with our new Yahoo ID and password. The form for our local business listing will now be displayed. When filling it out, we will be sure to include our full web address (http://www.companyname.com). We will include a description of our Boutique Hotel services in the description section, but avoid hype or blatant advertising, to get the listing to pass Yahoo's editorial review. We will also be sure to select the appropriate business category and sub categories.
Example: Dog Boutique Hotel   https://local.yahoo.com/info-17263802

Sales Reps/Account Executives

_____ (company name) will use independent commissioned sales reps to penetrate corporate markets outside of _____ (city/state). Management will work to keep in constant communication with the sales reps to ensure that their service is professional and timely. Independent sales representatives will provide the best mode for distribution in order to maintain pricing controls and higher margins. Independent sales reps are not full-time employees, thus benefits are not necessary. Independent sales reps receive a flat commission based on gross sales. Our sales reps are set at a commission rate of __ (15?)% of gross sales. The average sales rep can service up to __ (#) accounts with the average location generating around $____ per year. We expect to have ___(#) independent sales reps covering ___ (#) states in place to sell the company's product. In addition to field calls, sales reps will represent the product line at all regional tradeshows, with the marketing director attending all national tradeshows. To generate business, our sales reps will seek memberships in women's organizations that focus on the culture of fine wines, handcrafted items, nature and travel.

Point-of-Purchase Displays (POP)

The term point-of-purchase, or POP, typically refers to the promotional graphics focused on influencing consumer behavior at the moment of the purchasing decision. These graphics serve to impact a buying decision in favor of a specific brand or product in-store where the purchase is imminent. POP is increasingly becoming one of the more important aspects of advertising and promotion, because of its efficiency in targeting the consumer in the actual buying environment, the decline of network television viewership and newspaper readership, and the stark reality of recession-sized ad budgets. Because of its impact, we will work with our gift distributor to secure the following types of items from gift item manufacturers:

1. Banners   2. Ceiling danglers
3. Themed wall coverings 4. Directional posters
5. Floor Decals   6. Props

Affiliate Marketing

We will create an affiliate marketing program to broaden our reach. We will first devise a commission structure, so affiliates have a reason to promote our business. We will give them ___ (10)% of whatever sales they generate. We will go after reunion event planner bloggers or webmasters who get a lot of web traffic for our keywords. These companies would then promote our products/services, and they would earn commissions for the sales they generated. We will work with the following services to handle the technical aspects of our program.

ConnectCommerce   www.connectcommerce.com/
Commission Junction www.cj.com
ShareASale   www.shareasale.com/
Share Results
LinkShare   www.linkshare.com
Clickbank   www.clickbank.com
Affiliate Scout   http://affiliatescout.com/
Affiliate Seeking   www.affiliateseeking.com/
Clix Galore   www.clixgalore.com/

Gift with Purchase (GWP)

A GWP is an item that is presented to our client when he or she spends above a specified amount on products or services. The Gift with purchase or free item could be anything from drink recipe books, hotel voucher, free bag of ice, bottle cap, product samples, etc. We will attach our marketing logo and business card to the gift and use it as means to thank the guest for their patronage. We will also explore the dramatic impact of a surprise gift with purchase, because an unexpected bonus item is often very appreciated and remembered.

HotFrog.com

HotFrog is a fast growing free online business directory listing over 6.6 million US businesses. HotFrog now has local versions in 34 countries worldwide.
Anyone can list their business in HotFrog for free, along with contact details, and products and services. Listing in HotFrog directs sales leads and enquiries to your business. Businesses are encouraged to add any latest news and information about their products and services to their listing. HotFrog is indexed by Google and other search engines, meaning that customers can find your HotFrog listing when they use Google, Yahoo! or other search engines.
Resource: http://www.hotfrog.com/AddYourBusiness.aspx

Local.com

Local.com owns and operates a leading local search site and network in the United States. Its mission is to be the leader at enabling local businesses and consumers to find each other and connect. To do so, the company uses patented and proprietary technologies to provide over 20 million consumers each month with relevant search results for local businesses, products and services on Local.com and more than 1,000 partner sites. Local.com powers more than 100,000 local websites. Tens of thousands of small business customers use Local.com products and services to reach consumers using a variety of subscription, performance and display advertising and website products.
Resource: http://corporate.local.com/mk/get/advertising-opportunities

Autoresponder

An autoresponder is an online tool that will automatically manage our mailing list and send out emails to our customers at preset intervals. We will write a short article that is helpful to potential Boutique Hotel buyers. We will load this article into our autoresponder. We will let people know of the availability of our article by posting to newsgroups, forums, social networking sites etc. We will list our autoresponder email address at the end of the posting so they can send a blank email to our autoresponder to receive our article and be added to our mailing list. We will then email them at the interval of our choosing with special offers. We will load the messages into our autoresponder and set a time interval for the messages to be mailed out.
Resource: www.aweber.com

Corporate Incentive / Employee Rewards Program

Our Employee Rewards Program will motivate and reward the key resources of local corporations – the people who make their business a success. We will use independent sales reps to market these programs to local corporations. It will be a versatile program, allowing the corporate client to customize it to best suit the following goals:
1.   Welcome New Hires
2.   Introduce an Employee Discount Program for our Boutique Hotel reservations.
3.   Reward increases in sales or productivity with an Employee Incentive Program
4.   Thank Retirees for their service to the company
5.   Initiate a Loyalty Rewards Program geared towards the customers of our corporate clients or their employees.

Database Marketing

Database marketing is a form of direct marketing using databases of customers or prospects to generate personalized communications in order to promote a product or service for marketing purposes. The method of communication can be any addressable medium, as in direct marketing. With database marketing tools, we will be able to implement guest nurturing, which is a tactic that attempts to communicate with each guest or prospect at the right time, using the right information to meet that guest's need to progress through the process of identifying a problem, learning options available to resolve it, selecting the right solution, and making the purchasing decision. We will use our databases to learn more about customers, select target markets for specific campaigns, through guest segmentation, compare customers' value to the company, and provide more specialized offerings for customers based on their transaction histories, demographic profile and surveyed needs and wants. This database will gives us the capability to automate regular promotional mailings, to semi-automate the telephone outreach process, and to prioritize prospects as to interests, timing, and other notable delineators. The objective is to arrange for first meetings, which are meant to be informal introductions, and valuable fact-finding and needs-assessment events.

We will use sign-in sheets, coupons, surveys and newsletter subscriptions to collect the following information from our clients:
1.   Name   2.   Telephone Number
3.   Email Address   4.   Home Address
5.   Birth Date   6.   Anniversary Date
7.   Favorite Newspaper   8.   Favorite Meals

We will utilize the following types of contact management software to generate leads and stay in touch with customers to produce repeat business and referrals:
1.   Act   www.act.com
2.   Front Range Solutions   www.frontrange.com
3.   The Turning Point   www.turningpoint.com
4.   Acxiom   www.acxiom.com/products_and_services/

We will utilize contact management software, such as ACT and Goldmine, to track the following:
1.   Dates for follow-ups.

2.   Documentation of prospect concerns, objections or comments.
3.   Referral source.
4.   Marketing Materials sent.
5.   Log of contact dates and methods of contact.
6.   Ultimate disposition.

Cause Marketing

Cause marketing or cause-related marketing refers to a type of marketing involving the cooperative efforts of a "for profit" business and a non-profit organization for mutual benefit. The possible benefits of cause marketing for business include positive public relations, improved guest relations, and additional marketing opportunities.

Cause marketing sponsorship by American businesses is rising at a dramatic rate, because customers, employees and stakeholders prefer to be associated with a company that is considered socially responsible. Our business objective will be to generate highly cost-effective public relations and media coverage for the launch of a marketing campaign focused on _____ (type of cause), with the help of the _____ (non-profit organization name) organization.

Resources:
www.causemarketingforum.com/
www.cancer.org/AboutUs/HowWeHelpYou/acs-cause-marketing

Courtesy Advertising

We will engage in courtesy advertising, which refers to a company or corporation "buying" an advertisement in a nonprofit dinner program, event brochure, and the like. Our company will gain visibility this way while the nonprofit organization may treat the advertisement revenue as a donation. We will specifically advertise in the following non-profit programs, newsletters, bulletins and event brochures: _____

_____

Speaking Engagements

We will consider a "problem/solution" format where we describe a challenge and tell how our expertise achieved an exceptional solution. We will use speaking engagements as an opportunity to expose our areas of expertise to prospective clients. By speaking at conferences and forums put together by professional and industry trade groups, we will increase our firm's visibility, and consequently, its prospects for attracting new business. Public speaking will give us a special status, and make it easier for our speakers to meet prospects. Attendees expect speakers to reach out to the audience, which gives speakers respect and credibility. We will identify speaking opportunities that will let us reach our targeted audience. We will designate a person who is responsible for developing relationships with event and industry associations, submitting proposals and, most importantly, staying in touch with contacts. We will tailor our proposals to the event organizers' preferences.

Speaking Proposal Package:
1.   Speech Topic/Agenda/Synopsis
2.   Target Audience: Community and Civic Groups

3. Speaker Biography
4. List of previous speaking engagements
5. Previous engagement evaluations

Possible Targets:

1. AARP Groups
2. Churches
3. YMCAs
4. JCC's
5. Trade Groups
6. Event Planners
7. Travel Agents

Possible Speech Topics:
1. New Trends in Boutique Hotel Amenities
2. How to Evaluate the Quality of Boutique Hotel Accommodations

Speech Tracking Form

Group/Class	Subject/ Topic	Business Development Potential	Resources Needed	Target Date

We will use the following techniques to leverage the business development impact of our speaking engagements:

1. Send out press releases to local papers announcing the upcoming speech. We will get great free publicity by sending the topic and highlights of the talk to the newspaper.
2. Produce a flyer with our picture on it, and distribute it to our network.
3. Send publicity materials to our prospects inviting them to attend our presentation.
4. Whenever possible, get a list of attendees before the event. Contact them and introduce yourself before the talk to build rapport with your audience. Arrive early and don't leave immediately after your presentation.
5. Always give out handouts and a business card. Include marketing materials and something of value to the recipient, so that it will be retained and not just tossed away. You might include tips or secrets you share in your talk.
6. Give out an evaluation form to all participants. This form should request names and contact information. Offer a free consultation if it's appropriate. Follow up within 72 hours with any members of the audience who could become ideal clients.
7. Have a place on the form where participants can list other groups that might need speakers, along with the name of the program chairperson or other contact person.
8. Offer a door prize as incentive for handing in the evaluation. When you have collected all of the evaluations, you can select a winner of the prize.
9. Meet with audience members, answer their questions and listen to their concerns. Stay after your talk and mingle with the audience. Answer any questions that come up and offer follow-up conversations for additional support.
10. Request a free ad in the group's newsletter in exchange for your speech.

1. Send a thank-you note to the person who invited you to speak. Include copies of some of the evaluations to show how useful it was.

Speaking Engagement Package

1.	Video or DVD of prior presentation.	2.	Session Description
3.	Learning Objectives	4.	Takeaway Message
5.	Speaking experience	6.	Letters of recommendation
7.	General Biography	8.	Introduction Biography

Resource: www.toastmasters.com

Meet-up Group

We will form a meet-up group to encourage people to participate in our boutique hotel programs.

Resource: www.meetup.com/create/

Examples: www.meetup.com/topics/hotels/all/

Marketing Associations/Groups

We will set up a marketing association comprised of complementary businesses. We will market our Boutique Hotel as a member of a group of complementary companies. Our marketing group will include a _____ (cycling?) club, an event planner, and a tourism agency. Any business that provides event services will be a likely candidate for being a member of our marketing group. The group will joint advertise, distribute joint promotional materials, exchange mailing lists, and develop a group website. The obvious benefit is that we will increase our marketing effectiveness by extending our reach.

BBB Accreditation

We will apply for BBB Accreditation to improve our perceived trustworthiness. BBB determines that a company meets BBB accreditation standards, which include a commitment to make a good faith effort to resolve any consumer complaints. BBB Accredited Businesses pay a fee for accreditation review/monitoring and for support of BBB services to the public. BBB accreditation does not mean that the business' products or services have been evaluated or endorsed by BBB, or that BBB has made a determination as to the business' product quality or competency in performing services. We will place the BBB Accreditation Logo in all of our ads.

Examples:

www.bbb.org/chicago/business-reviews/hotels/ivy-boutique-hotel-in-chicago-il-
        88573698/customer-reviews/

Sponsor Events

The sponsoring of events, such as golf tournaments, will allow our company to engage in what is known as experiential marketing, which is the idea that the best way to deepen the emotional bond between a company and its customers is by creating a memorable and interactive experience. We will ask for the opportunity to prominently display our company signage and the set-up of a booth from which to handout sample products and sales literature. We will also seek to capitalize on networking, speech giving and workshop presenting opportunities.

Sponsorships
We will sponsor a local team, such as our child's little league baseball team, the local soccer club or a bowling group. We will then place our company name on the uniforms or shirts in exchange for providing the equipment and/or uniforms.

Patch.com
A community-specific news and information platform dedicated to providing comprehensive and trusted local coverage for individual towns and communities. Patch makes it easy to: Keep up with news and events, Look at photos and videos from around town, Learn about local businesses, Participate in discussions and Submit announcements, photos, and reviews.
Ex: http://vahi.patch.com/articles/clermont-hotel-clermont-lounge#video-14519630
http://lakeview.patch.com/groups/business-news/p/2-lake-view-hotels-ranked-as-some-of-best-in-chicago

MerchantCircle.com
The largest online network of local business owners, combining social networking features with customizable web listings that allow local merchants to attract new customers. A growing company dedicated to connecting neighbors and merchants online to help build real relationships between local business owners and their customers. To date, well over 1,600,000 local businesses have joined MerchantCircle to get their business more exposure on the Internet, simply and inexpensively.

Mobile iPhone Apps
We will use new distribution tools like the iPhone App Store to give us unprecedented direct access to consumers, without the need to necessarily buy actual mobile *ads* to reach people. Thanks to Apple's iPhone and the App Store, we will be able to make cool mobile apps that may generate as much goodwill and purchase intent as a banner ad. We will research Mobile Application Development, which is the process by which application software is developed for small low-power handheld devices, such as personal digital assistants, enterprise digital assistants or mobile phones. These applications are either pre-installed on phones during manufacture, or downloaded by customers from various mobile software distribution platforms. iPhone apps make good marketing tools. The bottom line is iPhones and smartphones sales are continually growing, and people are going to their phones for information. Apps will definitely be a lead generation tool because it gives potential clients easy access to our contact and business information and the ability to call for more information while they are still "hot". Our apps will contain: directory of staffers, publications on relevant issues, office location, videos, etc.

We will especially focus on the development of apps that can accomplish the following:

1. **Mobile Reservations:** Customers can use this app to access mobile reservations linked directly to your in-house calendar. They can browse open slots and book appointments easily, while on the go.
2. **Appointment Reminders:** You can send current customers reminders of regular or special appointments through your mobile app to increase your yearly revenue per customer.
3. **Style Libraries**
    Offer a style library in your app to help customers to pick out a _____ style. Using a simple photo gallery, you can collect photos of various styles, and have customers browse and select specific _____.
4. **Customer Photos**
    Your app can also have a feature that lets customers take photos and email them to you. This is great for creating a database of customer photos for testimonial purposes, advertising, or just easy reference.
5. **Special Offers**
    Push notifications allow you to drive activity on special promotions, deals, events, and offers. If you ever need to generate revenue during a down time, push notifications allow you to generate interest easily and proactively.
6. **Loyalty Programs**
    A mobile app allows you to offer a mobile loyalty program (buy ten ___, get one free, etc.). You won't need to print up cards or track anything manually – it's all done simply through users' mobile devices.
7. **Referrals**
    A mobile app can make referrals easy. With a single click, a user can post to a social media account on Facebook or Twitter about their experience with your business. This allows you to earn new business organically through the networks of existing customers.
8. **Product Sales**
    We can sell gift products through our mobile app. Customers can browse products, submit orders, and make payments easily, helping you open up a new revenue stream.

Resources:	http://www.apple.com/iphone/apps-for-iphone/
	http://iphoneapplicationlist.com/apps/business/
Software Development:	http://www.mutualmobile.com/
	http://www.avenuesocial.com/mob-app.php#
	http://www.biznessapps.com/

Example:
 The Altius Hotel has become the first top end hospitality player in the region to have created an engineering masterpiece–called 'The Altius App'. The mobile app is slated to make interactions of customers with the up-market Hotel, which boasts of Chandigarh's highest roof top restaurant, and vice versa a complete cake-walk. Once a user registers with the Hotel by downloading the App on his or her I-Phone or Android based mobile phone, the App has been designed to give users a clear and high quality 360 degree virtual tour of the Hotel.

Transit Ads
According to the Metropolitan Transportation Authority, MTA subways, buses and railroads provide billions of trips each year to residents. Marketing our Boutique Hotel in subway cars and on the walls of subway stations will be a great way to advertise our business to a large, captive audience.

Restroom billboard advertising (Bathroom Advertising)
We will target a captive audience by placing restroom billboard advertising in select high-traffic venues with targeted demographics. A simple, framed ad on the inside of a bathroom stall door or above a urinal gets at least a minute of viewing, according to several studies. The stall door ads are a good choice for venues with shorter waiting times, such as small businesses, while large wall posters are well-suited to airports or movie theatres where people are more likely to be standing in line near the entrance or exit. Many new restroom based ad agencies that's specialize in restroom advertisement have also come about, such as; Zoom Media, BillBoardZ , Flush Media , Jonny Advertising, Insite Advertising, Inc, Wall AG USA, ADpower, NextMedia, and Alive Promo (American Restroom Association, 9/24/2009).
Resources: http://www.indooradvertising.org/   http://www.stallmall.com/
              http://www.zoommedia.com/

Tumblr.com
Tumblr will allow us to effortlessly share anything. We will be able to post text, photos, quotes, links, music, and videos, from our browser, phone, desktop, email, or wherever we happen to be. We will be able to customize everything, from colors, to our theme's HTML.
Examples: http://boutique--hotels.tumblr.com/

Gift Certificates
We will offer for sale Gift Certificates via our website. This will provide an excellent way to be introduced to new clients and improve our cash flow position. An e-commerce platform for small businesses. BoomTime protects info with 256-bit SSL encryption when transmitting certain kinds of information, such as financial services information or payment information. An icon resembling a padlock is displayed on the bottom of most browser windows during SSL transactions, which you can also verify by looking at the address bar, which will start with "https://" instead of just "http://". The information you provide will be stored securely on BoomTime servers.
Resources:
    Boom Time   https://ps1419.boomtime.com/lgift
    Gift Cards   www.giftcards.com
    Gift Card Café   www.TheGiftCardCafe.com
    Allows companies to create their own special deals and discount services,
    and send it to just the contacts in their client database.

Examples:
https://shop.mrandmrssmith.com/us/shop-collections/vouchers
http://www.slh.com/gift-certificates/hotel-vouchers/

thumbtack.com
A directory for finding and booking trustworthy local services, which is free to consumers.
Resource: www.thumbtack.com/postservice
Examples:
www.thumbtack.com/mt/bozeman/party-rentals/lodge-hotel-fly-fishing-lodge

Citysearch.com
Citysearch.com is a local guide for living bigger, better and smarter in the selected city. Covering more than 75,000 locations nationwide, Citysearch.com combines in-the-know editorial recommendations, candid user comments and expert advice from local businesses. Citysearch.com keeps users connected to the most popular and undiscovered places wherever they are.

Publish e-Book
Ebooks are electronic books which can be downloaded from any website or FTP site on the Internet. Ebooks are made using special software and can include a wide variety of media such as HTML, graphics, Flash animation and video. We will publish an e-book to establish our Boutique Hotel expertise, and reach people who are searching for ebooks on how to make better use our products and/or services. Included in our ebook will be links back to our website, product or affiliate program. Because users will have permanent access to it, they will use our ebook again and again, constantly seeing a link or banner which directs them to our site. The real power behind ebook marketing will be the viral aspect of it and the free traffic it helps to build for our website. ebook directories include:
    www.e-booksdirectory.com/
    www.ebookfreeway.com/p-ebook-directory-list.html
    www.quantumseolabs.com/blog/seolinkbuilding/top-5-free-ebook-directories-
        subscribers/
Resource: www.free-ebooks.net/
Examples: http://italy.charmingitaly.com/top-boutique-hotels-in-sicily
        http://ebook.hiphotels.com/

e-books are available from the following sites:

Amazon.com	Createspace.com
Lulu.com	Kobobooks.com
BarnesandNoble.com	Scribd.com
AuthorHouse.com	

Hotel Signage
Hotel signage will help to generate revenue by promoting an upcoming event, restaurant offer, or information about our Boutique Hotel. Signage will be effective when it

combines eye-catching imagery and clear messaging, and creates a way of capturing our guests' attention and conveying our message or offer.

Business Card Exchanges
We will join our Chamber of Commerce or local retail merchants association and volunteer to host a mixer or business card exchange. We will take the opportunity to invite social and business groups to our offices to enjoy wine tastings, and market to local businesses. We will also build our email database by collecting the business cards of all attendees.

Hubpages.com
HubPages has easy-to-use publishing tools, a vibrant author community and underlying revenue-maximizing infrastructure. Hubbers (HubPages authors) earn money by publishing their Hubs (content-rich Internet pages) on topics they know and love, and earn recognition among fellow Hubbers through the community-wide HubScore ranking system. The HubPages ecosystem provides a search-friendly infrastructure which drives traffic to Hubs from search engines such as Google and Yahoo, and enables Hubbers to earn revenue from industry-standard advertising vehicles such as Google AdSense and the eBay and Amazon Affiliates program. All of this is provided free to Hubbers in an open online community.

Resource: http://hubpages.crabbysbeach.com/blogs/
http://hubpages.com/learningcenter/contents

Pinterest.com
The goal of this website is to connect everyone in the world through the 'things' they find interesting. They think that a favorite book, toy, or recipe can reveal a common link between two people. With millions of new pins added every week, Pinterest is connecting people all over the world based on shared tastes and interests. What's special about Pinterest is that the boards are all visual, which is a very important marketing plus. When users enter a URL, they select a picture from the site to pin to their board. People spend hours pinning their own content, and then finding content on other people's boards to "re-pin" to their own boards. We will use Pinterest for remote personal shopping appointments. When we have a customer with specific needs, we will create a board just for them with items we sell that would meet their needs, along with links to other tips and content. We will invite our customer to check out the board on Pinterest, and let them know we created it just for them.

Examples: http://pinterest.com/luxacc/boutique-hotels/
http://www.pinterest.com/pin/518406607079389571/
Resource: http://www.pinterest.com/pin/277675133245517749/

Pinterest usage recommendation include:
1.   Conduct market research by showing photos of potential products or test launches, asking the customer base for feedback.
2.   Personalize the brand by showcasing style and what makes the brand different, highlighting new and exciting things through the use of imagery.

3. Add links from Pinterest photos to the company webstore, putting price banners on each photo and providing a link where users can buy the products directly.
1. Share high-quality pictures or property images and put links back to our blog/website.
2. Make Boards interesting with hotel décor photos.
3. Showcase beautiful pictures of homes listed and include a link back to our website or blog.
4. Focus on educating followers and sharing what they would like to see, like images from a design company, interior designs, and room decor websites.
5. Ask happy clients to pin pictures of themselves in their rooms.
6. We will create a video and add a Call to Action in the description or use annotations, such as check my YouTube article, for the viewers to Pin videos or follow our Pins on Pinterest.
7. Encourage followers' engagement with a call to action, because 'likes', room décor questions, comments and 'repins' will help our pins get more authority and visibility.
8. Optimize descriptions with keywords that people might be looking for when searching Pinterest, as we can add as many hashtags as we want.
9. Be consistent by pinning regularly.
10. Let people know we are on Pinterest by adding "Pin it" and "follow" buttons to our blog and/or website.

Topix.com

Topix is the world's largest community news website. Users can read, talk about and edit the news on over 360,000 of our news pages. Topix is also a place for users to post their own news stories, as well as comment about stories they have seen on the Topix site. Each story and every Topix page comes with the ability to add your voice to the conversation.

Survey Marketing

We will conduct a door-to-door survey in our target area to illicit opinions to our proposed business. This will provide valuable feedback, lead to prospective clients and serve to introduce our Boutique Hotel business, before we begin actual operations.

'Green' Marketing

We will target environmentally friendly customers to introduce new customers to our business and help spread the word about going "green". We will use the following 'green' marketing strategies to form an emotional bond with our customers:
1. We will use clearly labeled 'Recycled Paper' and Sustainable Packaging, such as receipts and storage containers.
2. We will use "green", non-toxic cleaning supplies.
3. We will install 'green' lighting and heating systems to be more eco-friendly.
4. We will use web-based Electronic Mail and Social Media instead of using paper advertisements.
5. We will find local suppliers to minimize the carbon footprint that it takes for deliveries.

6.   We will use products that are made with organic ingredients and supplies.
7.   We will document our 'Green' Programs in our sales brochure and website.
8.   We will be a Certified Energy Star Partner.
9.   We will install new LED warehouse lighting, exit signs, and emergency signs.
10. We will install motion detectors in low-traffic areas both inside and outside of warehouses.
11. We will implement new electricity regulators on HVAC units and compressors to lower energy consumption.
12. We will mount highly supervised and highly respected recycling campaigns.
13. We will start a program for waste product to be converted into sustainable energy sources.
14. We will start new company-wide document shredding programs.
15. We will use of water-based paints during the finishing process to reduce V.O.C.'s to virtually zero.

Sticker Marketing

Low-cost sticker, label and decal marketing will provide a cost-effective way to convey information, build identity and promote our company in unique and influential ways. Stickers can be affixed to almost any surface, so they can go and stay affixed where other marketing materials can't; opening a world of avenues through which we can reach our target audience. Our stickers will be simple in design, and convey an impression quickly and clearly, with valuable information or coupon, printed optionally as part of its backcopy. Our stickers will handed out at trade shows and special events, mailed as a postcard, packaged with product and/or included as part of a mailing package. We will insert the stickers inside our product or hand them out along with other marketing tools such as flyers or brochures. Research has found that the strongest stickers are usually less than 16 square inches, are printed on white vinyl, and are often die cut. Utilizing a strong design, in a versatile size, and with an eye-catching shape, that is, relevant to our business, will add to the perceived value of our promotional stickers.

We will adhere to the following sticker design tips:
1.   We will strengthen our brand by placing our logo on the stickers and using company colors and font styles.
2.   We will include our phone number, address, and/or website along with our logo to provide customers with a call to action.
3.   We will write compelling copy that solicits an emotional reaction.
4.   We will use die-cut stickers using unusual and business relevant shapes to help draw attention to our business.
5.   We will consider that size matters and that will be determined by where they will be applied and the degree of desired visibility to be realized.
6.   We will be aware of using color on our stickers as color can help create contrast in our design, which enables the directing of prospect eyes to images or actionable items on the stickers.
7.   We will encourage customers to post our stickers near their phones, on yellow page book covers, on event invitations, on notepads, on book covers, on gift boxes and product packaging, etc.

8.   We will place our stickers on all the products we sell.

USPS Every Door Direct Mail Program
Every Door Direct Mail from the U.S. Postal Service® is designed to reach every home, every address, every time at a very affordable delivery rate. Every business and resident living in the ____ zip code will receive an over sized post card and coupon announcing the _____ (company name) grand opening 7-days before the grand opening:
Resource: https://eddm.usps.com/eddm/customer/routeSearch.action

Mirror Ads
When a traveler walks into select airport bathrooms, he or she will see movie poster-style ad displays over the sinks. Some are still images, while other are high definition videos. As the traveler walks to the sink to wash his or her hands, the full-frame ads shrink into the corner to "reveal" a mirror. Sensors detect when a traveler steps in front of the mirror and track how long they stand there, but no cameras watch or record reactions to the mirror ads. Clear Channel Airports is the marketer behind the advertising at Chicago O'Hare. Airports share in the ad revenues, giving them an incentive to let Clear Channel take over the mirrors.
Resource: Mirrus

Google Calendar   www.google.com/calendar
We will use Google Calendar to organize our mobile Boutique Hotel seminar schedule and share events with friends.

ZoomInfo.com
Their vision is to be the sole provider of constantly verified information about companies and their employees, making our data indispensible — available anytime, anywhere and anyplace the customer needs it. Creates just-verified, detailed profiles of 65 million businesspeople and six million businesses. Makes data available through powerful tools for lead generation, prospecting and recruiting.

CitySlick.net
CitySlick.net's unique approach to *online local advertising* helps distribute search traffic for local businesses. We will get more local customers through the internet via CitySlick's local citation network.

Zipslocal.com
Provides one of the most comprehensive ZIP Code-based local search services, allowing visitors to access information through our online business directories that cover all ZIP Codes in the United States. Interactive local yellow pages show listings and display relevant advertising through the medium of the Internet, making it easy for everyone to find local business information

Hold Biggest Fan Contest
Do you love _____ (company name)? Do you have a great story about how the team at

____ (company Name) helped you "get there" to achieve your goals? Well, then ____ (company name) wants to hear from you! _____ (company name) has launched the "Biggest Fan Contest" on its Facebook Page at the beginning of ____ (month), inviting current and former customers to share why they are _____'s (company name) "Biggest Fan." Participants are eligible to win a number of prizes including: _____.
To enter, visit www.facebook.com/_____ (company name), "like" the page, and click the "Biggest Fan Contest" tab on the right hand side. Participants are then asked to write a short blurb or upload a photo sharing why they love _____ (company name). If you have a story to tell or photo to share, enter today. Contest ends _____ (date). See contest tab for full details.

BusinessVibes   www.businessvibes.com/about-businessvibes
A growing B2B networking platform for global trade professionals. BusinessVibes uses a social networking model for businesses to find and connect with international partner companies. With a network of over 5000+ trade associations, 20 million companies and 25,000+ business events across 100+ major industries and 175 countries, BusinessVibes is a decisive source to companies looking for international business partners, be they clients, suppliers, JV partners, or any other type of business contact.
Examples:
https://www.businessvibes.com/companyprofile/Portland-Boutique-Hotels

Yext.com
Lets companies manage their digital presence in online maps, directories and apps. Over 400,000 businesses make millions of monthly updates across 85+ exclusive global partners, making Yext the global market leader. Digital presence is a fundamental need for all 50 million businesses in the world, and Yext's mission is perfect location information in every hand. Yext is based in the heart of New York City with 350 employees and was named to Forbes Most Promising Companies lists for 2014 and 2017, as well as the Fortune Best Places to Work 2014 list.

Google+
We will pay specific attention to Google+, which is already playing a more important role in Google's organic ranking algorithm. We will create a business page on Google+ to achieve improved local search visibility. Google+ will also be the best way to get access to Google Authorship, which will play a huge role in SEO.
Resources:
https://plus.google.com/pages/create
http://www.google.com/+/brands/
https://www.google.com/appserve/fb/forms/plusweekly/
https://plus.google.com/+GoogleBusiness/posts
http://marketingland.com/beyond-social-benefits-google-business-73460
Examples:
https://plus.google.com/+LatoBoutiqueHotelHotel/posts

Travel Aggregators

We will list our boutique hotel on aggregator websites like SkyScanner and Kayak. Although these websites charge fees for inclusion, it will be worth adding our boutique hotel to access a large and lucrative audience. Since travel aggregators dominate the search results for most hotel or flight-related keywords, it will be easy to work with them to improve our occupancy rate.

Inbound Marketing

Inbound marketing is about pulling people in by sharing relevant boutique hotel information, creating useful content, and generally being helpful. It involves writing everything from buyer's guides to blogs and newsletters that deliver useful content. The objective will be to nurture customers through the buying process with unbiased educational materials that turn consumers into informed buyers. Resource: www.Hubspot.com

Google My Business Profile   www.google.com/business/befound.html

We will have a complete and active Google My Business profile to give our boutique hotel a tremendous advantage over the competition, and help potential customers easily find our company and provide relevant information about our business.

Reddit.com

An online community where users vote on stories. The hottest stories rise to the top, while the cooler stories sink. Comments can be posted on every story, including stories about startup boutique hotel companies.
Examples:
https://www.reddit.com/r/hotel/
www.reddit.com/r/nashville/comments/48mc5o/boutique_hotel_planned_for_historic_
    james/
https://www.reddit.com/r/TravelPorn/

Exterior Signage

We will make effective use of the following types of signage: (select)
1.   **Channel Letter**
       Channel letters can be illuminated by LED or neon and come in a variety of colors and sizes. Front-lit signs are illuminated from the letter face, while reverse-lit signs are lit from behind the sign. Open-face channel letters lit by exposed neon work well to create a night presence.
2.   **Monument Signs**
       Monument signs are usually placed at the entrance to a parking lot or a building. This sign can easily be installed on a median or lawn. The size for a monument sign is typically based on city regulations for the specific location. These signs can be illuminated or non-illuminated, single- or double-sided.
3.   **Pylon Signs**

Also known as pole signs, they soar high above a business location to set the business apart from other businesses. They get attention from highway motorists who are still a distance away.

4. **Cabinet Signs**

Commonly called "wall" or "box" signs, they are a traditional form of signage. They effectively use a large copy area and eye-popping graphics. This type of signage can highlight our business day or night because we have the option to add illumination. The background can be the element that lights up, and the copy can be lit or non-lit.

5. **Sandwich Signs**

This sign will be placed on the sidewalk in front of our business to attract foot traffic.

6. **Vehicle Roof-top and Side-panel Signage**

6.4.1   Strategic Alliances

A strategic alliance is a type of cooperative agreements between different firms, such as shared research, formal joint ventures, or minority equity participation. The modern form of strategic alliances is becoming increasingly popular and has three distinguishing characteristics:

1. They are frequently between firms in industrialized nations.
2. The focus is often on creating new products and/or technologies rather than distributing existing ones.
3. They are often only created for short term durations.

We will focus our efforts on building strategic relationships within the community that we serve. We will form strategic alliances to accomplish the following objectives:

1. To share marketing expenses.
2. To realize bulk buying power on wholesale purchases.
3. To engage in barter arrangements.
4. To collaborate with industry experts.
5. To set-up mutual referral relationships.

We will also seek referrals from the following types of businesses and set-up mutual referral links and negotiated reciprocal discounts on business websites:

1.	Catering Services	2.	Wedding Planners
3.	Hospital Auxiliaries	4.	Attorneys
5.	Funeral Directors	6.	Maternity Shops
7.	Nursery Schools	8.	Restaurants
9.	Attraction Businesses (Colleges)	10.	Pony Trekking Centers
11.	Canoe Hire Shops	12.	Arts and Craft/Art Festivals
13.	Convention Centers	14.	Trade Exposition Management
15.	Ski resorts	16.	Golf courses

17.   Shopping malls   18.   Whitewater rafting expeditions

We will offer deals to the businesses that they can then pass on to their own customers. Our plan is to build a steady stream of clients, while serving and supporting other community businesses.

Strategic relationship with the University of _____.
We will develop a partnership with the university so when the school is in need of finding rooms for guests they will use our Boutique Hotel. We will also be advertising with the university so when students are searching for places for their parents to stay, they will come across our Boutique Hotel in school-related publications and feel more comfortable with booking a reservation sight unseen because of the trust bond they have formed with the university.

We will assemble a sales presentation package that includes sales brochures, business cards, and a DVD seminar presentation. We will print coupons that offer a discount or other type of introductory deal. We will ask to set-up a take-one display for our sales brochures at the business registration counter. We will give the referring business any one or combination of the following reward options:
1.   Referral fees
2.   Free services
3.   Mutual referral exchanges

We will monitor referral sources to evaluate the mutual benefits of the alliance and make certain to clearly define and document our referral incentives prior to initiating our referral exchange program.

6.4.2   Monitoring Marketing Results

To monitor how well _____ (company name) is doing, we will measure how well the advertising campaign is working by taking guest surveys. What we would like to know is how they heard of us and how they like and dislike about our services. In order to get responses to the surveys, we will be give discounts as thank you rewards.

Response Tracking Methods
    Coupons: ad-specific coupons that easily enable tracking
    Landing Pages: unique web landing pages for each advertisement
    800 Numbers: unique 1-800-# per advertisement
    Email Service Provider: Instantly track email views, opens, and clicks.

Our financial statements will offer excellent data to track all phases of sales. These are available for review on a daily basis. _____ (company name) will benchmark our objectives for sales promotion and advertising in order to evaluate our return on invested marketing dollars, and determine where to concentrate our limited advertising dollars to realize the best return. We will also strive to stay within our marketing budget.

Key Marketing Metrics

We will use the following two marketing metrics to evaluate the cost-effectiveness of our marketing campaign:

1. The cost to acquire a new guest: The average dollar amount invested to get one new client. Example: If we invest $3,000 on marketing in a single month and end the month with 10 new customers, our cost of acquisition is $300 per new guest.
2. The lifetime value of the average active guest. The average dollar value of an average guest over the life of their business with you. To calculate this metric for a given period of time, we will take the total amount of revenue our business generated during the time period and divide it by the total number of customers we had from the beginning of the time period.
3. We will track the following set of statistics on a weekly basis to keep informed of the progress of our business:
    A. Number of total referrals.
    B. Percentage increase of total referrals (over baseline).
    C. Number of new referral sources.
    D. Number of new customers/month.
    E. Number of Leads

Key Marketing Metrics Table

We've listed some key metrics in the following table. We will need to keep a close eye on these, to see if we meet our own forecasted expectations. If our numbers are off in too many categories, we may, after proper analysis, have to make substantial changes to our marketing efforts.

Key Marketing Metrics	2017	2018	2019
Revenue			
Leads			
Leads Converted			
Avg. Transaction per Customer			
Avg. Dollars per Customer			
Number of Referrals			
Number of PR Appearances			
Number of Testimonials			
Number of New Club Members			
Number of Returns			
Number of BBB Complaints			
Number of Completed Surveys			
Number of Blog readers			
Number of Twitter followers			
Number of Facebook Fans			

Metric Definitions

1. Leads: Individuals who step into the store to consider a purchase.
2. Leads Converted: Percent of individuals who actually make a purchase.

3. Average Transactions Per Customer: Number of purchases per customer per month. Expected to rise significantly as customers return for more and more _____ items per month
4. Average $ Per Customer: Average dollar amount of each transaction. Expected to rise along with average transactions.
5. Referrals: Includes customer and business referrals
6. PR Appearances: Online or print mentions of the business that are not paid advertising. Expected to be high upon opening, then drop off and rise again until achieving a steady level.
7. Testimonials: Will be sought from the best and most loyal customers. Our objective is ___ (#) per month) and they will be added to the website. Some will be sought as video testimonials.
8. New Loyalty Club Members: This number will rise significantly as more customers see the value in repeated visits and the benefits of club membership.
9. Number of Returns/BBB Complaints: Our goal is zero.
10. Number of Completed Surveys: We will provide incentives for customers to complete customer satisfaction surveys.

6.4.3   Word-of-Mouth Marketing

We plan to make use of the following techniques to promote word-of-mouth advertising:

1. Repetitive Image Advertising
2. Provide exceptional guest service.
3. Make effective use of loss package leaders.
2. Schedule activities, such as cooking demonstrations or special events.
3. Make trial easy with a coupon or introductory discount.
4. Initiate web and magazine article submissions
5. Utilize a sampling program
6. Add a forward email feature to our website.
7. Share relevant and believable testimonial letters
8. Publish staff bios.
9. Make product/service upgrade announcements
10. Hold contests or sweepstakes
12. Have involvement with community events.
13. Pay suggestion box rewards
14. Distribute a monthly newsletter
15. Share easy-to-understand information (via an article or seminar).
16. Make personalized marketing communications.
17. Structure our referral program.
18. Sharing of Community Commonalities
19. Invitations to join our community of shared interests.
20. Publish Uncensored guest Reviews
21. Enable Information Exchange Forums
22. Provide meaningful comparisons with competitors.
23. Clearly state our user benefits.

24.   Make and honor ironclad guarantees
25.   Provide superior post-sale support
26.   Provide support in the pre-sale decision making process.
27.   Host Free Informational Seminars or Workshops
28.   Get involved with local business organizations.
29.   Issue Press Release coverage of charitable involvements.
30.   Hold traveling company demonstrations/exhibitions/competitions.
31.   Stay in touch with inactive clients.

6.4.4   Guest Satisfaction Survey

We will design a guest satisfaction survey to measure the "satisfaction quotient" of our Boutique Hotel customers. By providing a detailed snapshot of our current guest base, we will be able to generate more repeat and referral business and enhance the profitability of our company.

Our guest Satisfaction Survey will including the following basics:
1.   How do our customers rate our Boutique Hotel business?
2.   How do our customers rate our competition?
3.   How well do our customers rate the value of our products or services?
4.   What new guest needs and trends are emerging?
5.   How loyal are our customers?
6.   What can be done to improve guest loyalty and repeat business?
7.   How strongly do our customers recommend our business?
8.   What is the best way to market our business?
9.   What new value-added services would best differentiate our business from that of our competitors?
10.   How can we encourage more referral business?
11.   How can our pricing strategy be improved?

Our guest satisfaction survey will help to answer these questions and more. From the need for continual new products and services to improved guest service, our satisfaction surveys will allow our business to quickly identify problematic and underperforming areas, while enhancing our overall guest satisfaction.

Examples:
http://www.wyndhamdeerfieldresort.com/guest-satisfaction-survey.aspx#gref
https://www.hotelbelleclaire.com/about/survey/
http://smallbiztrends.com/2007/06/the-small-biz-7-survey.html
Resources:
https://www.survata.com/
https://www.google.com/insights/consumersurveys/use_cases
www.surveymonkey.com
http://www.smetoolkit.org/smetoolkit/en/content/en/6708/Customer-Satisfaction-Survey-
      Template-

http://smallbusiness.chron.com/common-questions-customer-service-survey-1121.html

We will also try to collect the following kinds of information from our customer surveys:

1. Demographic Profile
   - Age   - Sex
   - Income   - Lifestyle
   - Household purchase penetration   - Education
   - Ethnicity   - Zipcode
   - Occupation
2. Purchase decision-making criteria.
3. Frequency of purchase
4. Pattern of purchase
5. Related purchases
6. Planned or Unplanned trip
7. Promotional materials exposed to.
8. Brand loyalty
9. Brand switching patterns
10. Hotel switching patterns.
11. Type of beverage preferred
    (Table, Sparkling, Premium, Non-alcoholic, Coolers, Sake)
12. Type of trip: Business or vacation
13. Color preferred
14. Hotel type preferred
15. Price range preferred
17. Brand preference
18. Where consumers most frequently visit
19. How and when (occasions) consumers use travel accommodations.
20. Loyalty factor
21. Learning about hotel selection methods
22. How much they want to learn.
23. Purchase decision influences.

6.4.5   Marketing Training Program

Our Marketing Training Program will include both an initial orientation and training, as well as ongoing continuing education classes. Initial orientation will be run by the owner until an HR manager is hired. For one week, half of each day will be spent in training, and the other half shadowing the Boutique Hotel's operation manager.

Training will include:
    Learning the entire selection of Boutique Hotel products and services.
    Understanding our Mission Statement, Value Proposition, Position Statement and
        Unique Selling Proposition.
    Appreciating our competitive advantages.

Understanding our core message and branding approach.
Learning our store's policies; returns processing, complaint handling, etc.
Learning our customer services standards of practice.
Learning our customer and business referral programs.
Learning our Membership Club procedures, rules and benefits.
Becoming familiar with our company website, and online ordering options.
Service procedures specific to the employee's role.

Ongoing workshops will be based on customer feedback and problem areas identified by mystery buyers, which will better train employees to educate customers. These ongoing workshops will be held _____ (once?) a month for _____ (three?) hours.

6.5   Sales Strategy

The development of our sales strategy will start by developing a better understanding of our customer needs. To accomplish this task we will pursue the following research methods:
1.   Join the associations that our target customers belong to.
2.   Contact the membership director and establish a relationship to understand their member's needs, challenges and concerns.
3.   Identify non-competitive suppliers who sell to our customer to learn their challenges and look for partnering solutions.
4.   Work directly with our customer and ask them what their needs are and if our business may offer a possible solution.

The _____ 's (company name) sales strategy is to harness the existing area's resort booking system that has been critical to the success of all of the area's lodges and inns. Room rates for the lodge will range from $____ to $_____ per night in peak season. In the off season prices will range from $_____ to $_____ per night.

_____ (company name) will sell its rooms directly to repeat customers, as well as via traditional travel agents and through the Internet. Repeat customers will have the privilege of priority reservations during the high season. We will also list _____ (company name) on www.worldres.com, which will make it available to millions of international tourists.

Sales in our business will result from quality personalized service. Our sales strategy is based on the selling of the following service benefits:
1.   Excellent quality of personalized service.
2.   Availability of one-stop support services
3.   Building effective interpersonal relationships

Our focus will be on making the services we offer of the highest possible quality. Only when those services are well-established, will we consider expanding our range of services offered.

Our clients will be primarily obtained through word-of-mouth referrals, but we will also advertise introductory offers, such as free wine and cheese with romantic weekend getaway package. The combination of the perception of higher quality, exceptional support and the recognition of superior value should turn referral leads into satisfied customers.

Internet Booking Companies
We will create a partnership with one key Internet Booking Company. We will choose the company that is most compatible with our hotels' needs, and offer them exclusive rates. By doing that, the internet company will be motivated to market the hotel by creating favorable placements and adding many "bells and whistle" to drive business into our boutique hotel.

The company's sales strategy will be based on the following elements:
Advertising in the Yellow Pages - two inch by three inch ads describing our services will be placed in the local Yellow Pages.
Placing classified advertisements in the regional editions of lifestyle magazines.
Word of mouth referrals - generating sales leads in the local community through guest referrals.
Use of reservation service organizations.

Our basic sales strategy is to:
Develop a website for lead generation by _____ (date).
Provide exceptional guest service.
Accept payment by all major credit cards, cash, PayPal and check.
Survey our customers regarding packages they would like to see added.
Sponsor charitable and other community events.
Provide tours of the facility.
Motivate employees with a pay-for-performance component to their straight salary compensation package, based on profits and guest satisfaction rates.
Build long-term guest relationships by putting the interests of customers first.
Establish mutually beneficial relationship with local businesses serving the needs of our targeted guest profile.

Direct Sales
Our Direct Sales strategy will be the most controllable and quantifiable element of our marketing effort. The emphasis of direct sales will be to create an account base of identified segments by prospecting for new business and to maintain existing business. As production of this identified business fluctuates, new accounts will be opened and closed to ensure that targeted goals are continuously reached. Budgets and needs will determine how many sales people are needed to impact particular markets. Direct Sales, properly structured, will be the most cost efficient element of our marketing plan.

We will hire well-trained sales professionals. We will get the most from the sales staff by creating an organized sales department and devising a proactive sales plan.

The goal of our direct sales department will to create and maintain a database of accounts that equals the budgets. All plans, goals, and strategies will stem from that quantified and specified goal i.e. room-nights, average rates, and revenues. In order to achieve the goals, each sales person will be accountable for results. Therefore, we will establish goals and targets which include sales activities i.e. sales calls and site inspections; new accounts; advanced bookings; as well as consumed business. We will also train other staff to handle the non-direct sales issues to maximize the sales effort.

6.5.1   Guest Retention Strategy

We will use the following techniques to improve guest retention and the profitability of our business:
1.   Keep the facility sparkling clean and well-organized.
2.   Ask the customers for feedback and promptly act upon their inputs.
4.   Tell customers how much you appreciate their business.
5.   Call regular customers by their first names.
6.   Send thank you notes.
7.   Practice good phone etiquette
8.   Respond to complaints promptly.
9.   Reward referrals.
10.   Publish a monthly opt-in direct response newsletter with customized content, dependent on recipient stated information preferences .
11.   Develop and publish a list of frequently asked questions.
12.   Issue Preferred guest Membership Cards.
13.   Hold informational seminars and workshops.
14.   Run contests.
15.   Provide an emergency hotline number.
16.   Publish code of ethics and our service guarantees.
17.   Publish all guest reviews.
18.   Help customers to make accurate competitor comparisons.
19.   Build a stay-in-touch (drip marketing) communications calendar.
20.   Keep marketing communications focused on our competitive advantages.
21.   Offer repeat guest discounts and incentives.
22.   Be supportive and encouraging, and not judgmental.
23.   Measure guest retention and look at recurring revenue and guest surveys.
24.   Build a community of shared interests by offering a website forum.
25.   Offer benefits above and beyond those of our competitors.
26.   Issue reminder emails and holiday gift cards.

We will also consider the following guest Retention Programs:

Type of Program	guest Rewards
Frequency Purchase Loyalty Program	Special Discounts

	Free Product or Services
Rebate Loyalty Programs	Credit Based on Percent of Incremental Sales from Prior Period.
'Best guest' Program	Special Recognition/Treatment/Offers
Affinity Programs	Sharing of Common Interests
	Accumulate Credit Card Points
guest Community Programs	Special Event Participation
Auto-Knowledge Building Programs	Purchase Recommendations based On Past Transaction History
Profile Building Programs	Recommendations Based on Stated guest Profile Information.

6.5.2   Sales Forecast

Our sales projections are based on the following:
1. Actual sales volumes of local competitors
2. Interviews with Boutique Hotel owners and managers
3. Observations of sales and traffic at competitor establishments.
4. Government and industry trade statistics
5. Local population demographics and projections.
6. Discussions with suppliers.
7. Ratio Trend Analysis of historical transaction data.
8. Local Attraction Operator attendance data describing seasonality trends and place of customer origin.

Our sales forecast is an estimated projection of expected sales over the next three years, based on our chosen marketing strategy, economic conditions and assumed competitive environment. Sales are expected to be below average during the first year, until a regular guest base has been established. It has been estimated that it takes the average Boutique Hotel business a minimum of two years to establish a significant guest base. After the guest base is built, sales will grow at an accelerated rate from word-of-mouth referrals and continued networking efforts. We expect sales to steadily increase as our marketing campaign, and contact management system are executed. By using reservation services, guidebook inclusions, advertising, especially introductory coupons, as a catalyst for this prolonged process, ____ (company name) plans to attract more customers sooner.

A solid rooms budget will be one laid out on a daily basis. It will incorporate demand factors and well-founded assumptions, by day, by market segment, with rooms and rates per segment. Each market segment has its own peaks and valleys on a daily basis as well as on a seasonal basis. This is the result of factors such as holidays, conventions, and seasonal trends. Incorporating all of these factors will create an accurate projection of occupancy and average rate when laid out on a daily basis as opposed to just using monthly totals and projections to establish budgets. This will also lay the foundation for improved budgeting in other departments, especially food and beverage. By accurately identifying and quantifying all potential segments on a micro basis and understanding each market segments' travel trends and needs, our boutique hotel will be able to make accurate sales forecasts and proactively solicit those specific markets, efficiently and cost-effectively, without wasting valuable resources, as well as understanding when to change course when market conditions change.

We will use the following methodology to estimate our occupancy, room rate and sales potential:

Project Market Area Annual Occupancy

A. Under a Area Hotels/hotels heading, list all of the competitive properties in our market area.
B. For each property, record the Days Open, Rooms in the property, and the estimated Occupancy Percent.
C. For each property, calculate and record the number of Rooms Available per year by multiplying Days Open by Rooms. Sum the Rooms Available column.
D. For each property, calculate and record the number of Rooms Sold per year by multiplying Rooms Available by Occupancy Percent. Sum the Rooms Sold column.
E. Calculate the current market occupancy by dividing the sum of Rooms Sold by Rooms Available.
F. Looking ahead to next year, record any additional rooms (new room supply) that will be added to the market area. If you are a prospective operator, include your planned facility.
G. For next year, record additional growth in room night demand (new room demand) that might occur as a result of improving economic conditions, tourism visitation, or simply as a result of having new lodging rooms added to the market area.
H. Record the total Rooms Available and Rooms Sold for next year (current year totals plus additions from steps F and G). Calculate next years market occupancy by dividing Rooms Sold by Rooms Available.

Project Average Room Rate

Effective pricing is critical in the lodging business as increases or decreases in rates have a major impact on the "bottom-line." Setting prices to maximize profit is important process that requires consideration of the rates charged by competitors and the price sensitivity of travelers to the area. The following four steps will help ensure that we are competitively prices relative to your competition.

1. Analyze your expected market segments. What factors do they consider when choosing a lodging facility (location, service, condition, affiliation...).
2. Compare your expected quality level and appeal with that of your competitors.
3. Analyze the room rates charged by our competitors. Consider single and double rates, discounting, and variations in rates by season. Estimate their average annual room rate.
4. Project our average annual room rate by considering the rates and quality levels of our competitors. Our rates must be acceptable to the market segments we are targeting.

Project Sales

After we have developed projections of occupancy and average room rate, we will be able to calculate our projected room revenue as follows:

Projected Annual Occupancy	_____%
x Number of Rooms in Boutique Hotel	_____
x Days Open	_____
x Average Daily Rate	_____
= Projected Annual Revenue	_____

Throughout the first year, it is forecasted that sales will incrementally grow until profitability is reached toward the end of year __ (one?). Year two reflects a conservative growth rate of __ (20?) percent. Year three reflects a growth rate of _____ (25?) percent. We expect to be open for business on ___ (date), and start with an initial registration of ___ (#) guests. With our targeted niche approach, along with our thorough and aggressive marketing strategies, we believe that sales forecasts are actually on the conservative side.

Table: Sales Forecast

	Annual Sales		
Sales	**2017**	**2018**	**2019**
Room Rentals			
Corporate Meetings			
Spa Treatments			
Health Club Fees			
Equipment Rentals			
Wedding Ceremonies			
Catering Services			
Special Events			
Facilities Rentals			
Attraction Ticket Sales			
Gift Sales			
Food Sales			
Clothing Sales			
Misc.			
Total Unit Sales			
Direct Cost of Sales:			
Room Rentals			
Corporate Meetings			
Spa Treatments			
Health Club Fees			
Equipment Rentals			
Wedding Ceremonies			
Catering Services			
Special Events			
Facilities Rentals			

Attraction Ticket Sales	_____
Gift Sales	_____
Food Sales	_____
Clothing Sales	_____
Misc.	_____
Subtotal Direct Cost of Sales	_____

6.6   Merchandising Strategy

Merchandising is that part of our marketing strategy that is involved with promoting the sales of our merchandise, as by consideration of the most effective means of selecting, pricing, displaying, and advertising items for sale in our Boutique Hotel business.

We will develop a merchandising strategy to sell handcrafted gifts and antiques to our guests. We will strive to feature merchandise, in actual lifestyle settings, that is not found in competitor stores and use proper and informative signage to help sell merchandise. We plan to group similar types of merchandise together for maximum visual appeal and encourage quests to interactive with the merchandise. Product presentation will be designed to lead the customers through the entire display area.

We will monitor our sales figures and data to confirm that products in demand are well-stocked and slow moving products are phased-out. We will improve the suggestive selling and consultative sales techniques of employees to boost sales.

We will encourage impulse purchases with the use of descriptive product labels and adjectives in our signage. We will attach our own additional business labels to all products to promote our line of services and location.

We will survey quests as to their product like and dislikes, and provide constructive feedback to the artisans that have provided their crafts to our Boutique Hotel on a consignment basis.

The décor of the merchandising area is extremely important to sales. Display units are primary, but lighting, furniture, wall surfaces, window treatments, carpeting, accessories and countertops will all play important supporting roles. We will monitor our sales figures and data to confirm that products in demand are well-stocked and slow moving products are phased-out. We will improve the telephone skills of employees to boost phone orders. We will attach our own additional business labels to all products to promote our line of services and location.

Video Displays
We will use video displays as effective marketing and merchandising tools. Actually seeing the product or service people in action will provide much needed information and incentive to buy. We will place a large flat-screen television with a DVD player in the

display area and use the instructional and educational videos, provided by the manufacturer or produced by our staff, to demonstrate the effectiveness of the items or the results of our service.

Themed Displays

We will create compelling and interactive themed displays. We will incorporate products our retail store is already selling to create holiday themed displays. This will increase our sales and help move our most profitable products. Creating holiday-themed merchandising displays will also help our store avoid costly leftovers that must be sold at highly discounted prices.

Interactive Displays

Providing free samples and creating a "try me" section in our retail store, will serve to create a place where customers can try out the latest products and buy only the ones they like the most. Creating a sample section will generate excitement and buzz among our existing customers, encouraging them to return to sample the latest products. A sample section will also build trust with new customers, since it shows that we are willing to let browsers sample products before making a purchase, and provide an opportunity to solicit immediate feedback. On the back end, providing free samples will reduce costly returns, since customers can make sure the item is what they need prior to purchase.

5.7 Pricing Strategy

When setting our room rates, we will need to take into account two major factors:
1. The price that the target market is willing to pay for your product.
2. The price offered by the competition.

Effective pricing will be critical for our Boutique Hotel, since pricing will have a major impact on the bottom line. High prices may maximize profits in the short run, but is likely to hinder repeat business in the long run. Setting prices to maximize profit in the short and long run is an important process that will require consideration of rates charged by competitors, the quality of our resort and the price sensitivity of travelers in the area.

Our pricing strategy will take into view the following factors:
1. Our firm's overall marketing objectives
2. Guest demand
3. Service quality attributes
4. Competitor pricing strategies
5. Market and economic trends.
6. Level of operating expenses
7. Desired profit margin
8. The tax savings associated with the owning of a Boutique Hotel business.
9. The perceived value of our amenities by quests.

We are not interested in being the low price leader, but we do plan to offer the following discounts for:

1.	Children	2.	Weekly/Monthly Stays
3.	Seniors	4.	Weekday Visits
5.	Business Club Members		

Our rates will be determined by the following specific factors:
1. Single or Double Occupancy on a weekday.
2. Double Occupancy on a weekend during the Off-Season.
3. Double Occupancy on a weekend during In-Season.
4. The particular room/amenities selected.
5. There will be a two night stay minimum on weekends.
6. Third person in the room: add $___ for child or $___ for adult.
7. State Sales Tax and Occupancy Taxes must be added to all published rates.
8. A ___ % gratuity will be added to all invoices.

We believe that in the second and third years we will be able to increase rates by 5 to 10% to reflect our prime location, unique ambiance, special amenities and personalized services.

Our pricing strategy plays a major role in whether we will be able to create and maintain customers for a profit. Our revenue structure must support our cost structure, so the salaries and other expenses we incur are balanced by the revenue we collect.

We will consider the following basic pricing strategies:

Quantity Discounts:	Bulk purchase breaks to increase sales volume.
Bundling Discounts:	Additive deal sweetners to differentiate product offering.
Version Pricing:	Degree of functionality pricing, from Basic to Premium
Loss Leaders	Attract first-time customer deals
Competitive Pricing	Reference point for product positioning.
Targeted Special Discounts:	For seniors, active military and students.
Time of Week/Month Discounts	Dependant on slow time of month or day of the week.
Continuity Discounts	Monthly automatic purchase plans for members.
Automatic Price Reductions	Monthly automatic markdowns of unsold dates.

Price List Comparison

Competitor	Service/Product	Our Price	Competitor Price	B/(W) Competitor

Resource: http://www.quikbook.com/

We will adopt the following pricing guidelines:
1.. We must insure that our price plus service equation is perceived to be an exceptional value proposition.

2.   We must refrain from competing on price, but always be price competitive.
3.   We must develop value-added services, and bundle those with our products to create offerings that cannot be easily price compared.
4.   We must focus attention on our competitive advantages.
5.   Development of a pricing strategy based on our market positioning strategy, which is ____ (mass market value leadership/exceptional premium niche value?)
6.   Our pricing policy objective, which is to _____ (increase profit margins/   achieve revenue maximization to increase market share/lower unit costs).
7.   We will use marketplace intelligence and gain insights from competitor pricing strategy comparisons.
8.   We will solicit pricing feedback from customers using surveys and informal interviews.
9.   We will utilize limited time pricing incentives to penetrate niche markets
10.   We will conduct experiments at prices above and below the current price to determine the price elasticity of demand. (Inelastic demand or demand that does not decrease with a price increase, indicates that price increases may be feasible.)
11.   We will keep our offerings and prices simple to understand and competitive, based on market intelligence.

Determining the costs of servicing business is the most important part of covering our expenses and earning profits. We will factor in the following pricing formula: Materials + Overhead + Labor + Profit = Price

Materials are those items consumed in the delivering of the service.
Overhead costs are the variable and fixed expenses that must be covered to stay in business. Variable costs are those expenses that fluctuate including vehicle expenses, rental expenses, utility bills and supplies. Fixed costs include the purchase of equipment, service ware, marketing and advertising, and insurance. After overhead costs are determined, the total overhead costs are divided among the total number of transactions forecasted for the year.

Labor costs include the costs of performing the services. Also included are Social Security taxes (FICA), vacation time, retirement and other benefits such as health or life insurance. To determine labor costs per hour, keep a time log. When placing a value on our time, we will consider the following: 1) skill and reputation; 2) wages paid by employers for similar skills and 3) where we live. Other pricing factors include image, inflation, supply and demand, and competition.

Profit is a desired percentage added to our total costs. We will need to determine the percentage of profit added to each service. It will be important to cover all our costs to stay in business. We will investigate available computer software programs to help us price our services and keep financial data for decision-making purposes. Close contact with customers will allow our company to react quickly to changes in demand.

We will develop a pricing strategy that will reinforce the perception of value to the guest and manage profitability, especially in the face of rising inflation. To ensure our success, we will use periodic competitor and guest research to continuously evaluate our pricing strategy. We intend to review our profit margins every six months.

6.8   Differentiation Strategies

We will use differentiation strategies to develop and market unique products and services for different guest segments. To differentiate ourselves from the competition, we will focus on the assets, creative ideas and competencies that we have that none of our competitors has. The goal of our differentiation strategies is to be able to charge a premium price for our unique products and services and/or to promote loyalty and assist in retaining our customers.

Differentiating will mean defining who our perfect target market is and then catering to their needs, wants and interests better than everyone else. It will be about using surveys to determine what's most important to our targeted market and giving it to them consistently.   It will not be about being "everything to everybody"; but rather, "the absolute best to our chosen targeted group".

Differentiation in our boutique hotel will be achieved in the following types of ways, including: Explanation
☐ Product features   _____
☐ Complementary services   _____
☐ Technology embodied in design   _____
☐ Location   _____
☐ Service innovations   _____
☐ Superior service   _____
☐ Creative advertising   _____
☐ Better supplier relationships   _____
Source:
http://scholarship.sha.cornell.edu/cgi/viewcontent.cgi?article=1295&context=articles

In developing our differentiation strategy will we use the following form to help define our differences:

1.	Targeted customer segments	_____
2.	Customer characteristics	_____
3.	Customer demographics	_____
4.	Customer behavior	_____
5.	Geographic focus	_____
6.	Ways of working	_____
7.	Service delivery approach	_____
8.	Customer problems/pain points	_____
9.	Complexity of customers' problems	_____

10.   Range of services   _____

We will use the following approaches to differentiate our products and services from those of our competitors to stand apart from standardised offerings:

1.   Superior quality
2.   Unusual or unique product features
3.   More responsive customer service
4.   Rapid product or service innovation
5.   Advanced technological features
6.   Engineering design or styling
7.   Additional product features
8.   An image of prestige or status

Specific Differentiators will include the following:
1.   Being a Specialist in one procedure
2.   Utilizing advanced/uncommon technology
3.   Possessing extensive experience
4.   Building an exceptional facility
5.   Consistently achieving superior results
6.   Having a caring and empathetic personality
7.   Giving customer s WOW experience, including a professional customer welcome package.
8.   Enabling convenience and 24/7 online accessibility
9.   Calling customers to express interest in their challenges.
10.   Keeping to the appointment schedule.
11.   Remembering customer names and details like they were family
12.   Assuring customer fears.
13.   Building a visible reputation and recognition around our community
14.   Acquiring special credentials or professional memberships
15.   Providing added value services, such as taxi service, longer hours, financing plans, and post-sale services.

Primary Differentiation Strategies:
Boutique Hotels differentiate themselves by personal service offerings and the general ambiance. Boutique Hotels usually have a sit down breakfast for their guests that is an elaborate spread of gourmet food such as quiche with portabella mushrooms, fresh roasted garlic and sun dried tomato omelettes, or fresh smoked fish. Guests of hotels are not just looking for a room to sleep in but a whole experience in staying in a lovely and secure setting, with interesting people to chat with, and people present to pamper them in any way possible.

One of our greatest differentiators will be our people, who will be vibrant and energetic, without being over the top or in your face. We use a series of visual cues to promote conversation with our guests. Inspired service will be a guest benefit as the result of interactions with fewer employees, as the guest recognizes and appreciates the same faces. Our employees will learn something about our guests through dialogue and interaction that allows them to create a customized experience that can have a stimulating influence upon the guest's emotions.

Our Boutique Hotel will feature a large central gathering room that allows travelers to socialize. The customers will receive the personal attention of the owners who will meet any need a traveler has. Our Boutique Hotel will provide a remarkable breakfast feast and that will meet any dietary restriction.

As Boutique Hotel keepers, we will be local experts and help our guests to skip tourist traps and truly enjoy the best the area has to offer at the most reasonable price. With this advice, which surpasses that of a concierge at even the priciest luxury hotel, our quality Boutique Hotel will be able to match any traveler's budget.

Our Boutique Hotel will feature made-to-order breakfasts, afternoon tea, hors d'oeuvres and wine.

During the weekends, guests will return to the Boutique Hotel in the evening and find cheese, fruit, and wine for snacking before turning in.

One of our key differentiating factors will be our location, and our proximity to a beautiful and interesting _____ (attraction description).

We will develop a registration questionnaire and use it to maintain a guest file, and keep track of individual guest favorites and preferences for future reference.

We will develop a referral program that turns our clients into commissioned referral agents.

We will use regular client satisfaction surveys to collect feedback, improvement ideas, referrals and testimonials.

We will promote our environmentally friendly "green" practices, and spend a lot of time and effort to educate the public on environmental and sustainability issues.

We will customize our offerings according to the cultural influences, customs, interests and tastes of our local market to create loyalty and increase sales.

Our low staff turnover rate translates to consistency of service level.

We will develop the expertise to satisfy the needs of targeted market segments with customized and exceptional support services.

We will develop a detailed 'Guest Needs Analysis Worksheet' to precisely understand

he needs, wants and preference of our individual guests to provide truly personalized
ervices.

Ve will develop an expertise in the _____ (Victorian) style of antiques and give
eminars to establish our credibility and trustworthiness.

Ve will develop mutually beneficial relationships with our networking partners and
uppliers.

nstead of rooms dedicated to different book themes, the rooms will be dedicated to
lifferent artists or composers. The wings of the Hotel will each be dedicated to Jazz,
)pera, Classical, or Contemporary music, plus the Hotel will feature an incredible music
ibrary of books, videos, and CDs for the guests' exploration and enjoyment.

5.9 Milestones

The Milestones Chart is a timeline that will guide our company in developing and
growing our business. It will list chronologically the various critical actions and events
hat must occur to bring our business to life. We will make certain to assign real,
ttainable dates to each planned action or event.

_____ (company name) has identified several specific milestones which
vill function as goals for the company. The milestones will provide a target for
chievement as well as a mechanism for tracking progress. The dates were chosen based
n realistic delivery times and necessary construction times. All critical path milestones
vill be completed within their allotted time frames to ensure the success of contingent
nilestones. The following table will provide a timeframe for each milestone.

Table: Milestones

Milestones	Start Date	End Date	Budget	Responsibility
Business Plan Completion				
Secure Permits/Licenses				
Locate & Secure Space				
Obtain Insurance				
Secure Additional Financing				
Get Start-up Supplies Quotes				
Obtain County Certification				
Purchase Office Equipment				
Renovate Facilities				
Define Marketing Programs				
Direct Mail Program				
Install Equipment				
Media Selection				

Technology Systems _____

Set-up Accounting System _____

Finalize Media Plan _____

Partnership Marketing _____

Create Facebook Brand Page _____

Open Twitter Account _____

Conduct Blogger Outreach _____

Develop Personnel Plan _____

Develop Staff Training Programs _____

Hire Staff _____

Train Staff _____

Press Release Programs _____

Implement Marketing Plan _____

Guidebook Inclusions _____

Get Website Live _____

Conduct SEO _____

Form Strategic Alliances _____

Purchase Inventory/Supplies _____

Press Release Announcements _____

Advertise Grand Opening _____

Kickoff Advertising Program _____

Join Community Orgs./Network _____

Monitor Sales Actions _____

Conduct Satisfaction Surveys _____

Achieve 20% Occupancy _____

Revenues Exceed $_____ _____

Monitor Social Networks _____

Respond Positively to Reviews _____

Measure Return on Marketing $ _____

Profitability _____

Totals: _____

7.0   Website Plan Summary

_____ (company name) is currently developing a website at the URL address www. (company name).com. Our Boutique Hotel website will be a powerful sales tool that allows our company to interact with the user and increase leads and sales. Our customer will arrive to our website with their own agenda and intention, and want to find information, make a reservation, or solve a problem. Our website will be easy to navigate, have a clear user interface, and provide relevant information to help the user to take action. We will design and develop our website so that it is functional for our users, effective in generating sales, and fully optimized for the search engines. We will use email to communicate with clients wishing to sign-up for specials and our newsletter.

Our website will be designed to take advantage of the trends in the digital world. Visitors to the site will find a layout designed to peruse while obtaining information and using tools to help guide consumers to plan and book their vacations. The site will be 100 percent smart phone friendly, and will offer the opportunity for content to be shared via all popular forms of social media.

We will develop our website to be a resource for web visitors who are seeking knowledge and information about the local area, with a goal to service the knowledge needs of our customers and generate leads. Our home page will be designed to be a "welcome mat" that clearly presents our service offerings and loyalty program benefits, and provides links through which visitors can gain easy access to the information they seek. We will use our website to match the problems our customers face with the solutions we offer.

We will use the free tool, Google Analytics (http://www.google.com/analytics), to generate a history and measure our return on investment. Google Analytics is a free tool that can offer insight by allowing the user to monitor traffic to a single website. We will just add the Google Analytics code to our website and Google will give our firm a dashboard providing the number of unique visitors, repeat traffic, page views, etc. This will help to stop wasting our company's money on inefficient marketing. Using an analytic program will show exactly which leads are paying off, and which ones to do without. We will find out what's bringing our site the most traffic and how to improve upon that.

We will seek to develop a website with the following state-of-the-art features:
1.   Innovative architecture facilitating fast download speeds
2.   Full compliance with the Google Panda and Freshness SEO updates.
3.   Ability to change the look-and-feel design of the hotel website with one click.
4.   Dynamic content personalization
5.   A suite of reservation conversion features
6.   Support of responsive design on the server side (RESS)

To improve the readability of our website, we will organize our website content in the following ways.
1.   Headlines   2.   Bullet points

3.   Callout text   4.   Top of page summaries

To improve search engine optimization, we will maximize the utilization of the following;
1.   Links   2.   Headers
3.   Bold text   4.   Bullets
5.   Keywords   6.   Meta tags

This website will serve the following purposes:

About Us	How We Work/Our Philosophy
History	Founders
Meet the Staff	Bios
What's New	
Area Attractions	Museums/Night Life/Sports/Outdoor Activities/ Golf/Dining/Festivals/Craft Fairs/Gambling/Tours
Contact Us	guest service contact info
Rooms and Rates	
Specials & Packages	
Amenities	
Golf Course	Reservation Forms
Health Club and Spa	
Weddings	
Corporate Meetings	
Concierge Services	Reservations/Laundry/etc.
Gift Catalog	Online Ordering
Schedule A Visit	Form
Book a Room Reservation	Online Availability Check.
Credit Card Authorization	Form
Local Events	Local Happenings/Reservations Link.
Customize Your Visit	Options Menu
Business Travelers Club	Benefits / Registration Form
Frequently Asked Questions	FAQs
Owner Profile	Bio/Resume
Newsletter Sign-up	Mailing List
Newsletter Archives	
Gift Certificates	Form
Accolades	Awards/PR/Articles/Videos
Our Competitive Advantages	
Upcoming Events	Seminar/Community Schedule
Testimonials	With Client Photos
Visual Tour/Photo Gallery	Facility, Rooms, Owners
Referral Program	Details
Directions	Location directions.
Guest Satisfaction Survey	Feedback
Press Releases	Community Involvement
Strategic Alliance Partners	Links

Transportation Schedules	
Guest Handbook	Policies, House Rules, Attractions
Our Blog	Area News/Diary/Accept comments
Refer-a-Friend	Viral marketing
YouTube Video Clips	Seminar Presentation/Testimonials
Service Guarantees	Cleanliness
Code of Ethics	
Mission Statement	
Email Alerts	Sign-up
Classified Ads	

Classified Ads

By joining and incorporating a classified ad affiliate program into our website, we will create the ultimate win-win-win. We will provide our guests with a free benefit, increase our rankings with the search engines by incorporating keyword hyperlinks into our site, attract additional markets to expose to our product, create an additional income source as they upgrade their ads, and provide our prospects a reason to return to our web site again and again

Resources:

App Themes	www.appthemes.com/themes/classipress/
e-Classifieds	http://www.e-classifieds.net/
Noah's Classifieds	http://www.noahsclassifieds.org/
Joom Prod	http://www.joomprod.com/

7.1 Website Marketing Strategy

Our online marketing strategy will employ the following distinct mechanisms:

1. Search Engine Submission

   This will be most useful to people who are unfamiliar with _____ (company name), but are looking for a local Boutique Hotel. There will also be searches from customers who may know about us, but who are seeking additional information.

2. Website Address (URL) on Marketing Materials

   Our URL will be printed on all marketing communications, business cards, letterheads, faxes, and invoices and product labels. This will encourage a visit to our website for additional information

3. Online Directories Listings

   We will make an effort to list our website on relevant, free and paid online directories and manufacturer website product locators.

   The good online directories possess the following features:

   Free or paid listings that do not expire and do not require monthly renewal.

   Ample space to get your advertising message across.

   Navigation buttons that are easy for visitors to use.

Optimization for top placement in the search engines based on keywords that people typically use to find hotels.

Direct links to your website, if available.

An ongoing directory promotion campaign to maintain high traffic volumes to the directory site.

4. Strategic Business Partners

We will use a Business Partners page to cross-link to prominent _____ (city) area tourism web sites as well as the city Web sites and local recreational sites. We will also cross-link with brand name gift suppliers.

5. YouTube Posting

We will produce a video of testimonials from several of our satisfied clients and educate viewers as to the range of our services and products. Our research indicates that the YouTube video will also serve to significantly improve our ranking with the Google Search Engine.

6. Exchange of links with strategic marketing partners.

We will cross-link to non-profit businesses that accept our gift certificate donations as in-house run contest prize awards.

7. E-Newsletter

Use the newsletter sign-up as a reason to collect email addresses and limited profiles, and use embedded links in the newsletter to return readers to website.

8. Create an account for your photos on flickr.com

Use the name of your site on flickr so you have the same keywords and your branded. To take full advantage of Flickr, we will use a JavaScript-enabled browser and install the latest version of the Macromedia Flash Player.

9. Geo Target Pay Per Click (PPC) Campaign

Available through Google Adwords program. Example keywords include Resort Hotel lodging, weekend getaway, accommodations, Hotel and _____ (city).

10. Post messages on Internet user groups and discussion forums.

We will get involved with Boutique Hotel related discussion groups and forums, posting relevant information and developing a descriptive signature paragraph. Ex: www.flyertalk.com/forum/talkboard-topics/640379-boutique-hotel-forum.html

11. Write up your own MySpace.com and Facebook.com bios.

Highlight your background and professional interests.

12. Facebook.com Brand-Building Applications:

As a Facebook member, we will create a specific Facebook page for our business through its "Facebook Pages" application. This page will be used to promote who we are and what we do. We will use this page to post alerts when we have new articles to distribute, news to announce, etc. Facebook members can then become fans of our page and receive these updates on their newsfeed as we post them. We will create our business page by going to the "Advertising" link on the bottom of our personal Facebook page. We will choose the "Pages" tab at the top of that page, and then choose "Create a Page." We will upload our logo, enter our company profile details, and establish our settings. Once completed, we will click the "publish your site" button to go live. We will also promote our Page everywhere we can. We will add a Facebook link to our website, our email signatures, and email newsletters. We will also add Facebook to the marketing mix by deploying pay-per-click ads through their advertising application. With Facebook advertising, we will target by specifying sex, age, relationship, location, education, as well as specific keywords. Once we specify our target criteria, the tool will tell us how many members in the network meet our target needs.

3. Blog to share our success stories and solicit feedback comments.
    Blogging will be a great way for us to share information, expertise, and news, and start a conversation with our customers, the media, potential partners, suppliers, and any other target audiences. Blogging will be a great online marketing strategy because it keeps our content fresh, engages our audience to leave comments on specific posts, improves search engine rankings and attracts links.
    Resource: www.blogger.com
4. Google Maps

7.2 Development Requirements

A full development plan will be generated as documented in the milestones. Costs that ____ (company name) will expect to incur with development of its new website include:

Development Costs
User interface design	$_____.
Site development and testing -	$_____
Site Implementation -	$._____

Ongoing Costs
Website name registration -	$_____ per year.
Site Hosting -	$_____ or less per month.

Site design changes, updates and maintenance are considered part of Marketing.

The site will be developed by _____ (company name), a local start-up company. The user interface designer will use our existing graphic art to come up with the website logo and graphics. We have already secured hosting with a local provider, _____ (business name). Additionally, they will prepare a monthly statistical usage report to analyze and improve web usage and return on investment. We will track the performance of our website identifying metrics, key performance indicators, and critical success factors. We will then compile this tracking information into digestible reports and analyze the data which will reveal what is working in our website and what is not.

The plan is for the website to be live by _____ (date). Basic website maintenance, including update and data entry will be handled by our staff. Site content, such as images and text will be maintained by _____ (owner name). In the future, we may need to contract with a technical resource to build the trackable article download and newsletter capabilities.

Resources: www.vizergy.com   www.web.com   www.1and1.com

7.3   Sample Frequently Asked Questions

We will use the following guidelines when developing the frequently asked questions for our the ecommerce section of the website:

1.   Use a Table of Contents: Offer subject headers at the top of the FAQ page with a hyperlink to that related section further down on the page for quick access.
2.   Group Questions in a Logical Way and group separate specific questions related to a subject together.
3.   Be Precise With the Question: Don't use open-ended questions.
4.   Avoid Too Many Questions: Publish only the popular questions and answers.
5.   Answer the Question with a direct answer.
6.   Link to Resources When Available: via hyperlinks so the customer can continue with self-service support.
7.   Use Bullet Points to list step-by-step instructions.
8.   Focus on Customer Support and Not Marketing.
9.   Use Real and Relevant Frequently Asked Questions from actual customers.
10.   Update Your FAQ Page as customers continue to communicate questions.

The following frequently asked questions will enable us to convey a lot of important information to our clients in a condensed format. We will post these questions and answers on our website and create a hardcopy version to be included on our sales presentation folder.

Where is _____ (company name) located?
We are located just north of _____ in the heart of _____, at the base of the _____ Mountains. We are in the small quaint town of _____. Just ___ miles north of _____ off the _____ Thruway at exit___; the Boutique Hotel is 5 to 10 minutes from the _____. Shopping can be found within minutes of ____ (city) in any direction.

What amenities and facilities are not included in your Standard Boutique Hotel Package?
• Gift Shop & Logo Shop
• Car rental. Tour desk.
• Telephone service. Internet services. Fax services.
• Laundry service. Money Exchange.
• Medical services available 24 hours a day, 6:00pm - 8:00am on call.
• Shuttle service to ___ (city) Clubs.
• Special wedding, honeymoon and anniversary packages.
• Baby sitting services
• A la carte wines.
• Spa services:

- Massages: Relaxing & anti-stress, Swedish, sports, reflexology & shiatsu.
- Facials: Deep cleansing, moisturizing, nourishing, revitalizing & oxygenating.
- Special body treatments: exfoliating body scrub, milk bath, thermal mud massage...
- Beauty salon: manicure, pedicure, braids.

What is included in my Super Deluxe All-Inclusive Package?

- Accommodations as selected.
- Welcome glass of sparkling wine or champagne
- All Gourmet meals and specialty bites
- Unlimited local and selection of international premium brands: Alcoholic and non-alcoholic beverages
- Daily and nightly activity program
- Live Music and shows
- Scuba Clinics in the pool
- Non-motorized water sports
- Beach Butler service
- Concierge/Hospitality Desk
- Taxes and gratuities included

What kinds of recreational activities are there?

We are always within driving distance to great activities happening all year round In the winter, there is _____ and many other winter activities occur during this time of the year. In the spring, summer and fall there is _____ and many other warm weather activities occur during this time of the year.

Is there any place to shop?

The shopping malls are very close by with a variety of shops. There are also many small gift shops and an abundance of antique shops at a very close location.

Is there any night life in the area?

There are a couple of lounges in the immediate area where you can enjoy a drink and some mellow music.

What is your pet policy?

We do ___ (not?) allow pets in the units. The only exception to this policy is licensed service animals. We would appreciate advanced notice for service animals. Any violations of this no-pet policy will result in a $___ fine and the immediate removal of the animal. There are several independent area kennels that may be able to provide you with pet boarding.

How's the food?

A stay at our Boutique Hotel will include a full breakfast in the morning, served in the dining room. We offer a tasty breakfast menu which includes orange juice, fresh fruits of the season, fresh homemade muffins, eggs of your choice and bacon, home made waffles with maple syrup, hot oatmeal and a selection of cold cereal. And of course, tea or coffee is also available. If you are wishing for lunch or dinner, they are available upon request.

Is there a computer connection in my room?
Yes. Every room has wireless High-Speed Internet Access. Wireless Notebook Adapters are available if needed.

Are there activities for my kids?
Yes. There is a small playground and volleyball court for the young and young at heart.

How much will all this cost?
We have a price range for everyone. Each room has the pricing listed on the room description page. You can also just call or stop in to pick your room/suite you desired and we will be happy to help you. Keep in mind that taxes are not listed in the room rates and are in addition at a combined rate of _____%

What are your telephone numbers?
Our phone number locally is _____ or toll free at _____ and our Fax number is _____. If you would like to write us our e-mail address is _____.

Do you have any certifications or approvals?
We are approved and a certified member of the following: Mobil Travel Guide, and Boutique Hotel Association. Each of these certification and memberships requires a regular and thorough inspection to assure compliance with the highest standards for safety, cleanliness and hospitality.

Are extras available and how much are they?
We have several extras available. Cribs and portable cribs are available. Portable small Crib are $___ per room/crib per night and large Cribs are $_____ per room/crib per night. Rollaway beds are available for $_____ per room per night. If you would like someone to join you for breakfast, a person not staying at the Boutique Hotel extra breakfasts are available for $_____ per person per breakfast.

Do you have non-smoking rooms?
Yes. In fact, all of our rooms, including the cottages and the Common Room, are non-smoking.

Do you have a business center?
Yes, we provide a business center and business services including fax, copy and printing. There may be a charge associated with these services.

Does ___ (company name) have a swimming pool?
We do not have a pool.

How close to my room can I park?
We have plenty of convenient parking and, with most of our rooms, you can park right outside your door.

Do you offer a Senior Discount Program?

Travelers 60 and older can save 10% at our Boutique Hotel. Simply request Senior Discount in the guest comments field when making your reservation. A request for this discount is applied at check-in and you will need to provide valid identification during the check in process to receive the discounted rate.

Which credit cards can be used to guarantee a reservation?

A credit card number is required to confirm/guarantee your reservation. We accept American Express, Diner's Club, Discover, MasterCard and Visa. Third party credit cards will not be accepted as payment.

7.4 Website Performance Summary

We will use web analysis tools to monitor web traffic, such as identifying the number of site visits. We will analyze customer transactions and take actions to minimize problems, such as incomplete sales and abandoned shopping carts. We will use the following table to track the performance of our website:

Category	2017		2018		2019	
	Fcst	Act	Fcst	Act	Fcst	Act
No. of Customers						
New Subscribers						
Unique Visitors						
Bounce rate						
Avg. Time on Site						
Page views/ Visit						
Total Page Views						
No. of Products						
Product Categories						
Number of Incomplete Sales						
Conversion Rate						
Affiliate Sales						
Customer Satisfaction Score						

8.0 Operations Plan

Operations include the business aspects of running our Boutique Hotel business, such as conducting quality improvement activities, auditing functions, cost-management analysis, customer service, management and skills trainings, strategic planning meetings, monthly operational auditing, implementing Sales & Marketing activities, conducting quality assurance tests, and supervising technical trainings on property management systems. Our operations plan will present an overview of the flow of the daily activities of the business and the strategies that support them. It will focus on the following critical operating factors that will make the business a success:

1. We will utilize the following property management system:

   _____

2. We will enjoy the following advantages in the sourcing of our inventory:

   _____

3. We will utilize the following technological innovations in the customer relationship management (CRM) process:

   _____

4. We will make use of the following advantages in our distribution process:

   _____

5. We will develop the following in-house training program to improve worker productivity: _____

6. We will utilize the following system to better control inventory carrying costs.

   _____

7. We will implement the following quality control plan:

   _____

Quality Control Plan

Our Quality Control Plan will include a review process that checks all factors involved in our operations. The main objectives of our quality control plan will be to uncover defects and bottlenecks, and reporting to management level to make the decisions on the improvement of the whole production process. Our review process will include the following activities:

   Quality control checklist
   Finished product/service review
   Structured walkthroughs
   Statistical sampling
   Testing process

We plan to work with the reservation service to ensure that there is match to guest needs and wants, and they conduct proper pre-screening interviews.

Operations Planning

We will use Microsoft Visio to develop visual maps, which will piece together the different activities in our organization and show how they contribute to the overall "value stream" of our business. We will rightfully treat operations as the lifeblood of our usiness. We will develop a combined sales and operations planning process where sales nd operations managers will sit down every month to review sales, at the same time reating a forward-looking 12-month rolling plan to help guide the product development nd manufacturing processes, which can become disconnected from sales. We will pproach our operations planning using a three-step process that analyzes the company's urrent state, future state and the initiatives it will tackle next. For each initiative, such as aunching a new product or service, the company will examine the related financials, alent and operations needs, as well as target customer profiles. Our management team vill map out the cost of development and then calculate forecasted return on investment nd revenue predictions.

Our Operating Policies

. Credit/Debit card in guests name is required at check-in for room security purposes. If you do not have a credit or debit card a $100 cash deposit is required for security purposes...No exceptions.

. Confirmation must be presented at the time of check-in.

. Payment in full is due upon arrival.

. Deposit Requirements: 1 to 3 days rental: 1 night deposit, 4 to 6 days rental: 2 night deposit, 7 days or more: 3 night deposit

. Deposit applies to last night's stay.

. Balance due on arrival in cash, travelers checks or money order. VISA, MASTERCARD & DISCOVER accepted.

. Deposits refunded if notified in writing two weeks in advance of arrival date subject to a 25% service charge.

. Deposits not transferable to future reservations.

. No refunds due to weather or early check-out.

0. All rates subject to state Sales and Tourism Tax.

1. Reservations held until 7 p.m. unless otherwise notified.

2. Rates listed apply only to advance reservations.

3. Misrepresentation voids reservation, and will be subject to forfeiture of all amounts prepaid.

4. One parking space per unit, strictly enforced, regardless of unit type.

5. No bicycles in rooms and No roller blades on premises.

6. As a matter of public health, children who are not fully potty trained must wear a "SWIM DIAPER" in pool.

7. No pets.

8. No Smoking in Rooms

Organizational Procedures

. We will keep all receivable accounts information in one place for easier employee access.

. We will develop a strict routine for housekeeping to alleviate stress and confusion.

. We will keep all guest records in a central location for at least one month after check out. This ensures the hotel has the guest's information readily available should there be any discrepancies once the guest has left the property.

215

4.   We will develop a housecleaning checklist and request that the housekeeper return a signed copy of the checklist at the end of each day.

We will develop a Guest Reservation Information Form, which we will use to build a guest information record in our database. It will include the following key info:

1.	Food preferences and allergies	2.	Interests and hobbies
3.	Key Reminder Dates	4.	Visit occasion
5.	Special requirements	6.	Entertainment preferences
7.	Reading preferences	8.	Guest Contact Information
9.	Preferred payment method	10.	Room and Package Preferences

We will develop a guest satisfaction survey, and include a request for improvement suggestions and possible referral candidates. We will develop a policies and procedures manual to insure that employees know how we want things done. It will include the following information:

1.   Reservation processing materials and policies.
2.   Check-in and check-out routines and policies.
3.   Cleaning checklists, schedules and procedures.
4.   Breakfast serving schedule, menu, recipes and room service policies.
5.   Guest relations, including how to handle common guest questions or complaints.
6.   Emergency handling procedures and contacts.
7.   House Rules
8.   Job Descriptions

Our operational controls will primarily involve keeping track of our revenue, expenses, repeat business percentage and guest satisfaction rating. We will conduct a quality improvement plan, which consists of an ongoing process of improvement activities and includes periodic samplings of activities not initiated solely in response to an identified problem. Our plan will be evaluated annually and revised as necessary. Our client satisfaction survey goal is a 98.0% satisfaction rating.

Control Costs

We will implement the following cost of goods profit controls and manage them consistently to have a profound impact on the profitability of the business.

1.   **Systematize Ordering** This means that the operation has an organized practice of procuring products each day. Components of that system include order guides, par levels, count sheets, inventory counts, a manager in charge of all procurement and a prime vendor relationship to reduce price and product fluctuations.
2.   **Check It In.** We will assign a teammate to check in every product that comes through the door using an organized process of time and date specific delivery windows. We will not only check product count but also vigorously demand and inspect the consistency of product quality and product price.
3.   **Store it well.** We will manage against profit erosion through theft, spoilage and other mishandling issues. We will ensure that each product has a specific home, that each product is labeled, that products are stored using the first-in, first-out storage method to ensure quality rotation and that products are locked and put

away until they are needed.

4. **Standardize.** We will create process standards that can be duplicated through consistent training and management of staff members.

5. **Manage the Cash Flow**. We will follow a strict process whereby every item that is sold is accounted for and paid for by the end-user. We will carefully manage voided checks.

Supply Chain Relationships

We will seek to establish good working relationships with our vendors and encourage suppliers to provide more special deals to help improve sales of products. We will also encourage our suppliers to provide in-store merchandising/marketing ideas, lower prices and other types of promotional support.

We will conduct pre-employment background checks on all potential staff. These checks will safeguard both us and the children in our care. There are two main reasons for performing this step. The first is to verify that the person applying for the position within our child care center is indeed the person they claim to be. The second reason is to research any criminal history that may pose an issue to the children and staff. Pre-employment background checks will also incorporate a drugs tests to determine if an individual has used recreational drugs.

We will develop an effective fire safety management policy, as fire safety is achieved via this policy combined with adequate fire safety features in our premises. Our goal is to effect whatever measures necessary to minimize the risk of a fire occurring and if a fire does breakout to ensure that staff and children are evacuated swiftly and safely. The fire safety program will detail what fire prevention measures are in place at our day care i.e. the steps we are taking to reduce or eliminate the risks of a fire occurring. We also plan to develop a list of specific interview questions and a worksheet to evaluate, compare and pre-screen potential suppliers. We will also check vendor references and their rating with the Hoovers.com.

We plan to write and maintain an operations manual and a personnel policies handbook. The Operating Manual will be a comprehensive document outlining virtually every aspect of the business. The operating manual will include management and accounting procedures, hiring and personnel policies, and daily operations procedures, such as opening and closing the store, and how to _____. The manual will cover the following topics:

- Community Relations	- Customer Relations
- Media Relations	- Employee Relations
- Vendor Relations	- Government Relations
- Competition Relations	- Equipment Maintenance Checklist
- Environmental Concerns	- Inventory Controls
- Intra Company Procedures	- Accounting and Billing
- Banking and Credit Cards	- Financing
- Computer Procedures	- Scheduling Procedures
- Quality Controls	- Safety Procedures
- Open/Close Procedures	- Security Procedures

- Software Documentation

Our plan is to automate our sales process, by developing an online registration calculator. We plan to adapt Quickbooks to track product inventory and sales. The plan is to place special emphasis on using technology to make the transaction with customers more efficient and to accept a wide range of automatic credit and debit card options. All systems are computer based and allow for accurate off-premises control of all aspects of our service business.

We plan to purchase a P.O.S. Software Package that will help us to accomplish the following objectives:
1.   Speed our order entry and database build processes.
2.   Assist in sales forecasting
3.   Allow us to provide a higher level of guest service.
4.   Lower our inventory costs.
5.   Improve overall operational efficiency.

Software Options

Quickbooks	//quickbooks.intuit.com/product/accounting-software/	
Applied Technologies	www.guestall.com	407-529-9072
AutoClerk, Inc.	www.asppms.com/autoclerk	925-871-1810
Hotel Software Systems	www.hssltd.com	503-404-0027
Innformed Solutions	www.innformed-manager.com	617-739-0306
Rezovation/Guest Tracker	www.rezovation.com	

DSPanel   www.dspanel.com/solutions/hospitality-solution/
This software system will help our company to increase its ROI, keep track of on-demand changes in room occupancy and create multiple budget and forecast scenarios. With 'Performance Canvas', we will create deployment scenarios that allow our managers to keep track of everything from top F&B sales, room occupancy and much more, right in their web browsers or mobile devices. Our revenue managers and financial professionals will be able to create and track multiple budgets, scenarios, and forecasts right in Excel without having to keep track of multiple spreadsheets.

9.0   Management Summary

The Management Plan will reveal who will be responsible for the various management functions to keep the business running efficiently. It will further demonstrate how that individual has the experience and/or training to accomplish each function. It will address who will do the planning function, the organizing function, the directing function, and the controlling function. We will also develop an employee retention plan because there are distinct cost advantages to retaining employees. It costs a lot to recruit and train a new employee, and in the early days, new employees are a lot less productive. We will need to make sure that our employees are satisfied in order to retain them and, in turn, create satisfied customers.

At the present time _____ (owner name) will run all operations for _____ (company name). _____ (His/Her) background in _____ (business management?) indicates an understanding of the importance of financial control systems. There is not expected to be any shortage of qualified staff from local labor pools in the market area.

_____ (owner name) will be the owner and operations manager of _____ (company name). His/her general duties will include the following:
1.   Oversee the daily operations
2.   Ordering inventory and supplies.
3.   Develop and implementing the marketing strategy
4.   Purchasing equipment and food supplies.
5.   Arranging for the routine maintenance and upkeep of the facility.
6.   Hiring, training and supervision of new employees.
7.   Scheduling and planning lessons and special events.
8.   Creating and pricing lesson programs and packages.
9.   Managing the accounting/financial aspect of the business.
10.   Contract negotiation/vendor relations.

The operations manager will take a monthly draw of $_____ month.

9.1   Organizational Structure

We will operate with an extensive management structure consisting of a General Manager which serves as the head executive, department heads that oversee various departments, middle managers, administrative staff, and line-level supervisors.
.

9.2   Owner Personal History

The owner has been working in the _____ () industry for over ____ (#) years, gaining personal knowledge and experience in all phases of the industry.

_____ (owner name) is the founder and operations manager of
_____ (company name). He/she began his/her career as a _____ .
Over the last ____ (#) years, _____ (owner name) became quite proficient in a
wide range of management activities and responsibilities, becoming an operations
manager for _____ (former employer name) from _____ to _____
(dates). There he/she was able to achieve _____.
_____, owner of _____ (company name), has a ____ degree in _____.
For ____ years he/she has managed a business similar to _____ (company name).
_____ (His/her) duties included _____.

Specifically, the owner brings _____ (#) years of experience as a _____ , as
well as certification as a _____ from the _____
(National _____ Association). He/she is an experienced entrepreneur with ____ years of
small business accounting, finance, marketing and management experience. Education
includes college course work in business administration, banking and finance,
investments, and commercial credit management.

The owner will draw an annual salary of $_____ from the business although most of
this goes to repay loans to finance business start-up costs. These loans will be paid-in-full
by _____ (month) of _____ (year).

9.3   Management Team Gaps

Despite the owner's and manager's experience in the _____ (?) industry, the company
will also retain the consulting services of _____ (consultant company name).
This company has over _____ (#) years of experience in the _____ industry, and
has successfully opened dozens of Boutique Hotel businesses across the country. The
Consultants will be primarily used for certification approval, market research, guest
satisfaction surveys and to provide additional input in the evaluation of new business
opportunities. The company also expects to retain the services of a local CPA to help the
owner manage cash flow. Additionally the business will make use of the following
advisory board to provide support for strategic planning and human resource related
issues.

The Board of Advisors will provide continuous mentoring support on business matters.
Expertise gaps in legal, tax, marketing and personnel will be covered by the Board of
Advisors. The owner will actively seek free business advice from SCORE, a national
non-profit organization with a local office. This is a group of retired executives and
business owners who donate their time to serve as business counselors to new business
owners.

Advisory Resources Available to the Business Include:

	Name	Address	Phone
CPA/Accountant			
Attorney			

Insurance Broker _____

Banker _____

Business Consultant _____

Wholesale Suppliers _____

Trade Association _____

Realtor _____

SCORE.org _____

Other _____

9.4   Management Matrix

Note: See appendix for attached management resumes.

Name	Title	Credentials	Functions	Responsibilities

9.5   Outsourcing Matrix

Company Name	Functions	Responsibilities	Cost

Note: Marketing and public relations will be handled mainly by the owner. If there is a greater need, a marketing consultant will be hired to help issue press releases and generate seminar and website content.

9.6.0   Personnel Plan

A top priority in managing our boutique hotel will be identifying and training staff who can be great personal ambassadors for the hotel. In addition to being skilled at the job they are hired for, above all they must be able to smile, converse and interact with guests. Properly trained staff attentive to guests' needs and expectations will also be crucial in understanding and making constructive use of customer feedback.

Employee Requirements:

1. **Skills and Abilities**
   Staff must have a high school education, be self-motivating, and have strong guest service skills. Previous experience as a _____ is preferred, along with an _____ Certificate, and First Aid and CPR Certificates.

2. **Recruitment**
   Experience suggests that personal referrals are an excellent source for experienced technicians. We will also place newspaper ads, use our Yellow Page Ad to indicate what types of staff we use and what types of customers we serve, and make effective use of our Newsletter to post positions available. We will give a referral bonus to existing employees.

3. **Training and Supervision**
   Training is largely accomplished through hands-on experience with

supplemental instruction. Additional knowledge is gained through our policy and operations manuals, and promotional materials. We will foster professional development and independence in all phases of our business. Supervision is task-oriented and the quantity is dependent on the complexity of the job assignment. Employees are called team members because they are part of Team _____ (company name). To help them succeed, employees will receive assistance with certification. They will also participate in our written training modules.

4.   Salaries and Benefits

Employees will be basically paid a wage plus commission. Good training and incentives, such as cash bonuses handed out monthly to everyone for reaching goals, will serve to retain good employees. An employee discount of __ percent on personal sales is offered. As business warrants, we hope to put together a benefit package that includes insurance, and paid vacations. The personnel plan also assumes a 5% annual increase in salaries.

9.6.1 Employee Scheduling

1.   We will prepare employee schedules for up to a month in advance. This will reduce scheduling conflicts and help employees if they need to request days off.
2.   We will have a specific place where employees can submit requests for days off. If this is viewable to other employees they may be able to work some details out among themselves, saving the manager time when making the schedule.
3.   We will hire one or two employees that do not mind working on an on-call basis. This can help alleviate stress when there is a need to fill a certain shift at the last minute.

9.6.1 Employee Productivity

1.   We will develop a specific guest check-in and check-out routine that all employees will be trained to follow. If employees have a strong understanding of policies and procedures they will be able to check guests in or out faster, resulting in a happier guest.
2.   We will reward our employees with incentives. A few good incentive ideas are a bonus for reaching a target amount for up-selling guests, raises based on performance and opportunities for advancement.
3.   We will listen to employees and be open to tips or suggestions from employees.

9.6.1   Job Descriptions

Our job descriptions will adhere to the following format guidelines:

1.	Job Title	2.	Reports to:
3.	Pay Rate	4.	Job Responsibilities
5.	Travel Requirements	5.	Supervisory Responsibilities
6.	Qualifications	7.	Work Experience
8.	Required Skills	10.	Salary Range
11.	Benefits	12.	Opportunities

Job Description   Boutique Hotel Manager

Resort managers oversee all resort staff members, from front desk clerks to janitorial services. Depending on the size of a resort, the resort manager may have several assistant managers helping to cover all needs of the facility. Typical job duties of resort managers include reviewing finances, overseeing hiring practices, holding meetings with the facility's various department heads, greeting and interacting with resort guests and checking on necessary supplies in various sectors of the resort.

Responsibilities

Because resort managers are responsible for the day-to-day running of a lodging facility, they must have a broad vision of the facility as well as an attention to detail. From knowing the number of poolside towels that are in stock, to recruiting, hiring and training new staff members, resort managers must keep track of all aspects of running a resort. Resorts can vary as to the types of recreation, entertainment, dining facilities and tourist attractions they offer. Because of this, resort managers may specialize in a particular brand of entertainment and amenities.

Customer Service

Resort managers ensure that resort employees comply with any customer service standards, policies, or initiatives. They also assist with resolving client complaints.

Budget

Resort managers track the spending of the location, ensuring that it operates within budgetary guidelines. They are also frequently in charge of setting rates for rooms, prices for meals, and fees for other services.

Supervision

Resort managers are responsible for supervising the resort staff. This includes hiring, training, coaching, disciplining, and assessing performance related to staff members' functions within the resort.

Job Description -- Security Manager

Ensuring the security of the Boutique Hotel, Security and Loss Prevention plays a crucial role. It is a function that affects not only the physical resorts, hotels, and operations centers, but the security of associates and guests as well. Security and Loss Prevention candidates will have a genuine concern for the safety and well being of others around them. Keys to success within this role: the ability to spot situations or surroundings that are out of the ordinary and the ability to interact in a friendly and courteous manner with both internal and external clients. Building both on experience and fundamentals, Security and Loss Prevention staff members begin as security guards at either a resort or business center. After this introduction, staff members progress, moving into supervisory or managerial roles in Facilities, Loss Prevention and Security.

Job Description -- Webmaster

Because our boutique hotel can benefit from the advanced technology allowing customers to book directly on-line, using our Website, we will make certain to hire a qualified webmaster. The webmaster will be involved with the planning and maintenance of our website. Therefore, to maximize the on-line booking capabilities, we will designate a staff member to ensure that rates, promotions, and room inventory are consistently up to date, and that the customer has the ease of booking, revising, and canceling reservation online. The webmaster will be charged with maintaining a most useful and helpful reservations system from the customer's perspective.

Job Description -- Public Relations Specialist
Our hotel's PR professional will handle communication with our local tourism board, convention bureau and business associations in order to maximize promotional opportunities.

Personnel Plan
1. We will develop a system for recruiting, screening and interviewing employees.
2. Background checks will be performed as well as reference checks and drug tests.
3. We will develop an innkeeper training course.
4. We will keep track of staff scheduling.
5. We will develop client satisfaction surveys to provide feedback and ideas.
6. We will develop and perform semi-annual employee evaluations.
7. We will "coach" all of our employees to improve their abilities and range of skills.
8. We will employ temporary employees via a local staffing agency to assist with one-time special projects.
9. Each employee will be provided a detailed job description and list of business policies, and be asked to sign these documents as a form of employment contract.
10. Incentives will be offered for reaching quarterly financial and enrollment goals, completing the probationary period, and passing county inspections.
11. guest service awards will be presented to those employees who best exemplify our stated mission and exceed guest expectations.

The following table summarizes our personnel expenditures for the first three years, with compensation costs increasing from $_____ in the first year to about $_____ in the third year, based on ____ (5?) % payroll increases each year and 100% enrollment. The payroll includes tuition reimbursement, pay increases, vacation pay, bonuses and state required certifications.

Table: Personnel Plan	Number of Employees	Hourly Rate	Annual Salaries		
			2017	2018	2019
General Manager					
Assistant Manager					
Revenue Manager					
Night Desk Staff					
Day Desk Staff					
Administrative Assistants					
Public Relations Specialist					

Office Staff _____

Gift Store Staff _____

Rental Shop Staff _____

Janitorial Supervisor _____

Housekeepers _____

Landscaper _____

Maintenance Supervisor _____

Maintenance Staff _____

Security Manager _____

Bookkeeper _____

Training Manager _____

Webmaster _____

IT Manager _____

Other _____

Total People: Headcount _____

Total Annual Payroll

Payroll Burden (Fringe Benefits)　(+)　_____

Total Payroll Expense　(=)　_____

According to the U.S. Bureau of Labor Statistics (BLS), the median salary for all types of lodging managers was $46,300 in 2009 (*www.bls.gov*). In addition to resort managers, these include management positions in hotels, motels, casinos and other areas of tourism and lodging. Growth in this field was expected to be slower than the average for other industries from 2008-2019, according to BLS statistics, growing at a rate of five percent. Some resort managers' benefits package may include on-premises lodging.

According to the job-search website Indeed.com, the average annual salary of a resort general manager in July 2010 was $49,000.

10.0   Risk Factors

Risk management is the identification, assessment, and prioritization of risks, followed by the coordinated and economical application of resources to minimize, monitor, and control the probability and/or impact of unfortunate events or to maximize the realization of opportunities. For the most part, our risk management methods will consist of the following elements, performed, more or less, in the following order.

1.   Identify, characterize, and assess threats
2.   Assess the vulnerability of critical assets to specific threats
3.   Determine the risk (i.e. the expected consequences of specific types of attacks on specific assets)
4.   Identify ways to reduce those risks
5.   Prioritize risk reduction measures based on a strategy

Types of Risks:

_____ (company name) faces certain risks inherent to a service business in the Boutique Hotel industry.

1.   Financial Risks

Our quarterly revenues and operating results are difficult to predict and may fluctuate significantly from quarter to quarter as a result of a variety of factors. Among these factors are:

   -Changes in our own or competitors' pricing policies.
   - Recession pressures.
   - Fluctuations in expected revenues from guests, sponsors and strategic relationships.
   - Timing of costs related to payments.

2.   Legislative / Legal Landscape.

Our participation in the lodging arena presents unique risks:

   - Malpractice and other related product liability.
   - Increased Federal and State regulations on privacy, occupancy and insurance, which we voluntarily meet as a result of our

memberships in certain organizations and participation in guidebook rating systems.

3.   Operational Risks

For the past __ (#) years the owner has been dealing with computers so he is comfortable with technology and understands a wide array of software applications. However, the biggest potential problem will be equipment malfunction. To minimize the potential for problems, the owner will be taking equipment repair training from the manufacturer and will deal with basic troubleshooting and minor repairs. Beyond that, we have identified a service technician who is located close-by.

To attract and retain client to the _____ (company name) community, we must continue to provide differentiated and quality services . This confers certain risks

including the need to:
- Anticipate to consumer preferences for amenities and service.
- Attract, excite and retain a large audience of guests to our community.
- Create and maintain successful strategic alliances with quality partners.
- Deliver high quality, "24/7" guest service.
- Build our brand rapidly and cost-effectively.
- Compete effectively against better-established lodging companies.

Market Risk
The entry of competition from another similar type of establishment poses a significant risk. This will require the building up of a loyal guest base and/or finding ways to co-market with the competitor to bring larger groups for the conference market.

Human Resource Risks
The most serious human resource risk to our business, at least in the initial stages, would be my inability to operate the business due to illness or disability. The owner is currently in exceptional health and would eventually seek to replace himself on a day-to-day level by developing systems to support the growth of the business.

Marketing Risks
Advertising is our most expensive form of promotion and there will be a period of testing headlines and offers to find the one that works the best. The risk, of course, is that we will exhaust our advertising budget before we find an ad that works. Placing greater emphases on sunk-cost marketing, such as our storefront and on existing relationships through direct selling will minimize our initial reliance on advertising to bring in a large percentage of business in the first year.

Business Risks
A major risk to retail service businesses is the performance of the economy and the small business sector. Since economists are predicting this as the fastest growing sector of the economy, our risk of a downturn in the short-term is minimized. The entrance of major chains into our marketplace is a risk. They will offer more of the latest equipment, provide a wider array of products and services, competitive prices and 24-hour service. This situation would force us to lower our prices in the short-term until we could develop an offering of higher margin, value-added services not provided by the large chains. It does not seem likely that the relative size of our market today could support the overhead of one of those operations. Projections indicate that this will not be the case in the future and that leaves a window of opportunity for ___ (company name) to aggressively build a loyal client base.

We will conduct on-site casualty loss control assessments. We will attend accident investigation and emergency preparedness training sessions to learn practical approaches for dealing with guest incidents as well as catastrophic events. We will also take steps to minimize our risk of bed bug infestation, and document processes for detection and routine inspection.

To combat the usual start-up risks we will do the following:
1. Utilize our industry experience to quickly establish desired strategic relationships.
2. Pursue business outside of our immediate market area.
3. Diversify our range of product and service offerings.
4. Develop multiple distribution channels.
5. Monitor our competitor actions.
6. Stay in touch with our customers and suppliers.
7. Watch for trends which could potentially impact our business.
8. Continuously optimize and scrutinize all business processes.
9. Institute daily financial controls using Business Ratio Analysis.
10. Create pay-for-performance compensation and training programs to reduce employee turnover.

Further, to attract and retain customers the Company will need to continue to expand its market offerings, utilizing third party strategic relationships. This could lead to difficulties in the management of relationships, competition for specific services and products, and/or adverse market conditions affecting a particular partner.

The Company will take active steps to mitigate risks. In preparation of the Company's pricing, many factors will be considered. The Company will closely track the activities of all third parties, and will hold monthly review meetings to resolve issues and review and update the terms associated with strategic alliances.

Additionally, we will develop the following kinds of contingency plans:
Disaster Recovery Plan
Business Continuity Plan
Business Impact and Gap Analysis
Testing & Maintenance

The Company will utilize marketing and advertising campaigns to promote brand identity and will coordinate all expectations with internal and third party resources prior to release. This strategy should maximize guest satisfaction while minimizing potential costs associated with unplanned expenditures and quality control issues.

10.1   Business Risk Reduction Strategy

We plan to implement the following strategies to reduce our start-up business risk:
1. Implement our business plan based on go, no-go stage criteria.

2. Develop employee cross-training programs.
3. Regularly back-up all computer files/Install ant-virus software.
4. Arrange adequate insurance coverage with higher deductibles.
5. Develop a limited number of prototype samples.
6. Test market offerings to determine level of market demand and appropriate pricing strategy.
7. Thoroughly investigate and benchmark to competitor offerings.
8. Research similar franchised businesses for insights into successful prototype business/operations models.
9. Reduce operation risks and costs by flowcharting all structured systems & standardized manual processes.
10. Use market surveys to listen to guest needs and priorities.
11. Purchase used equipment to reduce capital outlays.
12. Use leasing to reduce financial risk.
13. Outsource manufacturing to job shops to reduce capital at risk.
14. Use subcontractors to limit fixed overhead salary expenses.
15. Ask manufacturers about profit sharing arrangements.
16. Pay advertisers with a percent of revenues generated.
17. Develop contingency plans for identified risks.
18. Set-up procedures to control employee theft.
19. Do criminal background checks on potential employees.
20. Take immediate action on delinquent accounts.
21. Only extend credit to established account with D&B rating
22. Get regular competitive bids from alternative suppliers.
23. Check that operating costs as a percent of rising sales are lower as a result of productivity improvements.
24. Request bulk rate pricing on fast moving supplies.
25. Don't tie up cash in slow moving inventory to qualify for bigger discounts.
26. Reduce financial risk by practicing cash flow policies.
27. Reduce hazard risk by installing safety procedures.
28. Use financial management ratios to monitor business vitals.
29. Make business decisions after brainstorming sessions.
30. Focus on the products with biggest return on investment.
31. Where possible, purchase off-the-shelf components.
32. Request manufacturer samples and assistance to build prototypes.
33. Design production facilities to be flexible and easy to change.
34. Develop a network of suppliers with outsourcing capabilities.
35. Analyze and shorten every cycle time, including product development.
36. Develop multiple sources for every important input.
37. Treat the business plan as a living document and update it frequently.
38. Conduct a SWOT analysis and use determined strengths to pursue opportunities.
39. Conduct regular guest satisfaction surveys to evaluate performance.

10.2   Reduce guest Perceived Risk Tactics

We will utilize the following tactics to help reduce the new guest's perceived risk of starting to do business with our company.   Status

1. Publish a page of testimonials.   _____
2. Secure Opinion Leader written endorsements.   _____
3. Offer an Unconditional Satisfaction Money Back Guarantee.   _____
4. Long-term Performance Guarantee (Financial Risk).   _____
5. Guaranteed Buy Back (Obsolete time risk)   _____
6. Offer free trials and samples.   _____
7. Brand Image (consistent marketing image and performance)   _____
8. Patents/Trademarks/Copyrights   _____
9. Publish case studies   _____
10. Share your expertise (Articles, Seminars, etc.)   _____
11. Get recognized Certification   _____
12. Conduct responsive guest service   _____
13. Accept Installment Payments   _____
14. Display product materials composition or ingredients.   _____
15. Publish product test results.   _____
16. Publish sales record milestones.   _____
17. Foster word-of-mouth by offering an unexpected extra.   _____
18. Distribute factual, pre-purchase info.   _____
19. Reduce consumer search costs with online directories.   _____
20. Reduce guest transaction costs.   _____
21. Facilitate in-depth comparisons to alternative services.   _____
22. Make available prior guest ratings and comments.   _____
23. Provide customized info based on prior transactions.   _____
24. Become a Better Business Bureau member.   _____
25. Publish overall guest satisfaction survey results.   _____
26. Offer plan options that match niche segment needs.   _____
27. Require client sign-off before proceeding to next phase.   _____
28. Document procedures for dispute resolution.   _____
29. Offer the equivalent of open source code.   _____
30. Stress your compatibility features (avoid lock-in fear).   _____
31. Create detailed checklists & flowcharts to show processes   _____
32. Publish a list of frequently asked questions/answers.   _____
33. Create a community that enables clients to connect with
    each other and share common interests.   _____
34. Inform customers as to your stay-in-touch methods.   _____
35. Conduct and handover a detailed needs analysis worksheet.   _____
36. Offer to pay all return shipping charges and/or refund all
    original shipping and handling fees.   _____
37. Describe your product testing procedures prior to shipping.   _____
    38. Highlight your competitive advantages in all marketing materials. _____

11.0   Financial Plan

The over-all financial plan for growth allows for use of the significant cash flow generated by operations. We are basing projected sales on the market research, industry analysis and competitive environment.

_____ (company name) expects a profit margin of over ____ % starting with year one. By year two, that number should slowly increase as the law of diminishing costs takes hold, and the day-to-day activities of the business become less expensive.

Sales are expected to grow at ____ % per year, and level off by year _____.
Our financial statements will show consistent growth in earnings, which provides notice of the durability of our company's competitive advantage.

The initial investment in _____ (company name) will be provided by _____ (owner name) in the amount of $ _____. The owner will also seek a ___ (#) year bank loan in the amount of $ _____ to provide the remainder of the required initial funding.

The funds will be used to renovate the space, purchase furnishings and to cover initial operating expenses. The owner financing will become a return on equity, paid in the form of dividends to the owner.

We expect to finance slow and steady growth through cash flow.

The owners do not intend to take any profits out of the business until the long-term debt has been satisfied.

Our financial plan includes:
   Moderate growth rate with a steady cash flow.
   Investing residual profits into company expansion.
   Company expansion will be an option if sales projections are met and/or exceeded.
   Marketing costs will remain below ___ (5?) % of sales.
   Repayment of our loan calculated at a high A.P.R. of ___ (10?) percent and at a 10-
      year-payback on our $_____ loan.

11.1   Important Assumptions

The financial plan depends on important assumptions, most of which are shown in the following table. The Personnel Burden is low because benefits are not paid to our staff.

The following basic assumptions need to be considered:
1.   The economy will grow at a steady slow pace, without another major recession.
2.   There will be no major changes in the industry, other than those discussed in the

trends section of this document.
3. The State will not enact 'impact' legislation on our industry.
4. Sales are estimated at minimum to average values, while expenses are estimated at above average to maximum values..
5. Staffing and payroll expansions will be driven by increased sales.
6. Rent expenses will grow at a slow, predictable rate.
7. Materials expenses will not increase dramatically over the next several years, but will grow at a rate that matches increasing consumption.
8. We assume access to equity capital and financing sufficient to maintain our financial plan as shown in the tables.
9. The amount of the financing needed from the bank will be approximately $_____and this will be repaid over the next 10 years at $_____ per month.
10. We assume that people in _____ (city) will be interested in learning how to dance and will give us the opportunity to provide such lessons.
11. We assume that the area will continue to grow at present rate of __ % per year.
12. Interest rates and tax rates are based on conservative assumptions.
13. We will not offer consumer credit, but will extend 30 days credit terms to our qualified business accounts.

Revenue Assumptions:

	Year	Sales/Month	Growth Rate
1.			
2.			
3.			

Resource:
www.score.org/resources/business-plans-financial-statements-template-gallery

11.2   Break-even Analysis

Break-Even Analysis will be performed to determine the point at which revenue received equals the costs associated with generating the revenue. Break-even analysis calculates what is known as a margin of safety, the amount that revenues exceed the break-even point. This is the amount that revenues can fall while still staying above the break-even point. The two main purposes of using the break-even analysis for marketing is to (1) determine the minimum number of sales that is required to avoid a loss at a designated sales price and (2) it is an exercise tool so that you can tweak the sales price to determine the minimum volume of sales you can reasonably expect to sell in order to avoid a loss.

Definition: Break-Even Is the Volume Where All Fixed Expenses Are Covered.

Based on projections, we will need an average of __ guests each month to breakeven.

Three important definitions used in break-even analysis are:
- **Variable Costs** (Expenses) are costs that change directly in proportion to changes in activity (volume), such as raw materials, labor and packaging.

- **Fixed Costs** (Expenses) are costs that remain constant (fixed) for a given time period despite wide fluctuations in activity (volume), such as rent, loan payments, insurance, payroll and utilities.

- **Unit Contribution Margin** is the difference between your product's unit selling price and its unit variable cost.
  Unit Contribution Margin = Unit Sales Price - Unit Variable Cost

For the purposes of this breakeven analysis, the assumed fixed operating costs will be approximately $ _____ per month, as shown in the following table.

Averaged Monthly Fixed Costs:		**Variable Costs:**	
Payroll	_____	Cost of Inventory Sold	_____
Rent	_____	Labor	_____
Insurance	_____	Supplies	_____
Utilities	_____	Direct Costs per Patient	_____
Security.	_____	Other	_____
Legal/Technical Help	_____		
Other	_____		
Total:	_____	Total	_____

A break-even analysis table has been completed on the basis of average costs/prices. With monthly fixed costs averaging $_____ , $____ in average sales and $_____ in average variable costs, we need approximately $_____ in sales per month to break-even.

Based on our assumed ____ % variable cost, we estimate our breakeven sales volume at around $ _____ per month. We expect to reach that sales volume by our _____ month of operations. Our break-even analysis is shown in further detail in the following table.

Breakeven Formulas:

Break Even Units = Total Fixed Costs / (Unit Selling Price - Variable Unit Cost)

· _____ = _____ / (_____ - _____)

·**BE Dollars = (Total Fixed Costs / (Unit Price – Variable Unit Costs))/ Unit Price**

_____ = (_____ / (_____ - _____)) / _____

·**BE Sales = Annual Fixed Costs / (1- Unit Variable costs / Unit Sales Price)**

_____ = _____ / (1 - _____ / _____)

Table: Break-even Analysis

Monthly Units Break-even	_____
Monthly Revenue Break-even	$ _____
Assumptions:	
Average Per-Unit Revenue	$ _____
Average Per-Unit Variable Cost	$ _____
Estimated monthly Fixed Cost	$ _____

Ways to Improve Breakeven Point:
1. Reduce Fixed Costs via Cost Controls
2. Raise unit sales prices.
3. Lower Variable Costs by improving employee productivity or getting lower competitive bids from suppliers.
4. Broaden product/service line to generate multiple revenue streams.

11.3   Projected Profit and Loss

Pro forma income statements are an important tool for planning our future business operations. If the projections predict a downturn in profitability, we can make operational changes such as increasing prices or decreasing costs before these projections become reality.

Our monthly profit for the first year varies significantly, as we aggressively seek improvements and begin to implement our marketing plan. However, after the first ___ months, profitability should be established.

We predict advertising costs will go down in the next three years as word-of-mouth about our Boutique Hotel gets out to the public and we are able to find what has worked well for us and concentrate on those advertising methods, and corporate affiliations generate sales without the need for extra advertising.

Our net profit/sales ratio will be low the first year. We expect this ratio to rise at least _____ (15?) percent the second year. Normally, a startup concern will operate with negative profits through the first two years. We will avoid that kind of operating loss on our second year by knowing our competitors and having a full understanding of our target markets.

Our projected profit and loss is indicated in the following table. From our research of the Boutique Hotel industry, our annual projections are quite realistic and conservative, and we prefer this approach so that we can ensure an adequate cash flow.

Key P & L Formulas:

Gross Profit Margin = Total Sales Revenue - Cost of Goods Sold

Gross Margin % = (Total Sales Revenue - Cost of Goods Sold) / Total Sales Revenue
This number represents the proportion of each dollar of revenue that the company retains as gross profit.

EBITDA =Revenue - Expenses (exclude interest, taxes, depreciation & amortization)

PBIT = Profit (Earnings) Before Interest and Taxes = EBIT
A profitability measure that looks at a company's profits before the company has to pay corporate income tax and interest expenses. This measure deducts all operating expenses from revenue, but it leaves out the payment of interest and tax. Also referred to as "earnings before interest and tax ".

Net Profit = Total Sales Revenues - Total Expenses

Pro Forma Profit and Loss

	Formula	2017	2018	2019
Revenue:				
Room Rentals				
Corporate Meetings				
Spa Treatments				
Health Club Fees				
Golf Course Fees				
Equipment Rentals				
Wedding Ceremonies				
Catering Services				
Special Events				
Facilities Rentals				
Attraction Ticket Sales				
Gift Sales				
Food Sales				
Clothing Sales				
Misc.				
Total Sales Revenue	A			
Direct Cost of Sales	B			
Other Costs of Goods	C			
Total Costs of Goods Sold	B+C=D			
Gross Margin	A-D=E			
Gross Margin %	E / A			
Expenses				
Payroll				
Payroll Taxes				
Sales & Marketing				
Conventions/Trade Shows				
Building Depreciation				
License/Permit Fees				
Dues and Subscriptions				
Reservation Service Commissions				
Rent				
Utilities				
Deposits				
Loan Repayment				
Data Processing				
Repairs and Maintenance				
Janitorial Supplies				
Office Supplies				
Housekeeping				
Landscaping service				
Leased Equipment				
Guest Entertainment				

Insurance
Location Rental
Towel/Linen Replacement
Contracted Spa Professionals
Professional Development
Guest Shuttle Services
Vehicle Expenses
Food and Beverages
Vending Expenses
Merchant Fees
Bad Debts
Miscellaneous

Total Operating Expenses   **F**

Profit Before Int. & Taxes $E - F = G$

Interest Expenses   H
Taxes Incurred   I
Net Profit $G - H - I = J$

Net Profit / Sales $J / A = K$

11.5 Projected Cash Flow

The Cash Flow Statement shows how the company is paying for its operations and future growth, by detailing the "flow" of cash between the company and the outside world. Positive numbers represent cash flowing in, negative numbers represent cash flowing out.

The first year's monthly cash flows are will vary significantly, but we do expect a solid cash balance from day one. We expect that the majority of our sales will be done in cash or by credit card and that will be good for our cash flow position. Additionally, we will stock only slightly more than one month's inventory at any time. Consequently, we do not anticipate any problems with cash flow, once we have obtained sufficient start-up funds.

A __ year commercial loan in the amount of $_____, sought by the owner will be used to cover our working capital requirement. Our projected cash flow is summarized in the following table, and is expected to meet our needs. In the following years, excess cash will be used to finance our growth plans.

Cash Flow Management:

We will use the following practices to improve our cash flow position:
1. Become more selective when granting credit.
2. Seek deposits or multiple stage payments.
3. Reduce the amount/time of credit given to clients.
4. Reduce direct and indirect costs and overhead expenses.
5. Use the 80/20 rule to manage inventories, receivables and payables.
6. Invoice as soon as the service has been performed.
7. Generate regular reports on receivable ratios and aging.
8. Establish and adhere to sound credit practices.
9. Use more pro-active collection techniques.
10. Add late payment fees where possible.
11. Increase the credit taken from suppliers.
12. Negotiate extended credit terms from vendors.
13. Use some barter arrangements to acquire goods and service.
14. Use leasing to gain access to the use of productive assets.
15. Convert debt into equity.
16. Regularly update cash flow forecasts.
17. Defer projects which cannot achieve acceptable cash paybacks.
18. Require a 50% deposit upon the signing of the reservation contract and the balance in full, due upon registration and check-in.

Cash Flow Formulas:

Net Cash Flow = Incoming Cash Receipts - Outgoing Cash Payments
Equivalently, net profit plus amounts charged off for depreciation, depletion, and amortization. (also called cash flow).

Cash Balance = Opening Cash Balance + Net Cash Flow
We are positioning ourselves in the market as a medium risk concern with steady cash flows. Accounts payable is paid at the end of each month, while sales are in cash, giving our company an excellent cash structure.

Pro Forma Cash Flow

	Formula	2017	2018	2019
Cash Received				
Cash from Operations				
Cash Sales	A			
Cash from Receivables	B			
Subtotal Cash from Operations	A + B = C			
Additional Cash Received				
Non Operating (Other) Income				
Sales Tax, VAT, HST/GST Received				
New Current Borrowing				
New Other Liabilities (interest fee)				
New Long-term Liabilities				
Sales of Other Current Assets				
Sales of Long-term Assets				
New Investment Received				
Total Additional Cash Received	D			
Subtotal Cash Received	C + D = E			
Expenditures				
Expenditures from Operations				
Cash Spending	F			
Payment of Accounts Payable	G			
Subtotal Spent on Operations	F+G = H			
Additional Cash Spent				
Non Operating (Other) Expenses				
Sales Tax, VAT, HST/GST Paid Out				
Principal Repayment Current Borrowing				
Other Liabilities Principal Repayment				
Long-term Liabilities Principal Repayment				
Purchase Other Current Assets				
Dividends				
Total Additional Cash Spent	I			
Subtotal Cash Spent	H + I = J			
Net Cash Flow	**E - J = K**			
Cash Balance				

239

11.6   Projected Balance Sheet

Pro forma Balance Sheets are used to project how the business will be managing its assets in the future. As a pure start-up business, the opening balance sheet may contain no values.

Note: The projected balance sheets must link back into the projected income statements and cash flow projections.

_____ (company name) does not project any real trouble meeting its debt obligations, provided the revenue predictions are met. We are very confident that we will meet or exceed all of our objectives in the Business Plan and produce a slow but steady increase in net worth.

All of our tables will be updated monthly to reflect past performance and future assumptions. Future assumptions will not be based on past performance but rather on economic cycle activity, regional industry strength, and future cash flow possibilities. We expect a solid growth in net worth by the year _____.

The Balance Sheet table for fiscal years 2017, 2018, and 2019 follows. It shows managed but sufficient growth of net worth, and a sufficiently healthy financial position.

Excel Resource:
www.unioncity.org/ED/Finance%20Tools/Projected%20Balance%20Sheet.xls

Key Formulas:

Paid-in Capital = Capital contributed to the corporation by investors on top of the par value of the capital stock.

Retained Earnings = The portion of net income which is retained by the corporation and used to grow its net worth, rather than distributed to the owners as dividends.

Retained Earnings = After-tax net earnings - (Dividends + Stock Buybacks)

Earnings = Revenues - (Cost of Sales + Operating Expenses + Taxes)

Net Worth = Total Assets - Total Liabilities
         Also known as 'Owner's Equity'.

Pro Forma Balance Sheet

	Formulas	2017	2018	2019
Assets				
Current Assets				
Cash				
Accounts Receivable				
Inventory				
Other Current Assets				
Total Current Assets	A			
Long-term Assets				
Long-term Assets	B			
Accumulated Depreciation	C			
Total Long-term Assets	B - C = D			
Total Assets	**A + D = E**			

Liabilities and Capital

	Formulas	2017	2018	2019
Current Liabilities				
Accounts Payable				
Current Borrowing				
Other Current Liabilities				
Subtotal Current Liabilities	**F**			
Long-term Liabilities				
Notes Payable				
Other Long-term Liabilities				
Subtotal Long-term Liabilities	**G**			
Total Liabilities	**F + G = H**			
Capital				
Paid-in Capital	I			
Retained Earnings	J			
Earnings	K			
Total Capital	I - J + K = L			
Total Liabilities and Capital	**H + L = M**			
Net Worth	**E - H = N**			

11.7   Business Ratios

The final column, Industry Profile, shows ratios for this industry as it is determined by the Standard Industrial Classification SIC Index, 7011, for comparison purposes.

Our comparisons to the SIC Industry profile are very favorable and we expect to maintain healthy ratios for profitability , risk and return. Use Business Ratio Formulas provided to assist in calculations.

Key Business Ratio Formulas:

EBIT = Earnings Before Interest and Taxes
EBITA = Earnings Before Interest, Taxes & Amortization. (Operating Profit Margin)

Sales Growth Rate =((Current Year Sales - Last Year Sales)/(Last Year Sales)) x 100
Ex: Percent of Sales = (Advertising Expense / Sales) x 100

Net Worth = Total Assets - Total Liabilities

Acid Test Ratio = Liquid Assets / Current Liabilities
Measures how much money business has immediately available. A ratio of 2:1 is good.

Net Profit Margin = Net Profit / Net Revenues
The higher the net profit margin is, the more effective the company is at converting revenue into actual profit.

Return on Equity (ROE) = Net Income / Shareholder's Equity
The ROE is useful for comparing the profitability of a company to that of other firms in the same industry. Also known as "return on net worth" (RONW).

Debt to Shareholder's Equity = Total Liabilities / Shareholder's Equity
A ratio below 0.80 indicates there is a good chance the company has a durable competitive advantage, with the exception of financial institutions, which are highly leveraged institutions.

Current Ratio = Current Assets / Current Liabilities
The higher the current ratio, the more capable the company is of paying its obligations. A ratio under 1 suggests that the company would be unable to pay off its obligations if they came due at that point.

Quick Ratio = Current Assets - Inventories / Current Liabilities
The quick ratio is more conservative than the current ratio, because it excludes inventory from current assets.

Pre-Tax Return on Net Worth = Pre-Tax Income / Net Worth
Indicates stockholders' earnings before taxes for each dollar of investment.

Pre-Tax Return on Assets = (EBIT / Assets) x 100
Indicates much profit the firm is generating from the use of its assets.

Accounts Receivable Turnover = Net Credit Sales / Average Accounts Receivable
A low ratio implies the company should re-assess its credit policies in order to ensure the timely collection of imparted credit that is not earning interest for the firm.

Net Working Capital = Current Assets - Current Liabilities
Positive working capital means that the company is able to pay off its short-term liabilities. Negative working capital means that a company currently is unable to meet its short-term liabilities with its current assets (cash, accounts receivable and inventory).

Interest Coverage Ratio = Earnings Before Interest & Taxes /Total Interest Expense
The lower the ratio, the more the company is burdened by debt expense. When a company's interest coverage ratio is 1.5 or lower, its ability to meet interest expenses may be questionable. An interest coverage ratio below 1 indicates the company is not generating sufficient revenues to satisfy interest expenses.

Collection Days = Accounts Receivables / (Revenues/365)
A high ratio indicates that the company is having problems getting paid for services.

Accounts Payable Turnover = Total Supplier Purchases/Average Accounts Payable
If the turnover ratio is falling from one period to another, this is a sign that the company is taking longer to pay off its suppliers than previously. The opposite is true when the turnover ratio is increasing, which means the firm is paying of suppliers at a faster rate.

Payment Days = (Accounts Payable Balance x 360) / (No. of Accounts Payable x 12)
The average number of days between receiving an invoice and paying it off.

Total Asset Turnover = Revenue / Assets
Asset turnover measures a firm's efficiency at using its assets in generating sales or revenue - the higher the number the better.

Sales / Net Worth = Total Sales / Net Worth
Dividend Payout = Dividends / Net Profit
Assets to Sales = Assets / Sales
Current Debt / Totals Assets = Current Liabilities / Total Assets
Current Liabilities to Liabilities = Current Liabilities / Total Liabilities

Lodging Ratios
Occupancy Percent   =   Number of Rooms Sold / Number of Room Available
Average Daily Room Rate = Total Room Revenue / Number of Rooms Sold

Business Ratio Analysis

	2017	2018	2019
Sales Growth			

Percent of Total Assets
- Accounts Receivable
- Inventory
- Other Current Assets
- Total Current Assets
- Long-term Assets
- Total Assets

- Current Liabilities
- Long-term Liabilities
- Total Liabilities
- Net Worth

Percent of Sales
- Sales
- Gross Margin
- Selling G& A Expenses
- Advertising Expenses
- Profit Before Interest & Taxes

Main Ratios
- Current
- Quick
- Total Debt to Total Assets
- Pre-tax Return on Net Worth
- Pre-tax Return on Assets

Additional Ratios
- Net Profit Margin
- Return on Equity

Activity Ratios
- Accounts Receivable Turnover
- Collection Days
- Inventory Turnover
- Accounts Payable Turnover
- Payment Days
- Total Asset Turnover
- Inventory Productivity
- Sales per sq/ft.
- Gross Margin Return on Inventory (GMROI)

Debt Ratios
Debt to Net Worth _____
Current Liabilities to Liabilities _____

Liquidity Ratios
Net Working Capital _____
Interest Coverage _____

Additional Ratios
Assets to Sales _____
Current Debt / Total Assets _____
Acid Test _____
Sales / Net Worth _____
Dividend Payout _____

Business Vitality Profile
Sales per Employee _____
Survival Rate _____

Boutique Hotel Ratios
Occupancy Percent _____
Average Daily Room Rate _____

12.0   Summary

_____ (company name) will be successful. This business plan has documented that the establishment of _____ (company name) is feasible. All of the critical factors, such as industry trends, marketing analysis, competitive analysis, management expertise and financial analysis support this conclusion.

Project Description: (Give a brief summary of the product, service or program.)

Description of Favorable Industry and Market Conditions.
(Summarize why this business is viable.)

Summary of Earnings Projections and Potential Return to Investors:

Summary of Capital Requirements:

Security for Investors & Loaning Institutions:

Summary of expected benefits for people in the community beyond the immediate business concern:

Means of Financing:
A. Loan Requirements: $_____
B. Owner's Contribution: $ $_____
C. Other Sources of Income: $_____
Total Funds Available: $_____

13.0   Potential Exit Scenarios

The Management has planned for the following three possible exit strategies:

The first strategy would be to sell the Company to a larger entity at a significant premium. Since, the hotel and resort industry maintains a moderate risk profile once the business is established; the Management feels that the Company could be sold for ten to fifteen times earnings.

The second exit scenario would entail selling a portion of the Company via an initial public offering (or "IPO"). After a detailed analysis, it was found that the Company could sell for twenty times earnings on the open market depending on the business's annual growth rate and strength of earnings. However, taking a company public involves significant legal red tape. _____ (company name). would be bound by the significant legal framework of the Sarbanes-Oxley Act in addition to the legal requirements set forth in form S1 of the Securities and Exchange Commission. The Company would also have to comply with the Securities Act of 1933 and the Exchange Act of 1934.

The last exit scenario would involve the use of a private placement memorandum to raise capital from private sources. This is also a significantly expensive process that requires the assistance of both an experienced securities law firm and an investment bank. Funds would be raised from private equity and merchant banking sources in exchange for a percentage of the Company's stock.

APPENDIX

Purpose: Supporting documents used to enhance your business proposal.

Tax returns of principals for the last three years, if the plan is for new business

A personal financial statement, which should include life insurance and endowment policies, if applicable

A copy of the proposed lease or purchase agreement for building space, or zoning information for in-home businesses, with layouts, maps, and blueprints

A copy of licenses and other legal documents including partnership, association, or shareholders' agreements and copyrights, trademarks, and patents applications

A copy of résumés of all principals in a consistent format, if possible

Copies of letters of intent from suppliers, contracts, orders, and miscellaneous.

In the case of a franchised business, a copy of the franchise contract and all supporting documents provided by the franchisor

Newspaper clippings that support the business or the owner, including something about you, your achievements, business idea, or region

Promotional literature for your company or your competitors

Product brochures of your company or competitors

Photographs of your product. equipment, facilities, etc.

Market research to support the marketing section of the plan

Trade and industry publications when they support your intentions

Quotations or pro-forma invoices for capital items to be purchased, including a list of fixed assets, company vehicles, and proposed renovations

References

All insurance policies in place, both business and personal

Operation Schedules

Organizational Charts

Job Descriptions

Additional Financial Projections by Month

guest Needs Analysis Worksheet

Helpful Resources:

Associations:

American Hotel and Lodging Association	www.ahla.com
Professional Society of Hospitality Consultants	www.ishc.com
Professional Association of Innkeepers International	www.paii.org
Travel Industry Association of America	www.tia.org
American Motel Association	www.abba.com
New England Resorts and hotels	www.newenglandinnsandresorts.com/
African American Association of Innkeepers Int'l	www.africanamericaninns.com
National Motel Association	

Boutique Hotel Guide Website

Pamela Lanier's Travel Guides Online	www.travelguides.com
Select Registry	www.selectregistry.com
Boutique Hotel motels Online	www.bbonline.com

Reservation Service Organizations

Boutique Hotel Reservations	www.bbreserve.com
National Network	www.go-lodging.com/Media.html

Publications

Arrington's Boutique Hotel Journal	www.bnbjournal.com
Boutique Hotel Times	www.theinntimes.com
Innsights	www.innsights.com
Yellow Brick Road Newsletter	www.yellowbrickroadnl.com

Miscellaneous:

Vista Print Free Business Cards	www.vistaprint.com
Free Business Guides	www.smbtn.com/businessplanguides/
Open Office	http://download.openoffice.org/
US Census Bureau	www.census.gov
Federal Government	www.business.gov
US Patent & Trademark Office	www.uspto.gov
US Small Business Administration	www.sba.gov
National Association for the Self-Employed	www.nase.org
International Franchise Association	www.franchise.org
Center for Women's Business Research	www.cfwbr.org

Made in the USA
Las Vegas, NV
16 December 2021

38268128R00146